Praise for *Why Youth is Not Wasted on the*

"What is childhood? What is it for? The usu............ ..... ine purpose of childhood is to set the stage for bigger things to come. *Why Youth is Not Wasted on the Young* turns this view on its head. In this clear and beautifully written account of the role of immaturity in human development and evolution, Bjorklund argues that children's minds are qualitatively different from those of adults. Indeed, children have special ways of learning and knowing that enable unique mastery of skills and invention of knowledge. This book should be required reading for anyone who is struggling with the question of how best to structure their children's lives in today's frantic world."

Bruce J. Ellis, University of Arizona

"In this accessible and provocative work, David Bjorklund argues that childhood is not just training for adulthood. Rather, it serves important adaptive functions that we need to acknowledge and value."

Professor Sir Michael Rutter, King's College London and author of *Genes and Behavior*

"A lively, insightful analysis of human behavior from a novel, evolutionary standpoint; this is essential reading for anyone seeking to truly understand childhood and today's children."

Glenn Weisfeld, Wayne State University

"The science of cognitive development is blessed with some very fine introductory textbooks. The Bjorklund text is quite simply the best of this outstanding group of books. Its coverage of the field is broad and yet does not sacrifice the details that are so crucial to scientific understanding. The writing is engaging and accessible. Students who are fortunate enough to take courses in which this text is assigned will receive a grounding in cognitive development that is both thorough and exciting."

Charles J. Brainerd, Cornell University

To my parents, Hank and Bev Bjorklund, with much love and appreciation

Why Youth is *Not* Wasted on the Young

Immaturity in Human Development

David F. Bjorklund

Blackwell Publishing

BLACKWELL PUBLISHING
350 Main Street, Malden, MA 02148-5020, USA
9600 Garsington Road, Oxford OX4 2DQ, UK
550 Swanston Street, Carlton, Victoria 3053, Australia

First published 2007 by Blackwell Publishing Ltd

1   2007

Library of Congress Cataloging-in-Publication Data

Bjorklund, David F., 1949–
  Why youth is not wasted on the young : immaturity in human development /
David F. Bjorklund.
    p. cm.
  Includes bibliographical references and index.
  ISBN: 978-1-4051-4951-8 (hardcover : alk. paper)
  ISBN: 978-1-4051-4952-5 (pbk. : alk. paper) 1. Children. 2. Child
development. I. Title.

  HQ772.B4795 2007
  305.231—dc22
                                                                          2006026654

A catalogue record for this title is available from the British Library.

Set in 10.5 on 12.5 pt Galliard
by SNP Best-set Typesetter Ltd, Hong Kong
Printed and bound in Singapore
by Markono Print Media Pte Ltd

The publisher's policy is to use permanent paper from mills that operate a sustainable
forestry policy, and which has been manufactured from pulp processed using acid-free
and elementary chlorine-free practices. Furthermore, the publisher ensures that the
text paper and cover board used have met acceptable environmental accreditation
standards.

For further information on
Blackwell Publishing, visit our website:
www.blackwellpublishing.com

Contents

Contents

Preface

My original title for this book was *The Youngest Species.* It was intended to capture the idea that humans are a youthful species in several senses of the term. First, we have been on this planet for a relatively brief period of time, and have been "civilized" for only a fraction of that time; second, we take a long time to grow up (we're the Peter Pans of the animal kingdom); and third, we maintain a "young-at-heart" perspective into our adult years. Unfortunately, this title did not give people who didn't already know what the book was about an idea of what to expect between the covers. "Is it about dinosaurs, or other extinct animals?" one friend asked. "Is this going to be a biology book?" asked another. "What's a child psychologist doing writing a biology book?"

This book is not about dinosaurs, nor is it a biology book (although it does include an evolutionary perspective). This is a book about children, childhood, and development. The thought and behavior of infants and children are the focus of this book, although references to adolescents and adults are made now and then, and there is even the occasional mention of chimpanzees, ferrets, rats, ducks, and bob-white quail (although invariably juvenile ones). This is not surprising, for I have spent more than 30 years conducting research with and writing about children. This book is about childhood, both in terms of the physical characteristics and limitations of youngsters and also how society views children and what it expects from its youngest members. Some aspects of human's slow march to adulthood are a product of biology, plain and simple, and although these features of childhood may have changed over evolutionary time, they characterize children worldwide today. Other aspects of childhood are more vari-able. How have parents in the past, from medieval Europe through most of the 20th century, viewed children and childhood, and is this view changing today? In other words, how have changes in society affected how we perceive and treat children, and how do these changes impact children's lives? And this book is about development. How we view development affects how we understand and treat children. The picture of development I paint here is a bit different from the one most readers will have encountered. I argue that not all aspects of childhood prepare children for adulthood; some facets of immaturity are well suited for the lives children live as children, in the here and now, and not as preparation for the distant lives they will lead as adults.

In this book, I examine the long period of physical, social, and intellectual immaturity that we humans go through on our way to adulthood, and propose that, although maturity is the desired end state, some aspects of immaturity may be adaptive (or may have been adaptive for our ancestors). The first chapter outlines my basic premises, arguing that contemporary society is rushing children through a childhood that has purposes of its own, and providing a new framework for how to view development, a framework informed by evolutionary theory. In Chapter 2 I look at human evolution, particularly the role that developmental immaturity may have played in the emergence of *Homo sapiens*, and in the evolution of childhood. Chapter 3 examines how an extended period of immaturity, in combination with a big brain and living in socially complex groups, led to the evolution of the modern human mind. I also examine how slow growth of the brain today provides the plasticity, or modifiability, for children to adapt to a range of uncertain environments and to permit the reversal of the effects of deleterious early environments. Chapter 4 illustrates ways in which children's immature thinking and behavior may be adaptive to their day-to-day functioning – adapting them to the niche of childhood – and Chapter 5 looks specifically at how children's overly optimistic view of their own abilities may provide them benefits. Chapter 6 examines children's play, which turns out not to be the "purposeless" activity it is customarily defined to be. Chapter 7 investigates research on early learning and education, and how parents and educators can take advantage of children's immaturity in preparing them for life in contemporary society. Chapter 8 examines the changing nature of childhood, as many families promote adult schedules and behaviors for their children to a degree that may not be beneficial either in the short or long run for children. In the Epilogue I review briefly the ground we covered, and also look at adults, arguing that, to a large extent, an extended youth makes us the species we are. We adults retain some juvenile characteristics that help us deal with the world, and these can be most readily seen in our playful attitude that we maintain into old age.

I have enjoyed the intellectual work it has taken to organize my thinking about children, childhood, development, and the role that immaturity has played in making us the species, and the people, that we are. I hope my insights about these issues, and some of the implications they raise about how we rear and educate children today, strike a chord with readers and perhaps cause people to view children and their long journey to adulthood a bit differently.

David F. Bjorklund
Jupiter, Florida

Acknowledgments

Depending on how one does the computation, it took me a little over a year to write this book, or perhaps a little over 30 years. I first had the idea of writing a book such as this in 1992, shortly after publishing an article in *American Psychologist* titled "The Adaptive Nature of Cognitive Immaturity" with then-graduate student Brandi Green. However, I began thinking about some of the ideas presented in this book as a graduate student at the University of North Carolina at Chapel Hill, stimulated by lectures and discussions with Gilbert Gottlieb, Bob Cairns, and Harriet Rheingold, among others. In the interval between graduate school and actually sitting down to write this book, my thinking about child development, the potential role of immaturity in development, and particularly an evolutionary perspective to understanding human development, was influenced by my interactions with many people. Prominent among these are Jesse Bering, Bruce Ellis, David Geary, Carlos Hernández Blasi, Tony Pellegrini, Todd Shackelford, and Wolfgang Schneider. I also want to thank my many friends, colleagues, and students who took the time to read and comment on several or all of the chapters in this book: Charlie Bernholtz, Courtney Bortot, Christopher Cormier, Charles Dukes, Jason Grotuss, Carlos Hernández Blasi, Tony Pellegrini, Justin Rosenberg, Wolfgang Schneider, Santo Tarantino, and Viviana Weekes-Shackelford. And my special thanks go to my wife Barbara Bjorklund, for her constant love and support, as well as for her insightful comments on my work.

1

The Benefits of Youth

Nature wants children to be children before they are men. If we deliberately depart from this order, we shall get premature fruits which are neither ripe nor well flavored and which soon decay. We shall have youthful sages and grown up children. Childhood has ways of seeing, thinking, and feeling, peculiar to itself; nothing can be more foolish than to substitute our ways for them.

Jean Jacques Rousseau, *Emile*

Too old too soon, too smart too late.

Amish saying

My grandmother (and likely yours) was fond of saying, "Youth is wasted on the young." By this, of course, she meant that young people don't appreciate the gifts they have – health, vitality, nearly unlimited horizons – and that an older and wiser person afforded those gifts would not fritter them away. Alas, by the time we realize what we had it is often too late, and the old can only look back wistfully at wasted opportunities. If only wisdom could develop a bit faster, we'd have the intelligence to make good use of the benefits of youth.

This not-too-serious viewpoint from popular culture (my grandmother was not a philosopher) actually reflects a more general and serious perspective on how we in society, including philosophers, educators, politicians, and psychologists, view children and childhood. We implicitly believe that the immaturity of childhood is a necessary evil, something that we must get through on our way to adulthood, where the real action of humanity takes place. Would that there were another way to get to adulthood rather than through a prolonged period of immaturity. Children's immature and inefficient ways of thinking and acting are viewed as "incomplete" or "unfinished" versions of the adult. The child is a "work in progress," and, like many jobs, the sooner work can be completed the better.

1

This is a wholly reasonable view. A long period of dependency in humans *is* necessary. There is no other animal on this planet (and I would venture on any other planet) that must learn so much in order to be a successful adult. And I'm not just talking about school learnin', but the mastering of everyday tasks and situations that our ancestors also faced for thousands (perhaps millions) of years. Human social communities are more complex and diverse than those of any other species. There's no way that children's brains could have been hard-wired by evolution so that they come into the world understanding the "do's" and "don'ts" of society with the need of only minimal experience. There's too much to learn, and this requires not only a flexible intelligence, but also time.

But does development have to be this way? In some sense it likely does. Animals with long lifespans also tend to have long juvenile periods. Humans are a long-lived species who have the time to master many skills, such as those required to read books about slow-developing and long-lived species. But why couldn't our slow physical growth be accompanied by a more rapid intellectual and social development? We'd then have children, still dependent on adults for their care and protection, who are able to learn more readily the ways of their world and would presumably do a better job of it. In fact, this makes great sense. Surely an intellectually mature organism can learn more and better than an intellectually immature one. But this is not the way the human animal is put together. The argument I make in this book is that this is not a coincidence or an oversight of nature, but has adaptive value for the developing child and has played a significant role in the evolution of *Homo sapiens.* Youth is not wasted on the young. Infants and children make good use of their unique features (particularly psychological ones) both to survive the niche of childhood and to prepare themselves for life as adults. In fact, some of the qualities of youth would be wasted on the old.

This book takes a not-frequently-encountered view of development. I believe that development is not something that should be rushed through, but rather the slow course of human growth is adaptive and, in fact, has been shaped through human evolution. This perspective has implications not only for how we view biological development but also for how we think of children, their education, and their well-being. The chapters that follow examine various ways human beings' slow growth and extended immaturity may be adaptive and ways this immaturity can be used to rear successful, well-adjusted adults.

In this first chapter, I provide some of the general premises of my argument. First, I argue that contemporary society (particularly, but not limited to, the United States) is inappropriately rushing children through a childhood that has purposes of its own. Next, I describe different views of development. How we view development influences how we treat children. I propose that although some aspects of infancy and childhood do indeed prepare children for adulthood, others serve to adapt children to their immediate environment and not to prepare them for a future one. I then present the wider theoretical perspective from which I view development: evolutionary biology and psychology. This perspective runs through the entire book and reflects a recent trend in the behavioral sciences. Human thought and behavior, just as human biology, cannot be properly understood except through the lens of evolution. This is as much true for understanding development and the behavior and thought of children as it is for understanding adults.

Rushing through Childhood

My argument is that there is a *purpose* to childhood. It's more than just a passage to adulthood, but an important part of human life in its own right. One of my concerns is that modern life is ignoring this fact, as we rush children through childhood, focusing only on the adults they will become and not the people that they are. Some of this rushing is made necessary by formal schooling. As cultures become more complex, there is an ever-increasing need for technological expertise. We've always been a technological species, and humans are the most educable of animals. But our children are not learning to hunt game or identify edible from inedible plants at the sides of their parents in apprenticeships extending over years. They are learning to read, write, and deal with numbers in classrooms with groups of other same-aged children removed from their parents and other kin. The skills they are learning are abstract, aimed chiefly at dealing with symbols rather than concrete entities. Knowledge of history, science, and other parts of the planet that they may never visit must be acquired. Eventually they must specialize. The most successful people in society do not just master their three Rs, but develop skills that permit them to manufacture products or provide services from plumbing to brain surgery that nonexperts cannot do for themselves.

The world of formal schooling is necessary for children to gain the skills they need to compete in contemporary society, but it is a world that is foreign to our species. Reading and writing are new to humankind, dating back fewer than 6,000 years. It has only been within the last century that a majority of adults on Earth are literate – many today still cannot read. Children's minds did not evolve to read, nor is sitting quietly in rows of desks something that comes naturally to children. But we are capable of such feats, and the technological explosion that occurred with the widespread advent of literacy has transformed how human beings make a living. To develop these abilities one must start early. This requires teaching children with an eye to the future and a focus on mastering complicated skills early so they can serve as the foundation for later learning. We cannot expect children to develop these skills on their own or simply by watching what adults do.

I am not bemoaning modern life or advocating a back-to-nature point of view. I spent a couple nights on a Virginia commune once, overlooking the Blue Ridge Mountains. It was lovely; I enjoyed the hiking and canoeing we did, but it was a vacation. I have no wish to catch my own game, grow my own vegetables, or spend my evenings by the campfire telling stories of the hunt, gossiping about those not present, and swatting mosquitoes on a full-time basis. Although I love visiting the wilderness and communing with nature from time to time, I don't want to live there and certainly don't want to repeal the industrial revolution or argue that the only way to save humankind is to move back to the forests.

What I am concerned about is that in our quest to educate children for the increasingly complex demands of modern life, we go about it in the wrong way. We treat them as little adults, assuming that their minds and emotions are the same as ours only smaller. We believe that the faster they learn the basics, the faster they'll get to the more advanced stuff, and the more successful they'll be as adults. I don't think this is true. My concern is not that of a person who has an overly romantic view of childhood, as a time when children in our not-too-distant past were carefree and innocent, ignorant of any of the dark side of life. In fact, I'm sure that children's lives in developed countries today are far better in most ways than children's lives were 200 years ago (as are the lives of most adults). But this doesn't mean that we adults are doing the best we can for our children. Education, both formal and informal, that takes advantage of children's natural abilities and inclinations will be the most successful in producing competent adults. Understanding that children are not simply miniature adults, that they are specially adapted to the niche of childhood, will go a long way in helping to create learning and living environments best suited to their needs.

It is not only in schools that children are being rushed. The lives of many American middle-class children (and children in other developed countries as well) resemble nothing of the childhoods many of us remember just a generation ago. In many middle-class neighborhoods, children are shuttled from appointment to appointment after school – tennis, karate, dance, piano. Boy and Girl Scout meetings on one night, recitals on another, a supervised play date with a friend on another. Baseball and soccer are not the pick-up games down the park or in the field that many of us remember, but organized by adults, cheered on by adults, and governed by adults. A disputed call? An adult will determine who gets the ball and who was safe or out.

All of us know of harried families and children who have little unstructured time during the week. These are affluent families, consciously doing what they believe is best for their children. They are preparing their children for lives as adults in a fast-paced culture. Elinor Ochs and her colleagues run the Center for Everyday Lives of Families (CELF) at UCLA. They are following 32 Los Angeles families who have two working parents and at least two children. Many of these families work hard at keeping their children busy. The parents of two preteen children believe that the rewards of modern culture go to multi-taskers – those who can switch from one task to the next seamlessly, with idleness being the devil's handmaiden. Says the 47-year-old father of two, "You know the old saying. If you want something done, give it to a busy person. They're learning how to be that. The kids are doing well. They're getting good grades. They're not obese. And at the end of the day, this is good for them."[1]

Maybe it is, but maybe it's not. Children may be capable of handling such schedules, but they may not be optimal for them. Children have their own intellectual and emotional ways of relating, and their lives should not emulate those of adults. I say this not because I get warm and fuzzy feelings thinking of little children playing in a field surrounded by flowers and frolicking with a puppy with floppy ears (although it is a nice image). I say this because I do not believe that all of childhood is simply a preparation for adulthood. I do not believe that children have the same understanding of people and events in their world as adults do. My view of development is a bit different from those of others, and how you view development affects how you view children and what you do to foster their development.

Views of Development

My view is counterintuitive to how most people, professionals and laypeople alike, typically think of development. We are accustomed to thinking of development as being progressive – from immaturity to maturity – with the adult being the product that "counts." This makes sense and surely reflects reality for many human characteristics. Immaturity is associated with inefficiency – a poorly functioning system that must develop further if true advancement is to occur. And it is the adult who is the finished product, who, from a Darwinian perspective, does the reproducing, the *sine qua non* of biological success. From this view, childhood is simply the road to adulthood, a trail that must be taken, and it is the final destination that truly matters. (I recall a job interview of a young child psychologist in which the Chair of the department said something to the effect, "OK, so what's so important about studying children? They start out stupid, they get smarter, and by 18 or so, maybe 16, they're like adults. That's what you need to study. How adults think. Something important." Needless to say, he wasn't offered the job.)

There are other ways to view development, however, that don't have this sense of a gradual progression from immature to mature. For example, many insects and amphibians metamorphose: from caterpillar to butterfly (larva to adult, or imago), or from tadpole to frog. One could not know based just on appearance that a caterpillar and butterfly were even the same species. A great transformation occurs between one stage of development and the next, and the animal at each stage has its own complex organization – its own integrity. The caterpillar often leads a life that is equally complicated and active as that of the butterfly. Entomologists cannot view the caterpillar merely as an immature form of the butterfly, but must view the caterpillar as an animal with its own organization and requirements that is adapted to its present environment, not to an environment it will live in as a butterfly. A butterfly is the inevitable product of a caterpillar, but the two are qualitatively distinct. The caterpillar is not just an immature version of the butterfly.

Humans, and mammals in general, do not metamorphose. On the surface, at least, our development seems much less interesting and complex than those of many "lower" species. But looking at infants and children as having an integrity of their own – as individuals with abilities and characteristics that are especially suited to the environments they inhabit – provides a different picture of immaturity. Seen from this vantage, immaturity is not a necessary evil, but may play an *adaptive* role in children's lives and development. Not all features or experiences of childhood are preparations for adulthood. Some have evolved to adapt children to their *current* environment and not necessarily to a future one.[2]

Although I don't think that there is anything particularly profound with this perspective, it is very different from how most psychologists and educators view development. Early experience (particularly early trauma) is seen as setting the stage for later development. I take no argument with this perspective, for it is surely accurate for many experiences and characteristics of childhood. But believing that all psychological development progresses this way can be misleading and can distort our view of children and their development.

There are three aspects of human childhood and development that I think are important for our discussion here. First, humans spend a disproportionate amount of time as juveniles, waiting almost two decades before they are ready to reproduce. This extended period of youth is necessary to learn the complexities of human life, mainly social complexity. Human beings are a social species, and their nature can only be understood when considered in the context of social groups. Second, and related to the first, children have been prepared by evolution to be sensitive to certain classes of stimuli or events that result in readying them for life as adults. I refer to these as *deferred adaptations.* And third, some characteristics of infancy and childhood have been selected over the course of evolution to serve an adaptive function at specific times in early development, and not necessarily to prepare children for adulthood. I refer to these as *ontogenetic adaptations.* (*Ontogenetic,* from *ontogeny,* refers to individual development and is distinguished from *phylogeny,* which refers to development of the species, or, more conventionally, evolution.) I think the first aspect of development – the long period of childhood necessary to learn the complexities of human life – is self-evident, and I will discuss this aspect of development in greater detail in the next two chapters. The concepts of deferred adaptations and ontogenetic adaptations, however, require further explanation.

Preparing for Adulthood: Deferred Adaptations

The idea that many aspects of childhood prepare children for adulthood is not novel. In fact, this is the implicit view that most people have about childhood. That's what childhood is *for.* The idea of deferred adaptations is that aspects of children's learning or social behavior have been shaped by evolution to make such preparations easier.[3] Some sex differences in children's behaviors may be good examples of deferred adaptations. Males and females of most species (including humans) have different self-interests, focused mainly

7

around issues of mating and parenting; as a result, they develop different psychologies. These psychologies are related to investing in children, competing for mates, and developing social networks of same-sex individuals with whom people will cooperate and compete as adults (at least in traditional societies and for our ancestors). These sex differences don't just "pop out" in adolescence or adulthood, but develop over childhood, and prepare boys and girls for the roles they will play as adults (or would have played in ancient environments).[4]

One robust sex difference found in childhood is an interest in infants. From an early age, girls in cultures across the world display greater interest in babies (particularly in nurturing them) than boys.[5] And despite the assumed greater social pressures for girls to take care of infants than for boys, in the one study that investigated maternal socialization of interest in infants, no such evidence of maternal socialization of this sex difference was found.[6] This sex difference in interest in infants is also seen in the juveniles of many primate species, as well as humans.[7] What function, if any, might such interest have for girls? One obvious possibility is that interest and interaction with infants serve to prepare girls for playing the role of mothers. Mammal females, including humans, don't just give birth to babies, but are solely responsible for feeding them until weaned, and, with few exceptions, are almost entirely responsible for their nurturing and care. Experience with infants provides girls with the skills they will need as mothers in the years ahead. That this may be the case is shown in research with monkeys. Female monkeys who lack social experience interacting with other monkeys show deficits in maternal behaviors; first-time monkey mothers are more likely to show clumsy maternal behavior or abandon their infants than multiparous (repeat) mothers; and first-time monkey mothers with experience interacting with infants are more competent mothers than monkeys without such experience.[8] The universality of greater female interest in infants, and the finding of similar sex differences in our genetic relatives, suggests that this is not a quirk of socialization, but an evolved adaptation. But it is an adaptation that, although influencing children's behavior, has little obvious impact on their current behavior, but rather prepares them for the future.

Is this focus on sex differences here an appropriate one? One often hears that most gender differences, other than the obvious physical ones, are determined by culture and not biology. There is a convention in academic psychology of referring to differences between males and females that are attributable chiefly to biology as "sex differences" and using the term "gender differences" for those that are attributable chiefly to culture. This is a distinction that may be well meaning, but it perpetuates a false nature–nurture dichotomy – the belief that the contributions of biology and culture (or genes and environment, or instincts and learning) can be neatly separated and packaged. The truth is not so simple. Genes, for example, are always expressed in an environment, and environmental effects change organisms' behavior by altering their genetic expression. Despite the enthusiasm that our increasingly sophisticated knowledge of human genetics is providing us, there are no "genes for" any behavioral trait. There are genes *associated* with behavioral traits and physical outcomes (hyper-aggressiveness or mental retardation, for example), but these genes are always expressed in some context. This is true of individual differences in proneness to violence (for instance, children with a particular combination of genes associated with high levels of delinquency are more prone to antisocial behavior only when reared in abusive homes[9]) or to differences between males and females. In fact, it is not always easy to determine when biology ends and culture begins. For instance, the presence of industrial waste chemicals in some communities is associated with precocious puberty in girls. Is this a biologic effect (chemicals affecting hormones) or a cultural effect (modern industry produced those chemicals)? Similarly, girls who come from father-absent homes reach puberty earlier than girls from father-present homes. Is this an effect of biology or culture?[10]

That being said, there is a large body of literature indicating that boys and girls not only possess different genes, but also have different prenatal experiences, and that these differences, in interaction with their childhood environments, bias them to behave and view the world in different ways. For example, Penn State developmental psychologist Sheri Berenbaum and her colleagues have followed a group of girls who were exposed prenatally to high levels of the male hormone androgen. As children, these girls are more likely to display male-typical play styles, although they still identify with female roles and are no more likely to wish they were boys than are typical girls.[11]

The different roles males and females usually have with respect to reproduction also seem to affect their psychologies, biasing them to different attitudes and actions when it comes to issues related to dating, mating, and child rearing. *Parental investment theory* was developed by Rutgers University biologist Robert Trivers to explain many sex differences in behavior across a wide range of species, including humans. Trivers noted, as had others before him including Darwin, that males and females of most species do not invest equally in their offspring. In most animals, females invest much more. In mammals, fertilization and gestation are internal, and following birth, it is the mother who provides the sole source of nutrition to the infant via nursing. The males of most mammals provide no childcare, nor even food for the nursing mother. Some do, with human males being one of the exceptions (although the males of a couple of South American monkey species devote more time and energy to their offspring than the average human guy). Human children have an extended period of dependency and require more care than the young of other animals. So it's to men's advantage to devote more time and resources to their children than males of other species do, because the survival and success of a man's children is related to how much he invests in them. From a strictly Darwinian perspective, it's in a man's self-interest to invest in his mate and his children. But even in humans, it is mothers, not fathers, in every culture of the world, who provide the vast bulk of care to infants and young children.

This sex difference in parental investment is associated with different self-interests in males and females of most species. Females, because they are the more investing sex, have more at stake for any act of sexual intercourse than do males. Having sex for a woman brings with it the potential of nine months of pregnancy and several years of nurturing a highly dependent infant. They are thus more reluctant to consent to having sex than are men, are highly attentive to signs that men have resources (a fancy nest if you're a Bower Bird, perhaps a Ford Thunderbird if you're a human), and whether men are willing to commit those resources to them and their offspring for the long term. Men, too, have their concerns. Because fertilization is internal in mammals, a man can never be certain that the baby his mate gives birth to is his. Mother's baby, father's maybe. Thus, males look for signs not only of beauty (associated with health and fertility in many species), but also fidelity. Men need to be watchful of their mates to insure that the children they spend their resources raising don't carry the genes of another man. Men are also more competitive among themselves for access to females. As the more investing sex, females are viewed as "valued resources." As a result, it is they, in most cases, who do the choosing. Males with features that females like (such as large and colorful tails in peacocks) get "selected." Such female choice has played an important role in evolution in many species. (Or, as my mother likes to say, "If it weren't for women, men would still be swinging by their tails from the trees."[12])

10

These are dispositions that are shared by males and females of most sexually-reproducing species. (As predicted by parental investment theory, in species where males invest more than females, the characteristic sex differences in behavior are reversed. It's not the sex, or gender, of the individuals, per se, that makes a difference, but their differential investment in offspring.) But these are only disposition, not the inevitable outcomes of evolution, genetics, or hormones. They are supported or not, to varying degrees, in different cultures and at different periods in history. Anyone who's read Tom Wolfe's novel *I am Charlotte Simmons*, about the life of an early 21st century college student, can appreciate that women can be as promiscuous and cavalier about sex as men can be. Birth control, equal education and economic opportunity (or aspirations toward such goals), parental and societal attitudes about the roles men and women play, and state support for childcare can mask inherent differences that might exist between men and women. But neither are male–female differences simply a matter of culture. Cultural determinism is as wrongheaded as biological determinism. Men and women are complicated beings, and attributing any differences between them – at the level of individuals or of the sexes – to simplistic causes does both men and women an injustice.

Getting Through the Here and Now: Ontogenetic Adaptations

One problem with thinking of development solely in terms of preparation for adulthood is that one gets the impression that the organism "knows where it's going" and is behaving in a way that may be irrelevant to its current surroundings but looking forward to the life it will lead as an adult. It's almost like the young animals or children are signing up for trade school or college, not because of the benefits it affords them now, but for the jobs it will get them some years down the road. We humans do things like that, and so do other animals that store food away when it's plentiful to eat when harsher times arrive. Development may actually work that way to an extent, but only to an extent. Children must survive in the here and now. If they spend too much of their limited resources in endeavors that will do them good only in the future, they may never get there. Deferred adaptations work because either they don't cost too much for a child to "waste" his or her time on these future-benefiting activities, or, more likely, they also serve to adapt children to their current environment.

11

Other characteristics of infancy and childhood may not have any delayed benefits, other than keeping children alive so they can get to the future. They function, rather, to adapt children to their immediate situation – getting them through a temporary rough spot in early life – and once that is achieved they disappear. These are ontogenetic adaptations (or sometimes *transient* ontogenetic adaptations, emphasizing their temporary nature). Perhaps the most straightforward examples come from prenatal physiology. For instance, mammal fetuses get their nutrition, including oxygen, through the placenta. Babies do not breathe in utero. In fact, they are engulfed in amniotic fluid, yet they do not drown. Upon birth, a radical transformation occurs and the newborn must now abandon its old way of getting oxygen and activate a new one, one that it will use for the rest of its life. The old, prenatal mechanism served its function well, keeping the fetus alive and oxygenating all its cells while it was living in a liquid environment. With birth, the old mechanisms disappear. Similarly, many embryonic birds have an "egg tooth" on the tips of their bills that they use to crack open the shell. This, too, is lost once its job is completed.[13]

After a little thought, you could likely come up with a number of ontogenetic adaptations for mammals and birds reflecting changes from life in the womb (or egg) to life on the "outside" (for example, eating and drinking, the yolk sack in birds). Several newborn reflexes provide relatively straightforward examples of postnatal ontogenetic adaptations. For instance, when newborns are stroked on the cheek, they turn their heads in the direction of the stimulation (*rooting reflex*). This is obviously adaptive in nursing. The rooting reflex disappears over the first several weeks of life as babies gain more voluntary control of their behavior. Other reflexes that may have some adaptive value early in life before infants can exert control over their own behavior include the *swimming reflex*, the *palmar grasping reflex*, in which babies curl their fingers around an object placed in their palms, and the *Moro reflex*, in which, in response to a loud noise or loss of support, infants will extend their arms, arch their backs, and bring their arms toward each other, as if to hold on to something to prevent a fall. Each of these reflexes disappears by 6 months or earlier.

It's a bit harder to come up with clear-cut psychological examples. The waxing and waning of infant and childhood fears may be good candidates for ontogenetic adaptations. For example, most infants develop a wariness of strangers and a fear of separation from their parents during the first year, which will persist through their second year or beyond. Most preschoolers and school-age children fear the dark and being alone, both situations that can bode ill for a young child. Although such fears may persist into adolescence and adulthood for some people, they wane in most children as they become more capable of fending for themselves.[14]

Let me provide another (perhaps somewhat speculative) example. In 1977 developmental psychologists Andrew Meltzoff and M. Keith Moore surprised the world of child psychology by demonstrating that human newborns could imitate facial expressions. Babies typically don't imitate facial gestures until nearly 12 months, so this was quite out of character for what people thought young infants were capable of doing. In Meltzoff and Moore's study, an adult would make a face to an alert newborn, for example, sticking out his tongue, and minutes later the baby would make a similar face. The effect is more subtle than this brief description suggests, and not all subsequent studies that have investigated this have found it. But it's been observed frequently enough over the past 30 years in babies around the world to believe that it's the real thing. Meltzoff and Moore contended that *neonatal imitation* is the basis of later "real" imitation. Newborns were able to observe an action of another person and translate that action to a self-generated behavior, something that requires, at the least, the rudiments of symbolic representation (that is, the ability to represent and store knowledge mentally). That is, the roots of imitative behavior can be found during the earliest stages of life. There are some quirks to the phenomenon, however, most prominently that it disappears around two months of age and is not usually seen again until late in the first year of life.[15]

An alternative view of neonatal imitation is that it has nothing to do with the imitation seen later in infancy and childhood but serves a specific function during the first weeks of life and disappears when it is no longer useful. That's why it declines to chance levels around 2 months of age. But what could that function be? Some have speculated that it may be useful in nursing (mothers often open their mouths as they bring baby to their breast, which may prompt mouth opening in their babies), or in nonverbal mother–infant communication. Newborns are not all that socially responsive and do not readily respond to some of the behaviors mothers provide, which typically generate some response in older infants and children (for example, maintaining eye contact, responding to language, smiling). Neonatal imitation may be a type of reflexive responding on part of the infant that facilitates social give-and-take at a time when infants cannot "intentionally" direct their own behavior. This fosters positive feelings on the part of the moms and helps seal the mother–infant social bond. As babies get older and better able to control their own behavior, the reflexes (or, more properly, *fixed-action patterns*[i]) fall out of the baby's repertoire of behaviors. Support for this latter interpretation comes from a study by Swedish developmental psychologist Michael Heimann who showed that babies who displayed greater levels of neonatal imitation also had higher levels of social interaction with their mothers three months later.[16]

Although I clearly favor this latter interpretation, I admit that there are data on both sides of the argument, and that this is not as clear-cut a case of an ontogenetic adaptation as the placenta is. However, the very fact that we entertain the possibility that some aspects of children's behavior and cognition may serve a specific purpose in childhood and not be preparation for later development (in this case, a hidden reflection of a more advanced ability) causes us to view children and development differently. It is this different perspective I ask the reader to keep in mind while reading this book, for I believe it has consequences for important decisions we make about children as parents, teachers, and members of a democratic society.

A Darwinian Perspective

I'm sure it is clear to all who have read this far that I approach this topic from an evolutionary perspective. I believe that infants and children have been prepared by evolution for life in a human group. Babies do not come into the world as blank slates waiting for the chalk of experience to give their lives form. Rather, babies enter the world

---

[i] A fixed-action pattern refers to a stereotypic behavior that is brought about by a specific environmental event. It's like a complicated reflex that has some adaptive value for the individual. A classic demonstration of a fixed-action pattern was provided by the ethologist Niko Tinbergen (1951). Male stickleback fish act aggressively when they see the red belly of another male stickleback fish. The red belly signals a readiness to mate. Tinbergen noticed that the fish would make aggressive displays when they saw other red objects, including a red truck passing the window where the fish tank sat. Tinbergen demonstrated through a series of experiments that it was the red spot that elicited the stereotypic aggressive behavior. This is normally highly adaptive in the wild, in that the presence of a red spot is typically a sign of a sexual competitor.

with biases, things they like to look at and listen to, for instance. For example, infants and children can easily make sense of some types of information, such as faces and language; they are oriented toward people, and as they develop they more easily learn to "read" social than nonsocial cues. Experience is still necessary for children to develop an understanding of their physical and social worlds, but they get some help. The minds and behaviors of infants and children have been shaped by evolution as much as those of adults, and a cursory understanding of evolutionary theory will be useful.

Darwin and Natural Selection

Most readers will be familiar with the basic premises of evolutionary theory, originally formulated by Charles Darwin in his 1859 book *The Origin of Species*. Darwin (1809–82) was not the first to propose an account of biological evolution. Perhaps the most influential pre-Darwinian evolutionary theorist was the French biologist Jean Baptiste Lamarck (1744–1829). Lamarck is remembered today for the discredited theory of *inheritance of acquired characteristics* (build it up and pass it on to your children). Changes in behavior or form achieved in one generation (a smallish giraffe, for example, lengthening her neck due to her constant stretching for leaves, or a blacksmith increasing the size of his bicep as a result of his constant hammering) can be directly transmitted to the next generation. Although the theory is correctly rejected today, Lamarck was influential in his time, and Darwin even adopted Lamarck's idea of acquired characteristics as one mechanism of evolution. But Darwin's claim to fame was the discovery of the mechanism of *natural selection*, which, nearly 150 years later, remains the centerpiece of evolutionary theory. (Evolution by natural selection was simultaneously discovered by Alfred Russel Wallace [1823–1913], although Darwin provided more evidence for the phenomenon and was the engine behind the subsequent revolution in biological thinking this discovery caused.[17])

At its heart, the concept of natural selection is a simple one with four main features. First, more members of a species are born in any generation than will survive, a phenomenon that goes by the mellifluous name of *superfecundity*. Second, individuals possess different combinations of traits (*variation*). Third, such variation in traits is inherited, passed from one generation to the next. Finally, individuals with characteristics associated with survival and greater reproduction pass those traits along to their offspring. In the parlance of

15

evolutionary theory, these traits are "selected" by the environment because they result in more or better-adapted offspring.[ii]

Although Darwin didn't know it at the time, the primary mechanism for inheritance is through the genes. Thus, genes associated with traits that promote survival get passed on to future generations, whereas genes associated with nonsurvival or with low levels of reproduction are not passed on, or at least not passed on at a very high frequency. Over many generations, genetically based differences in physical or psychological characteristics interact with the environment. These characteristics change in frequency as a result of differential survival and reproduction and eventually result in species-wide changes.

Let me provide an example of natural selection in action. Princeton University biologists Peter and Rosemary Grant have studied finches on the Galápagos islands and have noted a relationship between beak size, availability of resources, and survival.[18] (Much of the data Darwin used to formulate his theory came from his extensive observations of species, including finches, on the Galápagos islands.) Beak size varies, from small to large, among one species of Galápagos

---

[ii] "Selected" is an active verb, and its use implies some intent on the part of the subject of the sentence, in this case "the environment." This is unfortunate, for neither natural selection nor evolution should be viewed as being intentionally directed by anything, be it God or some mystical force of nature. Similarly, evolutionists sometimes speak of features of an animal being "designed by natural selection," by which they mean that the mechanisms described by Darwin produced an adaptive solution to deal with some recurrent problem faced by a species' ancestors. Yet, the subtle implication is that natural selection knew what it was doing. It didn't. Natural selection and evolution are blind processes, producing adaptive responses in plants and animals to current environments, not necessarily to future ones. Evolution isn't directional; it does not know where it is going. The English language does not make it easy to discuss evolution without these subtle implications of intentionality. I have tried to use language carefully to avoid this pitfall, while still making the text readable. So, for instance, I avoid writing sentences such as "Evolution has prepared children..." and use the more awkward passive voice, writing, "Children have been prepared by evolution..." More appropriate yet would be "Children have been prepared through the processes of evolution...", but such writing, while perhaps more semantically accurate, is rhetorically cumbersome. Just keep in mind that evolution or natural selection never truly "selects" or "designs" anything. These are fine words, and they may capture metaphorically the products of natural selection and evolution, but, just as the book of Genesis, they are not to be taken literally.

finches (*Geospiza fortes*). Large beaks are better suited to cracking large seeds, whereas the small beaks are better suited to handling small seeds. In a period of drought, there were fewer small-seed plants, giving the larger-beaked birds an advantage over the smaller-beaked ones. Even those small-beaked birds that survived were at a mating disadvantage to their bigger-beaked cousins, however. Small-beaked males were less healthy, weaker, and less vigorous in their courtship displays than large-beaked males, and, as a result, attracted fewer females. Over the period of the drought, the number of large-beaked birds increased and the number of small-beaked birds decreased. Several years later, however, the climate changed, and small plants with small seeds proliferated, giving the foraging advantage to the small-beaked birds. Over several generations, the distributions changed, and small-beaked birds outnumbered the large-beaked ones.

This simple example of *microevolution* (changes within a species) reveals how changes in the environment result in some members of a species having a better "fit" with their surroundings than others and living to pass on those heritable characteristics to their offspring. Note, in this case, that neither the large-beak nor the small-beak variation is inherently better than the other. It depends on which environment a bird is hatched into, and this cannot be anticipated by the genes.

The idea is truly a simple one. One of Darwin's colleagues and his most ardent supporter, the biologist Thomas Henry Huxley, after learning of the theory, is purported to have said, "How extremely stupid not to have thought of that!" But it is also an extremely elegant idea, making sense of all of biology, from bacteria through human beings. Darwin's polymath cousin Francis Galton wrote to his cousin: "Your book drove away the constraint of my old superstition as if it had been in a nightmare." In the 20th century, biologist Theodosius Dobzhansky, one of the founders of the Modern Synthesis – the integration of Darwin's concept of natural selection and genetic theory – wrote that "nothing in biology makes sense except in the light of evolution"[19] – a sentiment most contemporary biologists would agree with.

But Evolution is Only a Theory

I am fully aware that evolutionary theory is controversial in America today, with many school districts attempting to supplement it with the divinely influenced theory of Intelligent Design. After all, evolution is just a theory and thus still has to be proven. Why should we rest our understanding of human behavior and development on such shaky grounds?

The purpose of science is to develop an accurate description of nature and how it works. We do this by collecting facts about nature (for example, when you drop an object it falls to the ground) and then formulating statements explaining those facts. These statements are theories. They can be stated in words, as Darwin did, or in mathematical formulae, as Newton did for gravity. Theories not only describe and explain already known facts but also make predictions of new findings. They get modified as new facts are discovered, and sometimes even rejected outright. The flat-Earth theory was popular for many years in Europe, but new discoveries made the theory untenable, and the only flat-Earth theorists around today are members of drinking clubs.

Contemporary scientists do not question the *fact* of evolution. It has occurred, over great stretches of time, as surely as the Earth revolves around the sun. The evidence collected over hundreds of years by thousands of scientists is just too overwhelming. But this does not mean that we know precisely *how* evolution occurred. Evolutionary theory is continually being debated and updated to produce a more accurate picture of nature. For example, the late Harvard biologist Stephen Jay Gould in his final book, *The Structure of Evolutionary Theory*, questioned three tenets of Darwin's theory: that evolution is gradual (there is evidence that it can occur rapidly – punctuated equilibrium – at least from the perspective of geologic time); that natural selection occurs only at the level of the individual (the possibility of group selection in social species – "for the good of the group" – has recently been suggested); and that natural selection is the engine of evolutionary change (other factors, such as developmental plasticity – we'll talk more about this in a later chapter – have been hypothesized as contributing significantly to evolutionary changes). But neither Gould, nor any other serious scientist, questions the *fact* of evolution. Evolution is as much a fact as any scientific discovery not directly observable can be, including the structure of atoms, the working of the immune system, or the movements of galaxies. (I write this with confidence, despite the fact that a 2006 Gallup Poll reported that 45% of Americans stated believing that God created humans, essentially in the form we exist now, within the last 10,000 years.)

So yes, evolution is a theory, but theories don't mean the same thing to scientists as they do to laypeople. Theories are accounts meant to describe, explain, and predict facts of nature, ideally in the most straightforward (or parsimonious) way. Because we humans are fallible, they are never perfect – in fact, theories are never absolutely proven. But they are not "just-so stories" or the fanciful renderings of a scientist's imagination. Evolution is as good a scientific theory as they come. It accounts for the state of the biological world, both present and past, using only a minimum number of assumptions, and is subject to modification as new facts come to light. Yes, evolution is only a theory, but what a theory it is!

Fear not an Evolutionary Orientation

Although evolutionary theory is the backbone of modern biology and has been adopted by many psychologists, some, particularly developmental psychologists, have been reluctant to jump on the evolutionary bandwagon. There are a number of reasons for this hesitancy, but perhaps the most important one is the belief that attributing evolutionary origins to children's behavior and thought smacks of biological determinism, or more specifically, *genetic determinism*. Put simply, if behavior is "in the genes," it is not subject to environmental modification. Evolution is based on genetic inheritance, thus attributing human behavior to evolutionary causes implies a form of genetic determinism – the fate of the individual is written in his or her DNA, which is as good as being written in stone. Developmental psychologists do not believe that this is how organisms, particularly human organisms, develop. Moreover, genetic determinism implies that if aggression, for example, is a "natural," or species-typical part of our biology, it is inevitable, not subject to education or change. Such a perspective strikes many developmentalists not only as factually incorrect but philosophically and ethically bankrupt.

If this were what an evolutionary perspective actually meant, I'd be inveighing against it myself. But it does not. Perhaps the hallmark of the human species is its flexibility, or *plasticity* – the ability to change in response to environmental conditions. Such behavioral and cognitive flexibility is also a result of evolutionary processes – the product of natural selection – as surely as our penchant for sweet-tasting food or our attraction to members of the opposite sex.

We are not infinitely flexible, of course. There is a range of likely behaviors we are able to emit or stimuli we can make sense of. But natural selection has not produced a one-trick pony. Humans, and most other animals, have evolved to be sensitive to a range of environments and to develop behaviors that are adaptive in a range of contexts. Biology and genetics may set the stage for life, but to become an adult one must go through infancy and childhood. That is, if evolutionary approaches assume that there is a human nature based in biology (which they do), that nature must develop, and development is shaped by experience as much as it is shaped by genes. There is no direct connection between genes and behavior for any human psychological characteristic worth talking about. For humans, more than any other species, the eventual outcome (that is, the adult) is dependent upon the experiences we have, beginning prenatally and continuing throughout life.

So fear not evolutionary explanations. They do not imply that we *Homo sapiens* are victims of our biology or strip us of human dignity. Just the opposite, I believe. I concur with Charles Darwin's view of evolution, as expressed in the final sentence of his seminal book: "There is a grandeur in this view of life with its several powers having been originally breathed by the creator into a few forms, or into one. And that whilst this planet has gone cycling on according to the fixed law of gravity from so simple a beginning, endless forms most beautiful and most wonderful have been, and are being evolved." An evolutionary perspective, rather than diminishing our species' place in the grand scheme of things, helps us understand the origins of our thoughts and behavior and what it means to be human.

I Come Not to Praise Immaturity

I realize that I could be viewed as a mush-minded romantic, yearning for a return to earlier times (that likely never existed) when children could be children and parents and teachers didn't have to worry about preparing them for an uncertain world. I certainly don't see myself that way. I come not to praise immaturity, but to argue that children's immature behaviors and styles of thought may have some advantages that are easily overlooked. I am not arguing for an artificial extension of youth by "babying" children. Perhaps the single most important job that adults in a society have is to see that their children grow up to be responsible adults themselves. Prolonging immaturity can have dire consequences, and maturity is still the goal of development. What I am suggesting is that there may be some adaptive values for immaturity that coexist with the maladaptive ones, at least at certain times in development.

2

The Youngest Species

Let's hope it's not true; but if it is true, let's hope that it does not become widely known.

Lady Ashley, on hearing Darwin's theory
that humans descended from apes

I would say that man, in his bodily development, is a primate fetus that has become sexually mature.

Louis Bolk[1]

"Don't say that, Uncle Hank. I'm not a monkey!" This is what my cousin Jean would invariably say when my father would utter, "Well, I'll be a monkey's uncle," usually in response to unexpected events, such as our beloved Boston Red Sox sweeping a four-game series from the much-hated New York Yankees. Although as a young child I found the image amusing, I later recognized it as an analogy: The likelihood of the Red Sox winning four in a row against the Yankees was as remote as my father being a close relative to a tree-swinging primate. Remote, but still within the realm of imagination. (For those not attuned to American popular culture, the "Curse of the Bambino" was exorcized in 2004 when the Red Sox defeated the Yankees in the American League Playoffs and went on to beat the St. Louis Cardinals in the World Series, much to the ecstasy of their long-suffering fans. Unfortunately, 2005 and 2006 didn't go quite as well.)

Now as a scientist, I realize that to be more accurate my father should have said, "Well, I'll be a chimpanzee's uncle," or "I'll be a gorilla's uncle," or even, "I'll be a nephew to an orangutan," for these great apes are our close biological cousins. In fact, the genetic make-up of humans and chimps is nearly identical; we share nearly 99% of our DNA with chimpanzees, and almost as much with gorillas.[2]

People and chimps are about as similar genetically as many inter-breeding species, such as horses and donkeys. Yet this genetic overlap belies enormous differences in anatomy and behavior, at least from the human's perspective. Humans walk upright, whereas chimps, when they're out of the trees, locomote hunched over, walking on the knuckles of their hands as well as their feet. Chimps can use their toes for grasping, whereas humans lost this ability when the feet evolved to support an upright body. Chimps have coats of fur, while humans are effectively naked. Perhaps the most important physical difference between apes and humans is the size of their brains. Although the human brain is not the largest in the mammalian world – those of elephants and whales are much larger – we have "more brain" per pound of body weight than any other land mammal. Furthermore, we are the only species who knows this fact and finds it impressive.[i]

Differences between apes and humans are even more dramatic when it comes to behavior and thought. Chimpanzees will strip the leaves off sticks and use these simple tools to gather termites; we humans build tools to make tools, construct permanent housing using available materials ranging from steel to snow, and build machines to do the work we're too scrawny to perform with our own muscles. Chimpanzees hunt cooperatively, conduct raiding parties on other troops of chimps, and communicate vocally and through gestures; humans harvest plants, domesticate animals, conduct warfare, and possess language that permits us not only to communicate more effectively but to represent reality in a way that transforms the mind, allowing us to remember the past, deal more effectively with the present, and plan for the future.

In this chapter I argue that one factor that contributed to human evolution was our slow growth, relative to our great-ape ancestors. Before delving into this issue I need to provide a brief history of our species over the last six to eight million years or so, including a look

---

[i] The relation between brain and body weight is assessed in terms of what brain weight would be *expected* for an animal of a specified body weight and is expressed as the *encephalization quotient* (*EQ*). Animals with "more brain" than expected given their body weight have an EQ greater than 1.0, and those with "less brain" than expected given their body weight have an EQ of less than 1.0. Thus, knowing the general relationship between brain and body weight when considering the entire family of mammals, one can evaluate how far out of line any particular species is. *Homo sapiens* is the species that has a brain weight most out of line from what it "should" have, with an EQ of a whopping 7.6 (Jerison, 1973, 2002; Rilling & Insel, 1999). Primates, in general, have larger brains than expected – for example, the EQ of chimpanzees is 2.3; but humans are the most discrepant.

at the likely lifestyles of our ancestors. I follow this with an examination of the evolution of childhood and the human developmental pattern in general. Human beings do not only differ from other animals and their ancestors in adulthood, but also in how they get there. I examine the possibility that humans added two stages to the basic mammalian pattern of development: *childhood* and *adolescence*. I next look at the onset of puberty and reproductive readiness, examining factors that seem to have resulted in girls reaching maturity faster than in the recent past. I then look at how differences in the *timing* of development – when a particular aspect of biological development begins or ends – can affect organisms and evolution, and particularly the role that changes in developmental timing likely played in the evolution of *Homo sapiens*.

A Brief Look at Human Evolution

Darwin himself did not use the term "evolution" in his 1859 book but rather the phrase "descent with modification." The word "descent" implies that current species descended (or evolved) from earlier species, that humans (or dogs, or stickleback fish, or nematodes) are related to earlier animals that are (in all likelihood) now extinct. With respect to humans, we did *not* evolve from chimpanzees, nor from the monkeys you see in the zoo. Rather, humans and chimpanzees evolved from a common ancestor, a chimp-like creature that lived between six and eight million years ago.

Having an idea of when two species last shared a common ancestor is directly related to how similar the two species are genetically. As I mentioned, chimpanzees (*Pan troglodytes*) and humans last shared a common ancestor about six to eight millions years ago and share nearly 99% of their genes. The line that eventually led to humans and chimpanzees diverged from the line that eventually led to gorillas about 10 million years ago, and both people and chimps have nearly 98% of their genes in common with the giant silverbacks of Africa.[ii]

[ii] Perhaps not surprisingly, many of the genes that differ between modern chimpanzees and humans are related to brain functioning. Patterns of genetic expression between the two species differ more in brain cells than in liver cells, for example (Enard et al., 2002). Also, a number of brain-related genes that have experienced substantial selection pressure from the time humans split from the rest of the ape line have been identified, although other than a gene associated with language (the FOXP2 gene), we're not certain exactly

23

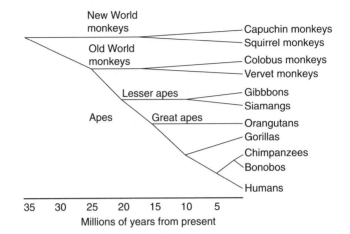

Figure 2.1 Evolutionary relationship among some living primates (from Bjorklund & Pellegrini, 2002). Reprinted with permission of the American Psychological Association.

(To put this in context, humans also share about 40% of their genes with bananas, so relatively small differences in genes can lead to enormous differences in the creatures they create.) As a scientist who is concerned primarily with *Homo sapiens* (call me a speciesist, if you must), looking at the degree to which a primate species is similar to humans gives us some clues as to what types of physiology, behaviors, or cognition we may have shared with a common ancestor and what in each species has uniquely evolved since we departed from that distant relative. Figure 2.1 presents a sketch of the evolutionary (or *phylogenetic*) relationship between some selected primates, including humans. As you can see, New World (South American) monkeys diverged from Old World (African and Asian) monkeys about 35 to 40 million years ago, meaning that we are only very distantly related to capuchin monkeys, the small and smart "organ grinder" monkeys

what these genes do. And brain-related genes apparently did not stop evolving once modern humans entered the world stage about 200,000 years ago. Recent research has identified two genes that are highly active in the brains of modern people, variants (or alleles) of which that differ in frequency among people in different parts of the world, that apparently evolved around 40,000 and 6,000 years ago, respectively. These times correspond to an explosion of symbolic expression and spread of civilizations, suggesting that they may have afforded their bearers a selective advantage (Evans et al., 2005; Mekel-Bobrov et al., 2005).

that once graced city streets. We are more closely related to the great apes – orangutans, gorillas, chimpanzees, and bonobos (or pygmy chimpanzees). It is because of this closeness that studies of the great apes, particularly of chimpanzees (*Pan troglodytes*) and bonobos (*Pan paniscus*), can be so informative for an understanding of human origins and nature. In fact, biologist and author Jared Diamond proposed that the differences among humans, chimpanzees, and bonobos are so small that our species should really be classified as the third chimpanzee (*Pan sapiens*, perhaps).[3]

Anyway, as most readers are likely aware, our kind did not simply emerge from the jungles of Africa – large-brained and hairless, walking upright, carrying a fine-crafted stone tool in one hand, an artist's brush in the other, and discussing plans for raiding the neighboring tribe – leaving our knuckle-walking and mute brethren behind in the trees. From the time we last shared a common ancestor with chimpanzees, the genetic line that led to modern humans underwent many changes and included many different species. How many intervening species (referred to collectively as *hominids*, or *hominins*) there were is debatable, based in large part on the incomplete fossil record, and also to the tendency of paleoanthropologists to disagree among themselves. Within this camp of scientists who study human origins, some are *splitters*, seeing differences in fossils as reflecting different species, whereas others are *lumpers*, lumping together a variety of specimens in a single species, believing that the differences reflect normal variation (such as differences between males and females). But all agree that the line of descent is not straight, that animals who were not quite human were the first to diverge from our common ancestor with chimpanzees, that at some time in the distant past several different hominid species (and several different species of humans – *Homo*) coexisted, and that all but one of these species (us) is extinct.[4]

The Fossil Record

Humans originated in Africa. A number of fossils of animals that may have been the "missing links" between the apes that eventually became chimpanzees and those that eventually became us date back to six million years ago, but their connection with humans is uncertain.[5] There is scant evidence for a species called *Ardipithicus ramidus* that most paleoanthropologists believe is in the human line, but the evidence doesn't become much better until a variety of species called australopithecines enter the fossil record. The best known of these species is *Australopithecus afarensis,* based mainly on the description of the nearly complete fossil called Lucy (purportedly named because on the evening of the discovery the Beatles song "Lucy in the Sky with Diamonds" was playing on the radio). Lucy and her kin walked upright, much as humans do and chimpanzees do not, was about 3.5 feet tall, and had a brain about the size of a modern chimpanzee (about 400 cc). So in the transition from ape to human, *bipedality* (walking on two legs) preceded big brains. A variety of other australopithecine species have been identified, some developing robust jaws and bodies, and others more *gracile* (that is, less robust) body types. It was the latter group that presumably evolved into the first humans, *Homo habilis,* who appear in the fossil record about 2.5 million years ago. They, too, lived only in Africa and had a bigger brain, about 650 cc.

Homo habilis translates roughly as "handy man," and these were the first hominids discovered to make and use stone tools. Tool use was once thought to be solely in the province of humans, but we know now that's not the case. Chimpanzees use stones to crack nuts and use sticks to fish for termites. They don't do much in the way of tool construction (they will strip the leaves off a potential termite-fishing rod, and they do seem to be selective in the stones and sticks they use as tools), but they (and a number of other species, including many birds) use tools to solve problems, chiefly (but not exclusively) to obtain food. But *H. habilis* obviously built tools and built them in a uniform way, developing a technology anthropologists refer to as *Olduwan* (named after the area of Africa where the tools were first found).[iii] *H. habilis's* genius was not only to develop the ability to construct useful stone implements but also to transmit this technology to other members of its kind and across generations. It's not simply that there was one *H. habilis* Einstein (or perhaps *H. habilis* Edison, more appropriately) who figured out how to build and use a better cutting tool; rather, once developed (whether by a lone Habilis Edison or by a committee of habili), this technology was passed to other members of the group, establishing unambiguous evidence of culture. We should be as impressed with the mind required

---

[iii] There's some evidence that a species of australopithecine, *Australopithecus garhi,* may have also used stone tools (Asfaw et al., 1999), and the use of wooden tools, such as sticks, surely predated the use and construction of stone tools. There is also some debate about whether *Homo habilis* may be better classified as a separate species of australopithecines rather than a member of the *Homo* genus.

to transmit such culture as we are with the invention of the tools themselves.[iv]

H. habilis presumably begat *Homo erectus* about two million years ago. (*Homo erectus* is sometimes divided into two species, *Homo ergaster*, which stayed in Africa, and *Homo erectus*, which left Africa and populated much of the Old World.) According to one scenario, *H. erectus* had a larger brain and created a more sophisticated tool kit (called *Acheulean*) than handy man. And some believe that *H. erectus* controlled fire by about three-quarters of a million years ago.[6]

Until this time, all the action on the hominid scene occurred in Africa. But sometime perhaps as early as two million years ago, *H. erectus* left Africa and made its way to Asia and Europe, where it existed, in some pockets, until as recently as perhaps 26,000 years ago,[7] meaning that it roamed the Earth with fully modern humans. In fact, one recent and fascinating finding is the discovery of dwarf humans on the Indonesian island of Flores. *Homo floresiensis* stood about 3 feet tall – the height of an average 3-year-old child – with head size proportional to body size (unlike modern pygmies, who are short in stature but have relatively large skulls), and presumably was a descendent of *H. erectus*. It's always exciting when a new species of humans is found, but what was so intriguing about *H. floresiensis* is that the fossils date back to just 12,000 years ago. That may seem like an eternity when put in reference to the typical human lifespan, but it's just a wink in geologic time and means that this dwarf species was alive at the same time as modern humans. Recent analysis of the endocast (inner surface) of one *flores* skull revealed that the small brain was organized much like the brains of modern people, with enlarged

---

[iv] I should also note here that humans, modern or ancient, aren't the only species with culture. Chimpanzees, orangutans, and even dolphins have been shown to pass on complex behaviors learned in one generation to the next (Rendell & Whitehead, 2001; van Schaik et al., 2003; Whiten et al., 1999). These include tool use, such as termite and ant fishing, forms of greetings, and forms of grooming. This is admittedly a liberal definition of culture – not quite the *Mona Lisa* or using the proper fork at a formal dinner party – but it reflects an ability to pass information learned in one generation to the next, suggesting that our common ancestor with chimpanzees also likely had the makings of a "cultural mind." Evolution doesn't create bodies or abilities from nothing, but works with what it's got in one generation to build the next; and our ancestors, even 7 million years ago, apparently had the right stuff.

temporal lobes, associated with language in living people, and enlarged frontal lobes, associated with "thinking" and complex problem solving.[8] All this suggests that this animal with the little brain may very well have had the intellectual wherewithal to create complex tools, use language, and think symbolically. Maybe size really doesn't matter. Not surprisingly, there is debate about the exact place of this Lilliputian creature in human history, with some believing it may be better classified as a new species of australopithecine and others thinking it may be an atypical *Homo sapiens* (one with microcephly, perhaps).[9] Stay tuned.

But where did *modern* humans (*Homo sapiens*, us) come from? The best evidence, both from fossils and DNA, suggests that we evolved from *H. erectus* that remained in Africa (see Figure 2.2). There is fossil evidence of a bigger-brained species (maybe several of them) with characteristics of both *H. erectus* and *H. sapiens*, which is sometimes referred to as *Archaic Homo sapiens* (and sometimes as *Homo heidelbergensis* or *Homo antecessor* or *Homo helmei* or a few other names). Our kind, with a brain capacity of about 1,300 cc, appeared in Africa as early as 160,000 years ago[10] and, about 100,000 years ago migrated out of Africa and replaced other human populations all over the globe (for example, Neanderthals in Europe, *H. erectus* in Asia), either by being better adapted to the changing climate, by out-competing them, or by killing them off.

It is not until about 40,000 years ago, however, that people who are undeniably "like us" are found in the archeological record. These people are best represented by the Cro-Magnons, named after an area in France where their remains were first discovered. Between 40,000 and 10,000 years ago, during the last Ice Age, these people lived in what is today Europe. They developed new stone technologies, far superior to what any of their predecessors had used. They buried their dead, made pottery and musical instruments, created statues that glorified (and exaggerated) the female form (likely fertility symbols), and painted beautiful scenes of animals and great hunts worthy of a Picasso on cave walls. They built huts using a variety of materials, but still lived as hunter-gatherers. With the end of the Ice Age 10,000 years ago, our nomadic ancestors began to settle down, domesticate plants and animals, and live in communities we would easily identify as cities and towns. Cultural evolution took off with the establishment of sedentary life, and history began. It is a mere wink of an eye between the last Cro-Magnon and us. Our kind has been "civilized" for less than one-half of one percent of the time the *Homo* genus has roamed this planet.

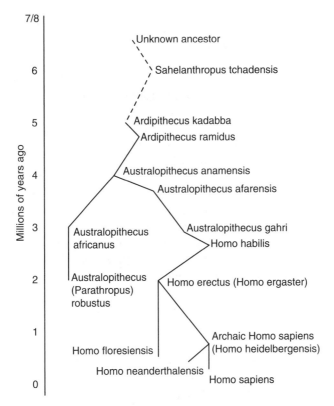

Figure 2.2 One possible phylogenetic tree of human evolution.

Cave Paintings

I have not seen the great cave paintings of Lascaux in France or Altamira in Spain, but I was fortunate to visit one of the many "lesser" caves with ancient paintings scattered throughout Spain. El Parc Cultural Valltorta-Gasulla is near the small town of Tírig in an olive-growing, mountainous area near the city of Castellón in eastern Spain. A guide led the small group of tourists from the parking lot onto a rugged landscape of small trees and bushes, with boulders scattered all about. After inspecting some stone huts used by herders hundreds of years ago, we moved to the edge of a canyon. Below we saw the steep cliffs rising hundreds of feet above a slow-moving river. The river was here in ancient times, too, larger and swifter and a source of water for man and beast alike, we were told. Deer and horses would come to the river, and the ancestors of the conquistadors would drive them into a canyon cul-de-sac and kill them with bows and arrows and spears. Proof of that is laid below.

We made our way down to the floor of the canyon and then climbed up again to a cave tucked into the side of a cliff about 100 feet above the river basin. Here, exposure to the elements was limited, as it apparently was in ancient times. The guide then pointed out faint figures on the walls. There are three hunters shooting arrows at deer. There are horses. And over here what looks like men getting ready to battle one another, or perhaps just celebrating the hunt. Like some paintings in the better-known caves, the figures were not literal representations of people and animals, but impressions. Not poor drawings intended to be realistic, but artistic interpretations that brought to mind some of the animals and humans that Picasso drew. These paintings did not go back to the earliest times of Cro-Magnon in Europe. They were about 5,000 years old, our guide said. But they were still special. I'd thought a lot about human prehistory over the years, and, in fact, am passionate about the subject. But seeing the faded paintings in the Cova dels Cavalls (Cave of the Horses), while standing in the same place as the artists did – looking over the canyon in one direction and the artful renditions of people and animals in the other – gave me a sense of deep history that was more primal and visceral than anything I'd experienced from books I'd read or the museum exhibits or photographs I'd seen.

The picture of human evolution is not nearly as simple as this brief sketch might imply. For example, Neanderthals (*Homo neaderthalensis*) apparently evolved from *H. erectus* or *Archaic Homo sapiens* stock and populated Europe and Eurasia beginning about 140,000 years ago, perhaps earlier. There's still debate about whether Neanderthals were a sub-species of modern humans (*Homo sapiens neaderthalensis* in contrast to *Homo sapiens sapiens*), or, like *H. erectus*, a unique hominid species. The genetic evidence suggests that *Homo sapiens* and Neanderthals last shared a common ancestor about 500,000 years ago.[11]

Whether Neanderthals and modern humans were the same species or not, they were clearly closely related and presumably could have interbred. What prevented them? Perhaps nothing. There has always been a group of paleoanthropologists who argue that Neanderthals and modern humans were members of the same species and thus surely did interbreed, meaning that Neanderthals are us (or at least a little bit of their DNA is part of us). In fact, most paleoanthropologists believe that two such closely related species as Neanderthals and *Homo sapiens* would almost certainly have had sex with one another. Horses and donkeys do it, lynx and bobcats do it, olive and hamadryas baboons do it, as well as many other closely related sister species of mammals. So it would be unlikely if Neanderthals and our *Homo sapiens* ancestors didn't also. (They apparently traded culture, and thus likely also traded mates.) Such inter-species matings sometimes produce hybrids, about a third of them fertile.

Until recently, this has been just speculation, as has the opposing argument that the two groups were different species and never interbred. Fossil remains found in what is today Spain suggest that at least some *Homo sapiens* and *Homo neanderthalensis* did produce offspring with physical characteristics of each species. But it seems this was not typical. If Neanderthals and modern humans had babies together, and those babies grew up to have babies, etc., there should be evidence of this in contemporary Europeans. There is no evidence from examination of DNA from populations around the world that Europeans have remnants of Neanderthal genes, which they should if the two species regularly interbred.

Why not? It's unlikely that the two species didn't interact, at least occasionally. One hypothesis is that key aspects of the appearance or behavior of members of the opposite sex of one species just turned off the other. Many animals are quite selective about whom they have sex with. For example, how a male looks, how he presents himself, dances, or builds a nest for his beloved, all can influence a female's reaction to a potential suitor. The wrong move, the wrong look, the wrong smell, or the wrong tie, and a potential mate becomes a rejected suitor. Some Neanderthals and fully modern humans likely did have sex and babies together, much as the *Homo sapien* Ayala did with her Neanderthal captors in Jean Aural's novel *Clan of the Cave Bear*. But the bulk of the evidence is that *Homo sapiens* and Neanderthals of 30,000 to 100,000 years ago mainly kept to themselves and didn't spawn a race of people who are still with us today.[12]

How Our Ancestors Made a Living

Perhaps as important as changes in brain size are to understanding human evolution (and in understanding the species we are today) is how our ancestors made a living. Based on fossil and archeological evidence and the lifestyles of modern hunter-gatherers, we can make an educated guess at how early humans lived. First, ancient humans, like our immediate hominid ancestors, have always been a social species.

Human nature can only be understood in light of our social nature. Since *Homo erectus* days, our ancestors likely lived in small, nomadic groups of between 30 and 60 people. They cooperated and competed with members of their group, and likely interacted with other nomadic groups, competing for resources such as food, trading goods and mates, and sometimes engaging in warfare. Warfare in one form or another is found in all groups of modern humans. Chim-panzees are the only other mammal known to engage in war parties, suggesting that the roots of war lie deep in our evolutionary history.[13]

Our ancestors made their living as hunters and gatherers on the savannahs of Africa. For food, they gathered fruits, nuts, vegetables, and tubers; scavenged meat left behind by larger predators; and hunted. There was surely a division of labor, with women doing most of the gathering and men doing most of the hunting, likely in coop-erative groups. The vegetation and prey animals early humans used as food surely varied over the past two million years, as reflected in the substantial climate changes that have occurred over this time.[14] This implies that humans had to learn to adapt to variable environments and required a flexible mind to do so.

Women likely gave birth every three or four years, which was also the likely time that babies were breast fed. Females likely reached puberty relatively late and gave their first birth in their late teens. Childcare was the responsibility of mothers, who were helped by other women (termed *alloparenting*), most particularly kin. Men likely pro-vided protection and resources to their children and their children's mothers. Ancient, like modern, humans were likely a marginally monogamous/marginally polygamous species, in which males com-peted with one another for access to females.[v] Most males likely had

---

[v] There are a number of physical factors that suggest that humans have always been a marginally monogamous/marginally polygamous species. These include: (a) the differences in physical size between males and females (*sexual dimorphism*), with males being only slightly larger than females. Males are substantially larger than females in species with male harems, such as gorillas, and differences are minimal in monogamous species, such as gibbons; (b) differences in testes size. Males in harem species have small testes relative to body size, such as gorillas, whereas males in promiscuous species have large testes relative to body size, such as chimpanzees. This difference is related to sperm competition (Baker & Bellis, 1995); there are no competing male sperm in the female reproductive tracts for harem-controlling male gorillas, whereas there is potentially great sperm competi-tion within the female reproductive tracts of promiscuous chimpanzees. Human testes size relative to body weight is intermediate between these two

a single mate at a time, although some of the higher-status males likely had several mates and others had little or no access to fertile females.

Why is it important to have an idea of how our ancestors lived? The reason is that it was during these ancient times that human thought and behavior were shaped by natural selection. Humans are primates and mammals, and so, not surprisingly, much of our behavior can be explained in terms of our "animal" heritage. But characteristics that distinguish us from our ape relatives have evolved since our species split with the line that led to modern chimpanzees, six to eight million years ago. Perhaps the period of greatest significance for understanding who we are as a species occurred in the more recent past, the last two million years or so, a period known as the *Pleistocene*. It was during this time that human nature, first expressed in the behavior of *Homo erectus*, was shaped. Human behavior continued to be molded by natural selection up until the emergence of civilization and beyond.

The important point here is that the human mind evolved to cope with conditions and challenges present in the Pleistocene, when our ancestors existed in small groups of nomadic hunter-gatherers. There was always culture within these groups, but the nature of that culture changed drastically when our kind became sedentary, domesticated plants and animals, and established cities and governments. The origins of such civilization go back only 10,000 years, far too little time for natural selection to have modified mind and behavior to adjust to such conditions. Human infants today are born with essentially the same brain that their infant ancestors 40,000 years ago were born with, and are "prepared" for the same type of lifestyle that their ancestors faced. Most children today, however, do not experience those environments, but are born into one unanticipated by more than a million years of human evolution.

This means that although infants and children continue to be well adapted for some aspects of human life (for example, basic social relations with both kin and peers), natural selection has not prepared

primate extremes (Short, 1979); (c) the number of different types of white blood cells, which are part of the immune system. More promiscuous species, such as chimpanzees, have a larger number of such types of cells than monogamous species, such as gibbons. The reason for this difference is related to the probability of contracting a sexually transmitted disease. Humans' immune system is more like the harem-based gorilla and monogamous gibbon (Nunn, Gittleman, & Antonovics, 2000).

them well for other aspects of modern life. A simple example involves our love of sweet and fatty foods. These taste signals tell us there are many calories in each bite, which are good for an animal that may not know where its next meal is coming from, but not as adaptive for one who has easy access to fast food and fights obesity and clogged arteries.[15] Other aspects of modern life and development may also be at odds with our evolved propensities. For example, children in modern cultures attend school, which is necessary for them to become successful adult members of their societies. We should not be surprised, however, that many children find formal schooling difficult, or at least unpleasant, given that much of what goes on in school is counter to their natural tendencies. Children did not evolve to sit quietly with large groups of same-age children and learn information from a previously unknown and unrelated adult about content that is not immediately relevant to their lives. Yet children do it, indicating that evolution has also provided them with a mind that is adaptable to unfamiliar environments.

The take-home message here is that we must keep in mind that human cognition, behavior, and development were adapted to a very different environment than most children live in today; and although natural selection continues to prepare children for life in a human group, some aspects of human nature may actually prove maladaptive to contemporary functioning.[16]

A Day in the Life of Hominids

Human lifetimes are measured in decades, not millennia, and as a result we often have difficulty appreciating the time course of human evolution. One way of getting a better idea of the timing of human evolution is to put it in a perspective we can relate to, such as equating evolutionary time with the length of a 24-hour day. Doing this, we set 12:01 a.m. as the time when humans last shared a common ancestor with chimpanzees (eight million years ago, or mya), 12:00 noon as 4 mya, and 12:00 midnight as today. One hour corresponds to about 333,333 years; one minute corresponds to about 5,555 years; and one second corresponds to about 93 years.

12:01 a.m. – Human's unknown last common ancestor with chimpanzees lived in Africa (8 mya)

3:00–9:00 a.m. – Several short (3–4 feet tall), bipedal hominids lived in Africa, including *Orrorin tugenensis*, *Sahelanthropus tchadensis*, and *Ardipithecus kadabba*. Their connection to later humans is unclear, but one of these hominids was likely the ancestor of modern people (5–7 mya).

1:30 p.m. – Lucy and her kind, *Australopithecus afarensis*, lived in Africa. *A. afarensis* walked upright much as humans do, but had the skull the size of a chimpanzee (3.5 mya).

4:30 p.m. – The first member of the *Homo* genus, *H. habilis* (handy man), lives in eastern Africa. They have a stone tool technology referred to as Olduwan (2.5 mya).

6:00 p.m. – *Homo ergaster* (or African *Homo erectus*) lives in Africa. They develop a more sophisticated stone tool kit called Acheulean (2 mya).

9:00 p.m. – *Homo erectus* leaves Africa and populates much of Europe and Asia (1 mya).

11:06 p.m. – *Archaic Homo sapiens*, having some features characteristic of both *H. erectus* and *H. sapiens*, live in Africa (300,000 years ago).

11:42 p.m. – Anatomically modern humans, *Homo sapiens*, live in African and migrate to other parts of the Old World (100,000 years ago).

11:54 p.m. and 36 seconds – Cro-Magnon people make cave paintings in Europe (30,000 years ago).

11:58 p.m. and 12 seconds – Agriculture, a sedentary lifestyle, and civilization begin in the Middle East (10,000 years ago).

11:59 p.m. and 22 seconds – The birth of Christ (2,000 years ago)

11:59 p.m. and 43.5 seconds – The fall of the Roman Empire (476)

11:59 p.m. and 57.5 seconds – Charles Darwin is born (1809).

11:59 p.m. 59.5 seconds – Watson and Crick discover the structure of DNA (1953).

11:59 p.m. 59.99 seconds – Boston Red Sox win the World Series (October, 2004).

The Evolution of Childhood

When most paleoanthropologists or biologists discuss human evolution, the focus is on adults. They describe the average *adult* skull size, for example, or the tool kit presumably used by adults to kill animals or prepare food. But our ancestors also developed, and issues of how they developed are of central concern to us here. The only way one can reach adulthood is to be born and stay alive through infancy, childhood, and adolescence. Adulthood may be where all the dating and mating take place – the essence of Darwinian success – but it is the young of a species that must be well adapted to their environment so that reproductive maturity *can* be reached. How we make the transition from birth to maturity seems to have been especially important in human evolution.

We take the course of human development for granted, and we generally don't think of it as anything really special. Like other mammals, we're born, have a period of infancy in which we're highly dependent on our parents for survival, enter childhood, then adolescence, and then become adults. It takes us longer to go through these stages than other mammals, but the basic pattern is the same. As it turns out, that's not the case, at least not in its entirety.

Zoologists and physical anthropologists typically describe three postnatal developmental stages for most mammals: infancy (sometimes with a separate neonatal period), the juvenile period (not found in all mammals), and adulthood. Infancy is the time between birth and weaning, and in mammals, is uniquely characterized by breast-feeding. The female mammary gland is the sole source of nutrition for most infant mammals. (In traditional societies, children nurse until 3 or 4 years of age. Their diets are, of course, supplemented with solid food, usually sometime during their first year, but weaning in traditional cultures is late-occurring relative to industrialized societies, extending human infancy to about 3 years of age.) Once an animal is weaned, it must feed itself. Sometimes a parent will prepare food and bring it to the weanling, but the juvenile must eat it itself. Although there is a wide range of behaviors and characteristics among different juvenile mammals, they are all more independent (sometimes totally) from their mothers than they were in infancy. (I say "mothers" here because fathers play a "parenting" role in only a small handful of all mammals.) Juvenile animals usually show increased vigor in behavior (often expressed as play, at least in social species), and they are not yet ready to reproduce. This comes with adulthood. Although this may sound familiar, it's not exactly the pattern that modern humans follow.

Childhood and Adolescence: Unique Human Stages of Development?

I have noted repeatedly in this book that humans are a slow-developing species and are dependent on their parents for a longer period of time than any other primate. In some respects, humans are not unique, but merely display an exaggerated pattern of primate development. The closer a species' common ancestor is with *Homo sapiens*, the longer is the period of immaturity: in lemurs approximately 2 years, in macaques approximately 4, in chimps approximately 8, and in humans approximately 15 years.[17] Thus, humans simply reflect an extension of the basic primate pattern.

Others have argued, however, that the human pattern of development is qualitatively different from that of other primates. University of Michigan – Dearborn anthropologist Barry Bogin argues that humans evolved two new stages of development: *childhood* and *adolescence*.[18] Most of us think of childhood as the time between infancy and adolescence, but Bogin is more specific. According to Bogin, childhood occurs between infancy and the juvenile period (about 3 to 7 years). What is unique about human childhood is that, although a child is weaned, it still cannot even minimally fend for itself. Food must be prepared for children. They cannot catch their own prey, gather the right kinds of fruits, vegetables, and gourds, and could not prepare these foods if they did. They not only lack the mental and motor abilities to achieve such feats, but also the teeth. Other animals have "milk teeth," or baby teeth, but these are replaced by adult teeth around the time of weaning, permitting juvenile animals to eat a diet similar to that of their parents. In fact, Bogin ties the end of childhood and the beginning of the juvenile period with the eruption of the first permanent molar (between 6 and 7 years of age).

Bogin's childhood stage also corresponds roughly to a period in cognitive development described by the renowned Swiss psychologist Jean Piaget as *preoperational*, when children's thinking is intuitive as opposed to logical. It is no coincidence that, in many societies, the end of this age period corresponds to children attaining new status as reflected in such things as the beginning of formal education, religious confirmation, or the possibility of legal responsibility for one's behavior. Before the age of 7 or so, it is nearly impossible to imagine a child fending for him- or herself. We don't expect too much more of an 8- or 9-year-old these days (and likely never did), but they seem to have both the minimal physical (for example, teeth) and intellectual skills to survive (if minimally) in a social group without substantial dependency upon adults. Think of the Artful Dodger from Dickens' *Oliver Twist*, and the millions of street children around the world today, who eke out an existence, often despite the actions of adults. (I will discuss the *cultural* evolution of childhood – how adults in a society view children – in Chapter 8.)

Turning to adolescence, its most familiar characteristic is its growth spurt, occurring earlier for girls than for boys. There is also an extended period of low fertility. Although adolescents may display the secondary sexual characteristics of adults, and may show signs of reproductive ability (menstruation in girls, ejaculation in boys), the likelihood of getting pregnant is low for about two to three years following *menarche* (a girl's first menstrual period). There is a similar period of low fertility for boys. (But *low* fertility is not infertility. Pregnancy can and does happen among adolescents.)

I've been using the terms "puberty" and "adolescence" almost interchangeably here, but technically there is a difference. *Puberty* refers to the suite of biologically paced changes that culminate in the adult body. Many of these changes have to do with secondary sexual characteristics (genital development, breast development in girls, muscle development in boys). *Adolescence* typically refers more to the psychological characteristics associated with these changes and how society members view people going through such changes. As such, different cultures treat young pubertal people differently. In fact, some claim that adolescence didn't really exist much before the 19th century. In earlier times, teenagers were commonly expected to take on adult responsibilities. In recognition of this, in many societies there are rituals associated with menarche for girls, or a certain age for boys (for example, Bar Mitzvah in Jewish tradition), that mark the end of childhood and the beginning of adulthood. Because the technological demands of earlier cultures did not require a long apprenticeship, there was no need for adolescence, the argument goes.

But this does not make adolescence a purely cultural invention. Although many less technologically advanced cultures had (and continue to have) coming-of-age rituals, rarely do the newly anointed adults take on real grown-up roles. They may partake more fully in adult life, but usually as apprentices, and they are rarely expected to take on the full responsibilities of adulthood. Adolescence describes a period of time associated with the transition from childhood to adulthood. Some of that transition is based on biologically governed mechanisms associated with attaining adult size and reproductive capacity. Cultures can confer adult status on their members at different times in development, depending on the tasks that are involved and the economic and social needs of the group.

Our own culture is conflicted about when to confer adult status on its offspring. On the one hand, the rates of sexual activity (and associated rates of sexually transmitted diseases) are quite high in the United States, a reflection of the grown-up roles we permit (or reluctantly tolerate) our adolescents to take. On the other hand, we encourage the most talented of our young to continue their education, effectively prolonging their adolescence well into their prime reproductive years. It's not easy being an adolescent in a post-industrial 21st century society, or, sometimes, even knowing if you are one.

Not all anthropologists agree that childhood and adolescence are unique to humans. For instance, even Bogin acknowledges that chimpanzees continue to nurse (although less often) after the eruption of their first permanent molar at about 3 years of age and spend the next 12 to 18 months learning how to find and process food (such as termite fishing or opening fruits with hard shells). These young chimps stay in close proximity to their mothers and learn, through observation and maybe even some deliberate teaching by their mothers, how to crack nuts or fish for termites. (For what it's worth, young females are more attentive to their mothers during tasks such as termite fishing, and, as adults, are more likely to use tools to get and process food than males.[19]) Much like human preschoolers, these 4- and 5-year-old chimpanzees would not survive if left to their own devices.

With respect to adolescence, chimpanzees and bonobos also show a period of low fertility following menarche, and other mammals have a period that could be described either as adolescence or as young adulthood, such as bachelor groups of gorillas or lions, who are not yet able to compete with older, stronger males for access to a harem of females. But if adolescence is not unique to humans, no other species displays quite the same pattern of physical changes as humans do. And recent findings from neuroscience indicate that adolescent brains really are different from the brains of children and those of adults. Neural tissue is significantly reorganized during adolescence, making the emotional and sometimes seemingly irrational behavior of teenagers understandable (if not easily tolerated).[20] (See discussion on adolescent brain development in Chapter 3.) To my knowledge, no other species shows signs of such brain reorganization in the years preceding adulthood, giving a special status to the stage of adolescence in *Homo sapiens.*

Whether one views the course of human development simply as an exaggeration of the basic primate pattern or as qualitatively different with the invention of new stages, the bottom line is the same. Human development takes a long time. The extended period of dependency and parental support affords the opportunity for extensive learning in preparation for adulthood, but also the risk of death before ever attaining reproductive maturity. This pattern surely brought with it new selection pressures (and of course was likely shaped by some of these same selection pressures) and influenced the body, behavior, and mind of human children and the adults they would become.

Becoming Adults: Are We Getting There Faster than Before?

It is not just our imaginations, but girls are reaching puberty earlier than in the past. The explanation for this must be examined at two levels – one looking at historical trends over the past two centuries, and the other looking at changes over the past decade or so. Taking the longer-term view, data on the age at which girls experience their first menstrual period (menarche) have been collected in parts of Europe going back to the 1830s. Although one has to be cautious in interpreting some of these older data sets, the trend is clear. The average age of menarche has been declining in Europe and the United States over the past 150 years, from between 14 to 16 years in the 19th century, to between 12 and 13 years in 1960.[21] There has been little or no change in age of menarche in the last 50 years. Worldwide today, the average age of menarche is between 12.5 and 13.5 years (about 12.5 years in the US).

Menarche is not the only (or even most important) sign of puberty, but it is the most reliable one. It is a specific event, the date of which many women can recall with precision years later. Other aspects of puberty occur earlier or later than menarche, they just aren't as easy to measure. For example, regular ovulatory cycles typically begin several years *after* menarche, accounting for the period of infertility following a girl's first menstrual period. Other aspects of puberty begin earlier, such as breast development (the beginning stages as early as 8 years), presence of pubic hair (11 years), and the adolescent growth spurt (9.5 years). These various indicators of sexual maturity are usually related to one another and reflect hormonal changes in a girl's body. From the data we have available, all of these indicators of puberty appear to be happening earlier than in decades past, not just menarche. The onset of puberty has significance because it signals, to the girl and to others, the advent of adulthood (or at least adolescence) with its accompanying behaviors and responsibilities. Girls who reach menarche early, on average, begin sexual activity earlier, which, of course, can lead to parenthood.

What's the reason for this decline over the past 150 years? The most obvious explanation is diet. Nutrition (at least in terms of number of calories consumed) has improved considerably over this time, and menarche is associated with the amount of body fat a girl has. This interpretation is supported by differences in the age of menarche in different cultures. For example, menarche for girls in some traditional groups in New Guinea where nutrition is poor is not until as late as 17 years. Earlier in the 20th century, in various countries around the world, menarche was achieved earlier for girls in urban, and presumably better fed, areas than for girls living in rural areas. And we know that obesity is related to earlier age of puberty onset in contemporary girls, which is a direct reflection of caloric intake.

But what about the more contemporary problem of girls becoming "mature" while still in elementary school? Is it merely a reflection of this more general historical trend I just described that we're just beginning to pay attention to, or is it something else with its own specific causes? In a 1997 study assessing over 17,000 girls between the ages of 3 and 12 years in the United States, Marcia Herman-Giddens and her colleagues reported that the age of onset of breast development and pubic hair has been decreasing in both White and African-American girls over the past 45 years. There has been little or no change in age of menarche, however. Although these average ages remain within the normal range (for example, beginning of breast development, 8.87 years for African-American girls, 9.96 years for White girls), many girls are showing signs of puberty very early. For instance, 3% of African-American girls and 1% of White girls showed signs of breast development by 3 years of age.

What is responsible for these changes? There have been a number of candidates suggested, obesity being tops on the list. As I mentioned earlier in explaining the long-term historical trend, girls who are overweight experience menarche sooner than other girls, and diet may also be associated with these others indicants of puberty. Environmental contaminants have also been identified as contributing to early puberty. Exposure to arsenic, polybrominated biphenyls (a fire retardant), insecticides, passive tobacco smoke, and chemicals used in common plastics have all been shown to be associated with onset of puberty. Exposure to estrogen-related hormones/chemicals has also been indicated. For example, certain shampoos and hair products contain estrogen, and this may be related to early pubertal onset. Exposure to sexually explicit contexts, either in "real life" or on television, has been hypothesized to be related to sexual development in girls. More general psychological factors have also been found to be related to age of menarche. Father absence, economic and social stress, and maternal depression are all associated with earlier onset of menarche and the subsequent beginning of sexual activity.[22]

Over the past two centuries, life has gotten easier for most people, at least in the Western world. Better diets and a more sedentary lifestyle have produced heavier children, which in turn has resulted in earlier age of menarche. Our contemporary society is contributing even more to this trend, with excess calories, environmental pollutants, chemicals and hormones in oft-used consumer products, and family stress, all factors associated with earlier age of sexual development in girls.

What is ironic is that attainment of some "adult" characteristics is occurring sooner in life, while attainment of true adulthood is being postponed. The demands of modern society require more extensive education and a functional extension of adolescence. Children who grow up too fast, in a society where formal education matters, are at a disadvantage. Being sexually active early may have made good Darwinian sense for our ancestors who lived in stressful, unpredictable worlds, and may even make sense in this "survival of the fittest" way today for some people. We view success as more than the number of children one has, however, but in the quality of the life one lives. Many girls are not only being robbed of their childhoods by precocious puberty, but, in some cases, of the quality of their adult lives and the lives of *their* children.

Childhood and Adolescence in Humans' Ancestors

What about our ancestors? If chimpanzees do not have full-blown childhoods or adolescence, when did these stages evolve? We can't know for sure, of course, but fossil evidence can give us some clues. First, based on skeletal and dental evidence, our hominid ancestors grew up faster than present-day humans do. For instance, the eruption of the first permanent molar in humans occurs at about 6.2 years. This developmental milestone occurs at 3.1 years in chimpanzees and is estimated to have been the same in *Australopithecus afarensis*, the species of which Lucy and her kind were members. *Homo habilis* children grew only a little more slowly than did Lucy, with their first permanent teeth erupting at about 3.8 years of age. By late *H. erectus*, children could chew on meatier stuff by about 5 years of age, about midway between the age of first permanent teeth for modern chimpanzees and humans.[23] Based on this and other fossil evidence, Bogin suggests that australopithecines, like chimpanzees, had no real period of childhood or adolescence. A brief period of childhood is first seen in *H. habilis*, increasing in length in *H. erectus*; and Bogin sees no evidence of adolescence except in *H. sapiens* and perhaps in Neanderthals (although other scientists aren't ready to rule out the possibility of an adolescent growth spurt in *H. erectus* and related species).[24]

But even Neanderthals, the *Homo* species that were most like modern humans, at least in brain size (in fact, Neanderthals had slightly larger brains – and bodies – than *H. sapiens*), presumably reached adulthood faster than we do (or did in the past). How can we know this? One way is to look at the relation between dental and bone development. For example, based on dental development, a well-preserved skeleton of a Neanderthal infant was believed to be about 2 years old when it died. Yet its skull size was equal to that of a 6-year-old child. This, and other fossil evidence, suggests that Neanderthals' brains, though larger than those of *H. sapiens*, reached their adult size considerably faster.[25] Archeologist and evolutionary theorist Steven Mithen has argued it's not just brain size that matters, but brain organization, and that it takes time, namely a prolonged childhood, to develop what Mithen refers to as *cognitive fluidity*, the ability of the mind to communicate with different parts of itself and bring to bear the mental prowess to solve novel problems. Based on the fossil evidence, it is only *H. sapiens* that has both a brain big enough and a period of youth long enough to produce cognitive fluidity.[26]

My description of human evolution and development suggests that there has been a lot of change over the past six to eight million years, when we last shared a common ancestor with chimpanzees. But recall that the absolute difference in DNA between chimps and contemporary humans is quite small – just over 1% by some assessments. How can so little DNA account for so enormous a difference? How can the body and mind of an ape be so different from those of a human when there's so little difference at the genetic level? The answer is: It's all a matter of timing.

Timing is Everything

Only a small percentage of DNA actually "builds" things. Most DNA in the genome is inactive throughout the life of an organism. Some genes, however, regulate development, turning other genes on and off, in this way playing a vital role both in *ontogeny* (the development of the individual) and in *phylogeny* (the evolution of the species).

Different parts of the body develop at different rates. Our sensory systems, for example, mature long before our intellectual capabilities do. Six-year-olds see and hear just fine, thank you, but don't expect them to drive a car, write the great American novel, or complete an IRS tax form. Rates of development can be accelerated or slowed down relative to how our ancestors developed, and such differences can have profound effects. Genetic-based differences in developmental timing are referred to as *heterochrony*. Of particular relevance for both human development and evolution is the type of heterochrony known as *neoteny*. Neoteny (literally "holding youth") refers to the slowing down, or retardation, of development, or, more specifically, to the retention into adulthood of ancestral embryonic or youthful stages.[vi] In other words, features associated with infancy or the juvenile period of an ancestor are now found to characterize adults of a species; an animal never "grows out" of what was a juvenile stage for an ancestor.

One of the earliest examples of the role that timing can play in the development of a species was for the salamander species axolotl.[27] As with salamanders in general, they start life in the water as tadpoles and then metamorphose into air-breathing, land-dwelling newts. But under certain conditions, when life in the water is good and looks to stay that way for a while, the tadpoles will mature sexually and repro-

---

[vi] Contemporary theorists have classified differences in heterochrony as either retarding development relative to an ancestor, termed *paedomorphosis*, or accelerating development, termed *peramorphosis*. Following McKinney and McNamara (1991), the three types of paedomorphosis, or retardation, are: (1) progenesis, or earlier onset of some aspect of development; (2) neoteny, or reduced rate of development; and (3) post-displacement, or delayed onset of development. For ease of reading, I do not differentiate between these three types of paedomorphosis here, often using the term neoteny to refer to retardation of development in general. The three forms of peramorphosis, or acceleration, are (1) hypermorphosis, or delayed offset of development; (2) acceleration, or increased rate of development; and (3) pre-displacement, or earlier onset of growth.

duce, still in the larval state. Some of the offspring may then go through the "normal" developmental sequence, from tadpoles to salamanders, while their parents remain larvae (albeit sexually active larvae). (This reminds me of the comments I've heard on several occasions from young children who are disgruntled with a decision made by their parent: "Just wait 'til I grow up and I'm *your* mommy!") Here, one system (organs of sexual reproduction) matures at a "normal" rate, but other systems (physical development in general) remain at juvenile stages. In this case, neoteny (retaining the juvenile larval stage) is an option an animal can take under certain environmental conditions. In other situations, it may serve as a way of changing important characteristics of a species, being an engine for evolution.

In the early years of the 20th century, evolutionary biologists such as Britain's Gavin de Beer and Walter Garstang, and the Netherlands' Louis Bolk proposed that the driving force of evolution is the change in the timing of ontogeny.[28] Of the early heterochrony theorists, Bolk was the one most concerned about human evolution (and the most extreme). Bolk saw as the primary difference between humans and apes the fetal character of the human body, believing that neoteny (or, using his term, *fetalization*) was the essence of humankind. People are apes who, bodily, have never grown up. According to Bolk: "There is no mammal that grows as slowly as man, and not one in which the full development is attained at such a long interval after birth...What is the essential in Man as an organism? The obvious answer is: The slow progress of his life's course."[29] The quote opening this chapter from Bolk presents his thesis in perhaps its most extreme form, suggesting that humans are essentially primate fetuses that have become sexually mature. (Although this is not quite as extreme as the axolotl larva becoming sexually mature, it may be a bit more disturbing for some of us *Homo sapiens* to imagine.)

Although few biologists today would likely go out on the same limb that Bolk set himself, many contemporary evolutionary biologists concur in principle, believing that the retarded rate of human development is responsible for our unique morphological form and behavioral characteristics.[30] Evolution has a lot in common with comedy – it all depends on timing. Take my DNA, please.

Changes in the pace of development should not be thought of as the *cause* of human (or any species') evolution, but rather as a description of how changes in development can contribute to changes in evolution. By retarding growth, other avenues, lost to faster-developing organisms, can be explored. Retarded development *permits* evolutionary innovations rather than causing them. The pressures for changing the pace of development can be found in the environment, with changes in the rate of development being a response to some of those pressures.

The viewpoint that differences in developmental timing play an important role in evolution was in reaction to an earlier long-held dogma of evolutionary theory that new species arise by the addition of features to the end-states of ancestral forms. So a recent species, such as humans, would be different from our chimp-like ancestor in terms of what we *added* to the fully formed ancestor. We are *more* than our ancestors. According to this theory, evolutionary changes are not associated with modifications early in development, only later in development (so called *terminal additions*). This was the central tenet of the *biogenetic law* as postulated by the German biologist Ernst Haeckel in the latter part of the 19th century.[31] The theory can be summarized in three words, which I learned in 10th grade biology class and have not been able to forget: "ontogeny recapitulates phylogeny." In plain English, this means that the development of the individual (ontogeny) goes through, or repeats, the same sequences as the evolution of the species (phylogeny). Evidence of these ancestral stages is most clearly seen during prenatal development. Or, as embryology goes, so went evolution. According to this theory, a thorough knowledge of embryology should provide the scientist with all he or she needs to know about the history of a species. The entire evolutionary past of a species can be discerned by looking (primarily) at embryological development, which is just a much speeded-up version of evolutionary history. What is new in evolution is what is added to the end-states of development.[vii]

[vii] I know that even well-developed embryos hardly seem like the end-state for an animal. But the point is that the basic body plan of an animal is formed during embryological development, and evolutionary changes were mostly additions to the end-state of ancestral embryos. Embryos wouldn't necessarily be a species' starting (or end) point for intellectual development, however, within a recapitulatory scheme. For example, some have speculated that stages of cognitive development have been added to the highest levels attained by earlier primates. Both monkeys and chimpanzees display the same level of cognitive development early in life, but, in the course of evolution, chimpanzees added a more advanced level of intellectual abilities relative to monkeys. Humans, in turn, added an even more advanced level (or two) of cognitive accomplishments to the basic structure possessed by chimpanzees, and presumably our common ancestor; see Parker & McKinney, 1999.

The biogenetic law, or *recapitulation theory*, was attractive, for one thing because it simplified the study of evolution. Examining old bones or the behavior of extant animals to get clues of ancient ancestors may be a nice pastime, but it eventually would be unnecessary. Seemingly, all that is needed to understand evolution is a detailed knowledge of embryological development.

Such a viewpoint also causes us humans to look at our genetic relatives a bit differently. From the perspective of the biogenetic law, what is unique about *Homo sapiens* is what we possess beyond the apes, not an unreasonable supposition. Clearly, we have added a larger brain, an upright stance, language, and a sense of morality to the basic anthropoid dispositions. We are *more* than apes in every way.

There were always problems with the biogenetic law – many exceptions that did not fit the rule. For example, the order in which a feature appeared in evolution did not always follow the same path in development. The development of teeth and tongues provides a good example. Teeth are an earlier evolutionary invention than tongues, but they appear later in the embryological development of present-day mammals than tongues.[32] By the mid-1920s, it was becoming clear that there were just too many exceptions. Although no one doubted that many evolutionary innovations were added to the end-states of an ancestor, there were many other paths that were also taken, some involving the retardation of certain aspects of development. In fact, neoteny seems to be a good strategy for evolutionary innovation, permitting, in the words of Robert Wesson, "a new beginning and relatively rapid change as the organism backs up evolutionarily to get a better start."[33] In a similar fashion, the paleontologist and evolutionary theorist Stephen Jay Gould wrote that

> the early stages of ontogeny are a storehouse of potential adaptations, for they contain countless shapes and structures that are lost through later [development]…When development is retarded, a mechanism is provided (via retention of fetal growth rates and proportions) for bringing these features forward to later ontogenetic stages.[34]

Using the chimpanzee as a model for what our distant ancestors may have been like, we find many features in *adult* humans that resemble those of *infant* chimps. For example, at birth, both humans and apes (and many other species) have large, rounded heads relative to the size of their bodies, with adult-sized eyes, round cheeks, a flat

nose, short arms, and relatively little hair.[viii] These infantile characteristics are endearing to adults; those helpless babies who keep adults
awake all night are so "cute," it's hard not to love them – a very adaptive characteristic, indeed. The grandfather of modern attachment
theory, John Bowlby, proposed that the immature features of human
infants promote caregiving by parents (and other adults). His arguments followed those of the Nobel Prize winning ethologist Konrad
Lorenz, who proposed that caretaking behaviors in many animals are
triggered by infants' immature features. These features are found not
only in infants, but also loveable cartoon characters (Mickey Mouse),
dolls (Cabbage Patch Kids), make-believe movie creatures (E.T.), and
the faces of many breeds of dog that have been deliberately bred to
display such features. In fact, sickly infants who are less likely to have
the full suite of infantile facial features, as well as infants with facial
malformations, are more likely to be victims of abuse sometime during
childhood.[35] These children are also slower to develop and their sickly
state may make interacting with them more stressful, so a lack of
infantile facial features may not be the only factor involved in their
abuse. But it does seem to contribute to how adults feel and behave
toward their babies.

Humans and apes actually look very much alike in infancy. We
maintain our youthful countenance more so than apes, with men
showing more "apelike" change than women. For example, men are
generally hairier than women, with more protruding jaws and pro-
nounced brow ridges. Science fiction writers and UFOlogists seem to
be aware of this evolutionary trend, typically describing futuristic
humans and visiting space aliens as short, hairless creatures with large
heads and big eyes. The implicit assumption here is that if human
evolution continued (or if evolution occurred elsewhere in the uni-
verse to produce a more intellectually advanced creature), the result
would be an even *more* infantile-looking adult. In fact, the prominent
British biologist J. B. S. Haldane, reflecting on the future course of
human evolution, wrote:

> If human evolution is to continue along the same lines as in the past,
> it will probably involve a still greater prolongation of childhood and

[viii] Facial differences between apes and humans may not have been attained
via literal retardation/neoteny, but via other means. Nonetheless, regardless
of the specific mechanisms, human adults look more like their infants than
is true for great apes, and this maintenance of infantile characteristics may
have had important consequences for human evolution.

retardation of maturity. Some of the characters distinguishing adult man will be lost. It was not an embryologist or palaeontologist who said, "Except ye...become as little children, ye shall not enter the kingdom of heaven."[36]

Modern human juveniles also apparently look a lot like the juveniles of our *Homo erectus* ancestors. Paleoanthropologists Susan Antón and Steve Leigh[37] examined the skulls of fossil *H. erectus* of different ages and saw great similarity between the skulls of *erectus* and *sapiens* juveniles. But the skulls of *H. erectus* went through much more change from the juvenile period to adulthood than do the skulls of *H. sapiens.* In fact, the shape of the cranium of modern humans is much like that of juvenile *H. erectus.* Antón and Leigh suggest that neoteny may be in play here. Over the course of hominid evolution, the juvenile shape of the skull was retained, while the actual size of the skull (and presumably the brain inside it) got larger.

There are many neotenous physical features that may have had a significant impact on the evolution of our species. For example, the angle at which our spines connect with our skulls is such that we can stand and walk upright on our legs (bipedality). Our skull sits on our backbone so that we're looking forward when we're standing up. This isn't the case for most other adult mammals. Rather, the spine enters the skull so that the animal is looking forward when it's on all fours. To get an appreciation of this difference, think of how you have to strain your neck to look straight ahead when you're on all fours, playing horsie with a child. But this is the difference between humans and other mammals, including chimpanzees, *as adults.* In contrast, the orientation of the spine to the skull in *embryonic* chimps and humans is the same. In both cases (and for other mammals as well), the spine enters the skull as it does for embryonic (and adult) humans. What happens is that in other mammals, the orientation shifts during prenatal development, while in humans, the embryonic orientation is retained – an adaptation that resulted in bipedality in our hominid forebears over six million years ago – the first major step in the development of *Homo sapiens.*[38] (You may not think of chimpanzees as being quadrupeds, like dogs and horses, but their primary mode of locomotion when on the ground is knuckle walking, using the knuckles of their hands to support their upper bodies.)

Another neotenous characteristic of humans is the orientation of the vagina. In chimpanzees as well as humans, the prenatal position of the vagina slopes toward the front of the body. In chimps, the slope of the vagina moves backward over prenatal development. As a result, copulation in chimpanzees is done from the rear. In humans, the position of the vagina does not change over the course of development, but retains its forward-sloping position from the embryonic period. This means that copulation can be done face to face. Such face-to-face lovemaking may have helped in the formation of pair bonds, with both the male and female working together to help raise their offspring. This is particularly important because human children are dependent upon their parents for so many years, making the establishment of stable "families" critical.[39]

Although bipedality and family bonds are clearly characteristics central to our definition of "human," perhaps our species' most outstanding trait is that of intelligence. Here, we have clearly developed beyond our evolutionary ancestors rather than having our development retarded to some earlier embryonic or infantile state. Because our survival depends so much upon learning, our brains must be larger in proportion to our bodies than for other species. When looking at mammals as a group, human brains are far larger than would be expected given their body size. In fact, as I mentioned previously, we are the brainiest creatures ever to grace this Earth, not in terms of absolute size, but in terms of brain size for body weight. This increased brain size in humans is selective, with some areas of the brain having evolved at a faster pace than others, most notably the neocortex, the area of the brain most centrally involved in higher cognitive activities.[40]

But what role could developmental retardation have played in our expanded brain development? The human brain grows beyond that of our ancestors; it is not retarded at some juvenile or embryonic phase. The answer, again, is timing. In all primates, stem neurons divide a certain number of times, producing all the neurons that an animal will have (or just about). This process stops, usually sometime late in prenatal development. Unlike other types of cells, neurons in most areas of the brain are not created after birth. The easiest way to create a bigger brain is to delay the offset of *neurogenesis* (the creation of new neurons). That is, instead of going through four or five cell divisions before ending neuron generation, extend the number of cell duplications by one or two. Each cell division essentially results in a doubling of the number of neurons. Many of these neurons will die. (In fact, neuronal death seems to be programmed into the brain, and if there is not a pruning of excessive neurons early in development, mental retardation can result.) This is what apparently happened repeatedly over the course of primate evolution, including in our *Homo* ancestors.[41]

Generating neurons is only part of what it takes to build a brain. Neurons must move, or migrate, to the area of the brain they "belong to," and, once in position, grow and make connections with other neurons. Such processes are found in all mammal brains and are especially rapid during prenatal development for all primates, including humans. The fetal brain develops rapidly in comparison to the rest of the body. Brain growth slows down quickly after birth for chimpanzees, macaque monkeys, and other primates, but not for humans. We continue the pace of brain development begun prenatally through our second year of postnatal life. By 6 months the human brain weighs 50% of what it will in adulthood; at 2 years about 75%; at 5 years, 90%; and at 10 years, 95%. In contrast, total body weight is about 20% of eventual adult weight at 2 years and only 50% at 10 years. So the brain, which grows rapidly before birth, continues its rapid development after birth. Thus, even when we develop "more brain" than other primates, we do it by retaining embryonic growth rates months after birth.[42]

If you think about it, it might seem that there would be an easier way to produce a bigger brain than to extend the rapid pace of brain development into infancy. Why not just build a bigger brain before birth and maintain the basic primate growth rate? The answer is that women are not built to carry babies with such large brains. If a species is going to have a big brain, it will also, of course, have a big skull. But the skull that houses a 2-year-old human brain is far too large to pass through a woman's birth canal. The evolutionary pressures that produced an enlarged brain required that the period of pregnancy be relatively short. If humans were as well developed bodily at birth as their simian cousins, their heads would never fit through the birth canal. There seemed to be two evolutionary options for dealing with bigheaded babies: (1) create wider hips for women, something that would make walking upright almost impossible (remember that bipedality evolved *before* big brains), or (2) premature birth.

We don't know if evolution experimented with wider-hipped women; but if it did, they and their progeny didn't survive. What did work was premature birth. It has been estimated that if human gestation followed the same time scale as the rest of human physical development, and infants were born with the same degree of neurological maturity as our ape relatives, pregnancy would last for 21 months.[43] Instead, human pregnancy lasts only 9 months and babies are physically immature. At birth they may be motorically and perceptually far behind the sophistication of other primate infants, but they have a brain that will continue to grow and eventually be capable of great things, including language and symbolic thought.

The necessity of giving birth to immature and slow-developing babies must have made things complicated for mothers. Not only must women carry their babies in their wombs for 9 months, they are solely responsible for their infants' nutrition and care for years ahead. Wenda Trevathan speculated that because of the prolonged immaturity of human infants, mothers of newborns required more social support than mothers of other mammal species. Some of that support may have come from the father, but other support from female relatives and "friends." In other words, "premature" birth and an extended period of offspring dependency co-evolved with increased sociality in hominid evolution.[44]

I don't want to give the impression that neoteny, or developmental retardation, was the sole, or even primary, mechanism in human evolution. Clearly, our cognition and the brain that underlies it are more advanced than those of chimpanzees, our common ancestor, and our *Homo* forebears. These are usually viewed as additions to or accelerations of development patterns and not as cases in which a retardation of development or retention of ancestral forms influenced evolution.[45] Nonetheless, the idea that all of evolution is a matter of acceleration and gain relative to our ancestors is a common one, and one that, taken alone, misrepresents human evolution. My principal point here is to demonstrate that (a) changes in the timing of development can have a substantial impact on evolution, and (b) that sometimes slowing down can be as consequential as speeding up, particularly in human evolution.

The Youngest Species

Homo sapiens is a young species. Although our ancient predecessors failed to leave us a time capsule to verify all the facts and dates, the earliest of our kind (*Archaic Homo sapiens*) appeared about 300,000 years ago, presumably evolving from *Homo erectus*, who had been around for nearly two million years. It wasn't until about 160,000 years ago, however, that evidence of fully modern people is found, and we didn't seem to make much of an impression (in terms of art and technology, anyway) until about 40,000 thousand years ago. So, in the big picture of things, we're babes in the biological woods. We're not literally the youngest species. There are species of fish, for example, that seem to date back only about 10,000 years, and if bioengineering is considered, there are species of bacteria that are very modern, indeed.

But humans are young in other ways. First, we are neotenous, in that we retain many juvenile characteristics that our evolutionary ancestors grew out of. Other species have done this, too, for differences in timing in individual development (heterochrony) is a much-used technique in evolution's bag of tricks. Neoteny fosters innovation, permitting nature to go back to an earlier phase and try something new. In our case, some of the innovations were walking upright, opportunities for face-to-face copulation, and a large brain for dealing with an increasingly complicated social world. Students of human evolution, such as Louis Bolk and Ashley Montagu,[46] listed a number of additional physical and functional human features that may have been the product of neoteny. These include the shape of the head and face, late eruption of teeth, the size and orientation of the pelvis, a delicate (or gracile) skeleton, and a nonopposable big toe, among others.

Humans are young in a second way. We are slow to grow up, and this has consequences for us today – not just for how we became the species we are, but for the men and women our children will grow up to be. Most critically, our slow-developing brains and extended childhoods give us the time to learn the complexities of human culture. This has important implications for how we live as a species and is the topic of the next chapter.

3

The Slow Rate of Growing Up

The long period of childhood is not just a time of fragile immaturity and vulnerability, not just a phase of development to be got through before the real show of humanity emerges on stage. It is the time when the human brain can set to work on language, on taste, on poetry and music, with centers at its disposal that may not be available later in life. If we did not have childhood, and were able somehow to jump catlike from infancy to adulthood, I doubt very much that we would turn out human.

Lewis Thomas, *The Fragile Species*

"I can't *wait* until I grow up! I'm so tired of being told what I can and can't do!" This was said by Brittany, a precocious 11-year-old, seemingly exhausted by the long trek to adulthood and independence. Such protestations are common among children and adolescents, and most parents can identify with them, for they were young once too. But parents realize, as this child will in the years to come (and she may actually now), that 11 years is far too young to be on your own. It takes a long time to reach adulthood, and this is not merely a reflection of modern society, but a characteristic of our species in general and one that contributed mightily to who we are as human beings.

We humans take many years before we reach reproductive maturity. Primates in general are slow to develop, with humans being the slowest, spending a greater proportion of our lives in childhood than any other mammal. The closer is the common ancestor with *Homo sapiens*, the longer is the period of immaturity: in lemurs approximately 2 years, in macaques approximately 4, in chimps approximately 8, and in humans approximately 15 years. And 15 years is, of course, not the typical age of first childbirth. Few 15-year-olds around the world get pregnant and give birth, and this was likely true for our ancestors as well. For example, the average age of first childbirth in traditional human groups is about 19 years. We humans may be capable of having children in our mid-teens, but it's likely that the average age of first childbirth was closer to 20 years in our ancestors.[1]

In this chapter I examine the generally slow rate at which humans develop and its consequences both in our species' history and today. I begin by looking at the risk that delayed development presented our ancestors. Having babies with heads that can just barely squeeze out of their mothers' birth canals and waiting nearly two decades before they are ready to reproduce themselves would seem to present some significant risks for survival – of mothers, babies, and the species. With such risks come great benefits, however, and the large and slow-developing brain that makes birth so difficult in humans also provides it with substantial advantages. I then look at three interacting factors that I believe are at the core of human intellectual evolution: big brains, social complexity, and slow development. This confluence of factors has resulted in a highly social species, centered around family, with individuals who are able to modify their behavior in response to the varied social and physical environments in which they find themselves. This latter characteristic, brain and cognitive *plasticity*, is perhaps our species' greatest claim to fame and is made possible by our slow rate of neural development.

The Gamble of Delayed Development

We in modern culture typically view 15 years old as too young to be having children. There is much justified concern about "children having children." Teenagers have their whole lives ahead of them, and burdening themselves with dependent offspring before they themselves are truly independent is not usually viewed as a wise or adaptive decision. In today's technological world, this is true. Modern women can expect to survive childbirth, and both men and women, once they reach their teen years, can anticipate another 60 years plus on this planet. This was not true, however, for our ancestors. Even today, the life expectancy of men and women in many third-world countries barely reaches 40 years (and actually doesn't reach this modest level for men in some of the most impoverished nations). In the United States, life expectancy as little as 150 years ago was only 38 years for white men and 40 years for white women.[i] Longevity is a modern phenomenon. The three score and ten years promised in the Bible forecasts a rosy future, not the typical life expectancy an ancient could realistically expect.

The 15- to 20-year wait that our hominid and hunter-gatherer forebears had before reaching reproductive maturity must have come at a great expense. Many must have died of disease or fallen prey to predators before ever having a chance to pass their DNA on to the next generation, and, given the risks of childbirth, many females must have died giving birth to their children, leaving the infants motherless and dependent upon the kindness of strangers. The greater longevity of women over men that is near universal today and is generally attributed to the heartier constitution of the "fairer sex" (associated with the higher metabolic costs of greater muscle mass in males) may not be new to the 21st century, but it wasn't always the case. It was not until the late Middle Ages, the 13th or 14th century, that women in Europe began to outlive men. Death during childbirth was common. Even in colonial America, it was estimated that 20% of the deaths of adult females was associated with childbirth, with one in 30 births resulting in the death of the mother.[2] The rates were surely higher for our large-brain predecessors, dating back at least 2 million years to *Homo erectus*, and possibly 2.5 million years to *Homo habilis*.

When looked upon in hindsight, our delayed maturation was quite a gamble. In fact, paleoanthropologists suggest that humans were close to extinction 100,000 to 200,000 years ago, with as few as 10,000 adults living worldwide.[3] How much this population bottleneck was due to too many women dying before ever giving birth is unknown, but it doesn't take a PhD in evolutionary biology to know that the longer one waits to reproduce the greater are one's chances of dying childless. And if this scenario characterizes an entire species, the possibility of extinction must have constantly loomed over the horizon. But, obviously, this was a gamble that paid off. There are six billion us alive on this planet right now, and we have achieved what some biologists refer to as "ecological dominance." We're the kings and queens of this hill, threatened by no other predator other than ourselves (if you discount the viruses that occasionally turn into pandemics).

[i] These figures may be a bit misleading, because infant mortality was particularly high in centuries past. For example, once a person reached the age of 15 in pre-industrial Europe, he or she could expect to live to age 55. See Geary, 2002a.

Evolutionary theorists propose that when there is great cost to some biological adaptation, such as delaying age of maturation, there should also be great benefit. Natural selection would not favor the development of a high-cost/low-payoff strategy. It may evolve, but the bearer of such adaptations would soon go extinct. So what were the compensatory advantages to humans of delayed maturation and a generally extended immature state?

At one level, the advantages of extended immaturity are obvious. Humans, more than any other species, depend on learning and behavioral flexibility for their success. The complexities of human societies are enormous and highly variable, and it takes an extended childhood to acquire all that must be learned to succeed. Because brain growth continues well into adolescence, connections among neurons are created and modified long after they have become fixed in other species. The result is a more "flexible" brain (in terms of what neural connections can be made), which means more flexible thinking and behavior – good characteristics for a slow, fangless, and not-too-strong land mammal to have. Additionally, an extended youth provides the opportunity to practice complex adult roles, which, because of their cultural variability, cannot be hard-wired into the brain.

There is some cross-species evidence that building big brains takes time. Although humans are the brainiest and slowest developing of all primates, we reflect only the extreme of what can be seen as a general tendency in primate evolution. Figure 3.1 shows the relation between brain size and the length of the juvenile period for seven different primates, including humans. As you can see, overall brain size is closely related to length of the juvenile period, with humans having both the largest brains and longest pre-reproductive period of any primate.[4]

Big Brains, Social Complexity, and Slow Development

Theorizing about the factors responsible for the evolution of human intelligence has a long history, and many candidates have been suggested, including tool use, hunting, food gathering, and climate change. Let me make it clear that there is no single cause for human evolution. Multiple factors acting synergistically surely are responsible for changes in body and mind that occurred within the human line over the last six million years. But one currently popular viewpoint

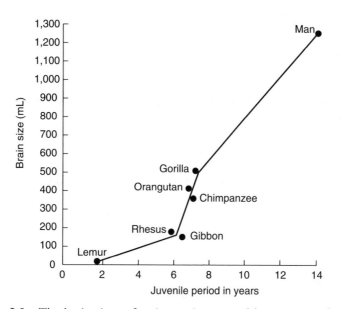

Figure 3.1 The brain sizes of various primates and humans as a function of the length of the juvenile period (from Bonner, 1988). Copyright © 1988 Princeton University Press. Reprinted by permission of Princeton University Press.

puts the spotlight not on factors that helped our ancestors acquire more and better food or avoid being lunch for predators, but on social factors within the human group.[5] According to this perspective, language and intelligence evolved to help individuals understand their social world – to foster cooperation and competition with our fellow humans. Changes from our australopithecine ancestors to *Homo sapiens* were not only in terms of physical characteristics, but also in terms of social sophistication.

Social complexity, in and of itself, is not enough to produce an intelligent species, otherwise ants may be running the world. Rather, I argue it was the confluence of three factors that is responsible for the modern human mind: social complexity, a big brain, and an extended juvenile period.[6] Our ancestors had the beginnings of these three characteristics at least six million years ago. Chimpanzees have the largest brain relative to body size of any land mammal other than humans, have a prolonged juvenile period, and live in socially complex groups, at least relative to other primates. So our common ancestor with chimpanzees surely also had the preconditions necessary for evolving human intelligence. In fact, there is a relationship among these three factors for primates in general. Anthropologist Tracey Joffe compared social complexity, measured in terms of size of the group, the length of the juvenile period, and the size of the neocortex (the "thinking" part of the brain) for 27 different primate species, including humans. Joffe reported a strong relation among these three factors: the larger the social group, the bigger the brain, and the longer the juvenile period tended to be.[7]

One factor (social complexity, for example) should not be viewed as *the* cause of human brain expansion, and by implication human intelligence. There is no simple cause and effect here; the relation among these three factors is synergistic, with changes in one factor being both a cause and a consequence of changes in related factors. But social complexity was a required ingredient in human cognitive evolution. It exerted selection pressure for a bigger brain and a prolonged childhood, which in turn permitted increased levels of social complexity to be attained.

But perhaps I'm overstating my case here. Sure, *modern* society is complex. It takes a long time to learn the skills necessary to become a brain surgeon, an investment banker, or an attorney, and even longer to figure out how to deal effectively with the IRS or the bureaucracies of large businesses and governments (and for men to understand women, and vice versa). But how complex was life one million (or even 100,000) years ago, when protohumans foraged around in small groups, never worrying about the possibility of a tax audit? In fact, how complex is life in contemporary hunter-gatherer societies? Was enhanced intelligence really necessary to be successful for "primitive" humans?

This was essentially the question posed by Alfred Russel Wallace, the co-discoverer with Charles Darwin of the principle of natural selection, when considering the intelligence of "savages." And his answer was "no." He proposed that the recently "discovered" African natives were far more intelligent than the demands of their lifestyle required. They survived by foraging and doing a little hunting, a way of living not too dissimilar from that of chimpanzees who shared the jungles with them. They were smarter than they needed to be. Given the racist views of Victorian England, Wallace was magnanimous when he admitted that the African natives were far more similar in intelligence to cultured Englishmen than they were to apes.

Wallace likely overstated the ease of making a living for early humans and modern hunter-gatherers. Based on the life of modern hunter-gatherers, the work of hunting for our ancestors was left mainly to men and gathering mainly to women. Surely hunting game that was usually faster and stronger than any single man required complex skills: tracking, a knowledge of the habits of these beasts, the making of tools enabling the capture and killing of animals, and substantial cooperation among group members. These all would seem to require a lot of time to learn. The work of gathering would seem to be less taxing, and some of it is. Chimpanzees and small children can easily learn to identify and gather ripe fruit from a tree, and if this were all there was to gathering, a long apprenticeship would not be necessary. But examinations of modern-day gatherers reveal a set of complex abilities that take years to master. Successful gatherers must be able to identify and differentiate scores of edible and poisonous forms of vegetation. They must know how to locate roots and gourds buried in the earth and how best to extract their nutrition. Hillard Kaplan and his colleagues[8] concluded that not only hunting, but gathering, involves a large set of complicated skills, and an extended childhood is necessary for them to be acquired. But even so, these skills do not seem to necessitate the level of intelligence humans possess. Wolves, for example, are successful pack hunters, and although they are undeniably intelligent animals, they pale in comparison to our own species.

Wallace's problem is that he mistook the technological genius that people sometimes display as the true reflection of intelligence. Such genius is rarely displayed in carrying out the everyday chores of life, however, either among stone-age primitives, modern industrial-age folks, or even chimpanzees. For example, psychologist Nicholas Humphrey, one of the first people to articulate the importance of social complexity in the evolution of human intelligence, wrote:

> Someone may retort that if an ethologist had kept watch on Einstein through a pair of field glasses he might well have come to the conclusion that Einstein too had a hum-drum mind. However, that is just the point: Einstein, like the chimpanzee, displayed his genius at rare times in "artificial" situations – he did not use it, for he did not need to use it, in the common world of practical affairs.[9]

The real complexities of human life are social, not technological, and it is in social intelligence that our kind excels. In all cultures, from the high society of Palm Beach, Florida to the hunter-gatherer societies of the San !Kung in the Kalahari Desert, social interactions and relations are complex and the core of human life. In fact, I would argue that what is especially impressive about the food-gathering technology of hunter-gatherers is that it is so easily passed along from one generation to the next, avoiding extinction of a complicated and life-supporting set of skills. The intelligence that is capable of insuring the preservation of these tools and techniques over generations is what we should marvel at. Such intelligence must be social in nature, permitting one individual to understand the perspective of another, enabling the explicit teaching of and veridical transmission of complex skills.

Cooperating and Competing

One consequence of increased social complexity in a group is the need for greater cooperation among members. It increases the likelihood of success in hunting and food gathering, and also in competition with other groups. During the course of evolution, groups of hominids that failed to cooperate could find themselves victims of other, better organized (that is, more cooperative) groups. This, of course, was the beginning of the "us versus them" feelings that persist today in modern humans.

What type of intelligence must develop in order to deal with these new social pressures? One useful intellectual skill is that of deceit. Being able to hide one's true feelings and to act trustworthy and kind when one's real motives are less than friendly is a consummate political skill, and one that likely developed via its success over millions of years of evolution.

The social pressures of cooperating and competing with other members of the group can be seen as a driving force of human intelligence. Humans are more intelligent than necessary to eke out an existence in the rain forests of Africa. Our intelligence developed not so much to meet the demands of a hostile external environment, but to meet the demands of hostile members of our own species. According to anthropologist Richard Alexander,[10] hominids essentially evolved a new hostile force of nature – themselves.

Such social intelligence, however, requires time to develop. Recognizing friends and foes, learning to cooperate and compete in situations that evolution could not anticipate, and learning the social roles and relationships that bind any group of people together, takes time. The complexity and variability of our social relationships far exceeds that of any other species, although serious hints of such complexity are found in other groups of primates. For example, deception has been observed in chimpanzees and baboons. In one observation, E. W. Menzel reported that a chimpanzee, Belle, was shown the source of some hidden food and would lead the other chimps to it. But when she did this when the dominant male, Rock, was present, he would take all the food for himself. Belle soon would wait until Rock left before uncovering the food, and on some occasions led the troop in the opposite direction. While Rock was searching, Belle double-backed and got the food. Jane Goodall reported that male chimps would sometimes suppress their distinctive cry during orgasm when copulating with a favorite female, avoiding having to share the female with other males. And Frans de Waal has documented coalitions among male chimpanzees that serve to grab and maintain social status in chimpanzee troops. So the roots of advanced social intelligence were surely present in our smaller-brained ancestors, making the jump to human social cognition possible.[11]

It could certainly be argued that the brain and the time needed to handle such complexity represented an evolutionary trade-off. Given how complex we are and how long it takes to learn the ways of our social world, it's amazing that we made it this far as a species. If one were making bets on the likely evolutionary success of a creature that eschews fur, tough skin, and strong bones and teeth in exchange for a brain that is almost too large to exit the birth canal and then takes nearly 20 years to reach maturity while learning the socially complex web of relationships that will vary from group to group, the odds, I imagine, would not be in our favor. Yet, we're here, and the complex series of factors responsible for our evolution and our place in the contemporary world is centered around our slow growth, without which we'd still be swinging in the trees. (Despite our hegemony as a species, we may still turn out to be a short-term evolutionary experiment. Fully modern humans date back only 40,000 to 160,000 years, depending on how you define "fully modern." Either way, this is just a blip in evolutionary time, and, in fact, only a fraction of the time that our predecessor *Homo erectus* walked the Earth.)

Family Matters

The second traditional argument for the importance of delayed development centers on the foundation of the human family and social structures. The human infant is totally dependent at birth and will remain dependent upon adults for years to come. Pair-bonding and some division of labor (both within and between family members) may have been a necessary adaptation to the pressures presented by the slow growth of offspring, increasing the likelihood that children would survive to have babies themselves. Because of the luxury of time children have to develop and the presence of (often) two parents to care for most of their immediate needs, human children are able to play and create new behavioral strategies to adapt to novel contexts. This is expressed by animal behaviorist Gordon Burghardt in his *surplus resource theory*, which argues that animals are most apt to play when there is an abundance of resources. For most other animals, this means being well fed and comfortable; this is also true for humans. But the many years before children have to take on adult responsibilities provides them with "temporal affluence," and the presence of parents to protect and nurture them years past weaning can be viewed as another resource not available to other animals.[12]

The immature appearance of human babies may also have played a role in the formation of the hominid family. Recall the discussion in the previous chapter of the infantile features of human infants and the positive feelings they bring out in adults. It is not only the infants' mothers and other women who become enamored with little babies, but also their fathers and other men. Often, in spite of cultural pressures, men think little babies are cute and become attached to them. Such an attachment would help keep the fathers around, looking after their tiny offspring. In fact evolutionary biologist Sarah Hrdy suggested that the father–child bond might have been the basis of the father–mother–child bonds in human families. Noting that male primates are unique in the mammal world in the attention and care they give to infants, perhaps this capacity preadapted "members of this order for the sort of close, long-term relationships between males and females that, under some ecological circumstances, leads to monogamy."[13]

This alone would not likely be enough for the formation of marginally monogamous families (or even small harems, with the male providing the role of provider for his mate and children). Something else must keep the male tied to the family, and increased female sexual receptivity likely played a role here. Unlike most other female mammals (the bonobo being the most obvious exception), human females are potentially sexually receptive nearly all the time, not just during a period of estrus, or "heat." But with the loss of estrus comes the loss of specific signals (such as swelling of the genital areas) to arouse males. Other signals may have evolved that instead attracted males to females on a more regular basis, and those signals may be associated with females' more juvenile, or neotenous, features.

As I mentioned in the previous chapter, adult human females retain more juvenile features than males. They have less and finer body hair, smaller hands and feet, more delicate facial features, and a higher pitched voiced. These are some of the features that men find so attractive in women (the skin-deep part of beauty). Thus, by becoming more childlike in appearance, females increased the strength of their bonds with the father of their children, securing assistance in the raising of their dependent offspring. The forward sloping of the vagina, encouraging face-to-face lovemaking, another neotenous feature, also likely played a role in establishing lasting bonds between males and females.

According to Robert Wesson, the more attracted males became to neotenous features of females the greater the pressure for slow development. "As neoteny progressed, it became still more necessary for the male to support his mate and the young; as the father became more important for the long-helpless young, there was more competition among females to secure and hold helpful mates, that is to make herself attractive, which meant more neotenic."[14] The long period of dependency also meant that the male's genetic success could not be measured just by how many females he inseminated or how many children he sired. His inclusive fitness would depend on how many of his offspring reached sexual maturity, assuring him of becoming a grandfather. To increase the odds of this happening, his help in rearing his children would be needed.

It is not only modern biologists who have considered the family a necessary condition for the success of our species. The theme is found in John Locke's 1689 *Second Treatise of Government*. Locke believed that an extended childhood did much to keep parents together: "[O]ne cannot but admire the wisdom of the great Creator who...hath made it necessary that society of man and wife should be more lasting than that of male and female among other creatures, that so their industry might be encouraged, and their interest better united, to make provision and lay up goods for their common issue."[15]

Slow Growth and Brain Plasticity

Slow growth may have been an evolutionary gamble that paid off over the past two million years or so, but what has it done for us lately? Although our slow rate of growing up (coupled with myriad other factors, of course) may have led to modern *Homo sapiens*, does it have any consequences for us today? Is it something that "got us here," so to speak, and now we just have to learn to live with its inconveniences? Or does it continue to serve an important role in shaping the adults

65

we become? We've seen the role that slow growth may have played in the evolution of the species, but what is the impact of slow growth for the development of the *individual*?

Such effects are many. For example, we still think that human infants are adorable because of their neotenous features, and this certainly doesn't hurt their chances for survival in environments that in many ways are equally as unpredictable and unstable as those our *Homo* ancestors lived in. But perhaps the most important aspect of slow growth for us today is related to the *plasticity*, or modifiability, of the brain and the consequences that has on our behavior.

Plasticity refers to the extent to which something can be changed or modified. The human brain, of course, is the seat of the human mind and the organ that controls our behavior. The degree to which the brain can be modified reflects the degree to which intelligence and behavior can be modified. How plastic, or pliable, is the human brain, and how does slow growth influence that plasticity?[ii]

Neuronal Plasticity

The building block of the brain is the neuron. Neurons are specialized brain cells that are connected to one another, producing an amazingly complex communication system. The adult brain has about 10 billion neurons. Neurons are connected to one another via *synapses*, which are small spaces between cells through which chemical and electrical messages are passed. A single neuron can have as many as 10,000 synapses (up to 100,000 in the prefrontal cortex), producing a system of almost unimaginable complexity (you do the math). The making of new synapses, termed *synaptogenesis*, is rapid during the prenatal period and continues at a frenetic pace in the months after birth. In fact, by the end of the first year, the infant brain has nearly twice as many synapses as the adult brain.[16]

Virtually all the neurons a person has were produced before birth. For most parts of the brain, neuron production ends by the fourth or fifth month after conception. There are some recently discovered

---

[ii] Using the term "plasticity" to refer to children's behavior strikes some people the wrong way, bringing to mind the connotation of "artificial." In fact, a reviewer for a previous book I wrote was much offended that I should refer to children in such a disparaging way. But it is the original meaning of the word, synonymous with "pliable," that is the proper connotation of plasticity, and I mean no disrespect to children or their brains when using the term.

exceptions, however. Neurons in the hippocampus, a part of the brain important in the formation of new memories, have been found to be generated by adults, both in animals and in humans.[17] So with this exception (which might be a very important one), there is essentially no plasticity of neurons, if plasticity is thought of only in terms of making new ones. In fact, newborns actually have considerably more neurons in their heads than adults do. The neurons are much smaller, of course, accounting for the ability of all those brain cells to fit into such a small skull. In this limited sense, newborns are "brainier" than adults. But they lose many of these "extra" neurons (and synapses) over the course of infancy and childhood in a process called *selective cell death*. Many neurons and their synapses die. Some seem programmed to die (a process known as *apoptosis*), but the fate of others is determined, at least in part, by their use. University of Illinois psychologist William Greenough and his colleagues proposed that specific experiences produce neural activity, which in turn determines which of the excess synapses will survive.[18] The brains of animals, including humans, have evolved to "expect" certain experiences. For example, the visual nervous system contains neurons that respond specifically to moving objects. Early experience of merely viewing a normal world, for instance, is sufficient for the visual nervous system to develop properly, resulting in normal vision. The sense organs of the ear and the nervous tissue associated with those organs are responsive to and "expect" a certain range of auditory stimulation. The auditory sense organs and brains of dogs "expect" a different range of sound stimuli, and the eyes and brains of bees "expect" a range of visual stimulation that humans are totally insensitive to. When an animal (a bee, a dog, or a human) gets stimulation in the species-typical range – that is, when it "sees" or "hears" stimuli that its ancestors saw and heard and that all normal members of the species will see and hear – the brain gets hooked up "as expected." These connections are not necessarily "pre-wired," the result of a simple reading-off of DNA; but they are all but inevitable. Evolution has produced a developing brain that is sensitive to certain stimuli that the individual can't help but get (at least in "normal" situations). When the developing brain gets the stimulation it "expects," it develops in a species-typical fashion.

So there's plasticity here, if not in terms of creating new neurons, at least in terms of creating new synapses. But not much, at least at this level. If you raise cats in darkness, for example, neurons in the eyes that are normally responsive to movement, angles, or cues of depth don't respond the way they're "supposed" to.[19] In fact, neurons in the auditory cortex that are surgically rewired to receive visual stimulation fire when shown visual stimuli (at least in ferrets). These animals can see, using neurons that were intended for hearing.[20] This is impressive evidence of neural plasticity, but let's face it, how many infant ferrets (to say nothing of people) are going to have their nervous systems surgically rewired?

But these are only a subset of neurons in the infant brain. Other neurons are not destined to be hooked up in a certain way under "normal" conditions. Rather, whether and how they connect to other neurons depends on the specific experiences they have. In fact, new synapses are being created throughout life. As you read these words your brain is changing. Some of those changes may be in terms of the amount of neurotransmitters (chemicals that influence communication between neurons) you have in the synapses between neurons, the ease with which a certain neuron will fire given a specific signal, or the creation (or destruction) of synapses.

What causes new synapses to form? Experience. Perhaps the most convincing evidence of the effects of experience on brain structures comes from studies providing environmental stimulation for laboratory animals. In studies dating back to the first half of the 20th century, psychologists have raised mice and rats in stimulating, or "enriched," environments and contrasted them with those raised in "deprived" environments. What's enriching for a laboratory rat? Mostly the company of other rats and a variety of objects to interact with, and even problems to solve (such as mazes). And what's considered "deprived" for a lab rat? Being raised alone in an essentially empty cage.

The differences between enriched and deprived rats are seen both in their behavior and in their brains. Enriched rats are better learners on a wide range of tasks, such as mazes, than are deprived rats. And this difference in rat intelligence is reflected in their brains. Enriched animals have bigger brains (usually 5% to 10% bigger), more synapses, and greater concentration of neurotransmitters than deprived animals. These effects are found not only in young animals, where plasticity is expected to be greatest, but also in old animals. Yes, you can teach an old rat new tricks, and change its brain in the process.[21]

Synaptic plasticity does decline with age, but it certainly doesn't disappear. Infants have the most to learn and so it's not surprising that their brains are the most pliable. As children age, some neurons die, and with their deaths synapses that could have been formed are now an impossibility. But human brains take a long time to fully mature, meaning that high levels of plasticity are also maintained. It is this plasticity, afforded by our extended period of neural immaturity, that gives humans the capacity to learn and modify their behavior throughout life, and is also likely to develop our unique ability to think in symbols and represent the world in a way no other animal on Earth can.

Adolescent Brain Development

Conventional wisdom not too long ago held that the brain develops gradually through childhood and is essentially complete by age 12 or 13. By this time, children have the neural machinery they need to think like adults. All they are lacking is the experience required for mature thought. The often-disruptive behavior seen in adolescence was thought to be due less to changes in brain organization than to changes in hormones. But despite the obvious hormonal changes that teenagers experience, specific relations between such changes and behavior were hard to come by. They play a role, clearly, but something else was underlying behavior changes seen in adolescence, and that something else turned out to be brain development.

Research by Jay Giedd of the National Institute of Mental Health and his colleagues led the way with new discoveries about changes in white and gray matter in the teenage brain.[22] Gray matter refers to the bodies of neurons, the brain cells involved in "thinking" and controlling behavior. White matter refers to brain tissue that is mainly involved with transmitting signals from one neuron to another (axons and dendrites). It is white because it is coated in *myelin*, a fatty tissue that insulates axons (the fibers that connect neurons) and speeds the rate at which electrical signals are transmitter from one neuron to the next. Giedd and his team reported that gray matter peaked in different areas of the brain at different times (for example, at 12 years in the frontal lobe, 16 years in the temporal lobe, and through age 20 in the occipital lobe). Some areas then went through extensive pruning, losing about 1% of gray matter each year in adolescence. At the same time, the total volume of white matter increases over adolescence. Some of this increase in white matter reflects increasing connections between different regions of the brain, suggesting changes in neural organization, or how different parts of the brain communicate with one another.

In other research, Beatriz Luna and her colleagues at the University of Pittsburgh reported that adolescents use different parts of their brains when solving certain problems than adults do. For instance, adolescents are more apt to activate portions of their frontal cortices when performing simple laboratory tasks, whereas adults use other parts of their brain, as well as the frontal cortices, when faced with the same tasks. In other research, teenagers were less apt to activate the frontal cortex than adults when processing emotional information, suggesting that they are less able to inhibit their reactions to emotional stimuli. The distribution of neurotransmitters in the brain also changes in adolescence. For example, the excitatory neurotransmitter GABA is reduced in the frontal cortex in adolescence at the same time dopamine increases.[23]

It is difficult to know exactly what to make of all the changes in the adolescent brain. It is obvious now that brain development is not a straight line from childhood to adulthood, but takes a nonlinear (some may say torturous) path through the teen years. Scientists cannot yet connect specific brain changes to specific behavioral changes, but they are confident stating that teenagers' brains are not like adults', nor like children's. This has important implications for how we view adolescent behavior and for holding them responsible for their often-erratic behavior. For instance, there is great debate about whether teenagers should be treated like adults in the criminal justice system. They are capable of committing adult crimes, but should they receive adult sentences for their actions? Do their developing brains provide them an excuse for their behavior, or should they pay the same price an older and neurologically more stable person pays for the same crime? These are issues that cannot be answered by brain scientists alone, but it is an area in which developmental research must be used to inform the justice system and help society make the difficult decisions associated with adolescent crime.[24]

Are Children Getting Smarter?

There are many ways to measure intelligence (and perhaps as many ways to define intelligence). One of the great accomplishments of 20th century psychology was the development of the IQ test, a standardized way of measuring intelligence that boils down the complications of "what is intelligence" to a single score. If you know a person's IQ, you know where that person stands with respect to others in the population with respect to intelligence as it is measured by the test.[iii]

[iii] A score on an IQ test is a *measure* of intelligence as understood in our society, not intelligence itself. It is often convenient to define intelligence as "what an IQ test measures," but this, of course, does not capture the full scope of human intelligence. Intelligence is a multifaceted thing, with many

IQ tests have been around since the second decade of the 20th century and are periodically revised, updating the test items, in part to reflect cultural changes. (Asking a child in the year 2007 what one should do if he or she misses the trolley on the way to school is unlikely to get a meaningful answer.) Another reason to revise the test is to insure that the average IQ remains the same, a score of 100. Although there are different ways in which IQ tests are constructed, all major tests require that an average score reflect the average intelligence of the people they are testing. An intellectually average 10-year-old should get just enough items correct on an IQ test to produce a score corresponding to the "average" of all 10-year-olds, which is set arbitrarily at 100. There's nothing magic about this. Test makers work very hard, testing many people, adding, deleting, and revising questions to insure that their tests reflect the "real" intelligence (as measured by IQ anyway) of individuals in their population.

What happens, then, when after 10 or 20 years the average score changes from 100, either up or down? What happens is that the test makers revise the test so that the average is back at 100. Australian psychologist James Flynn observed that these periodic changes in average IQ scores over the last century were not random. Instead, Flynn found that IQ tests had to be revised periodically because the average scores were consistently heading upward at a rate of about 3 to 5 points per decade, a phenomenon that now goes by the name of the *Flynn effect*. The effect seems to be larger for people on the low end of the IQ range and there is some evidence that the effect is slowing down or has stopped in recent decades.[25]

This is a bit perplexing, for, on the surface, it suggests that average people today are much smarter than they were 50 years ago. I don't want to get into the debate about what the Flynn effect means about the nature of intelligence or about IQ tests, but I am convinced that the effect is real and that it does indeed mean something. Why the

components, some that are interrelated with one another, and others that are not. I've always liked Robert Sternberg's definition of intelligence as "the mental activities necessary for adaptation to, as well as shaping and selecting of, any environmental context...(I)ntelligence is not just reactive to the environment but also active in forming it. It offers people an opportunity to respond flexibly to challenging situations" (1997, p. 1030). IQ is derived from a well-standardized test that purports to measure individual differences in intelligence, and I believe that it does capture much of what people in our culture take to be "smarts." But it is not equivalent to intelligence, only an imperfect measure of it.

improvement? There are a lot of possible reasons, including greater access to education, improved medical care, and better nutrition. But there's another catch. IQ can be divided into two broad types; the first, called *crystallized*, refers to abilities that vary with experience and education and are assessed by tests of cultural knowledge and verbal fluency, such as vocabulary. The second is called *fluid*, and refers to skills that are believed to be more biologically based and less influenced by individual differences in experience and education and is reflected in tests such as memory span and those that measure spatial thinking.

Which type of abilities shows the most change over the decades? When I first learned of the Flynn effect, my guess was crystallized abilities, because these skills are subject to change from education, which was my first choice for the reason for the IQ increase over the last century. Good guess, but wrong. Counterintuitively, it is fluid abilities that run the Flynn effect.[26]

One explanation for this pattern is that the 20th century has seen a drastic change in the complexity of life, particularly the amount and nature of visual images people must deal with.[27] The 20th century saw the advent of photographs, glossy magazines, billboards, movies, television, VCRs, computers, and now video games. Children grow up inundated with visual information that must be sorted out and comprehended.

Further evidence that fluid intelligence is pliable and influenced by exposure to visual/spatial experience comes from a study examining cognitive abilities in Greek and Chinese children. University of Cyprus developmental psychologist Andreas Demetriou and his colleagues gave Greek and Chinese children between the ages of 8 and 14 years of age an extensive battery of cognitive tasks. Although there were no differences in measures of general intelligence, the Chinese children outperformed the Greek children on all measures involving visual/spatial processing. They attributed these substantial differences to the Chinese children's extensive practice with their logographic (pictorial symbols) writing system, in contrast to the phonetic system used by Greek children.[28]

Our ancestors may have gazed at the occasional buffalo painted on the cave wall, but otherwise they did not have to deal with visual representations of other things. When they saw an object or an event it was the real thing – not a representation of something or an imaginary happening recorded in an ersatz environment halfway across the world. But children have the neural plasticity to learn to make sense of this plethora of visual messages, and as a result they apparently increase their IQ scores.[29]

Whether this has any impact on real-world functioning is debatable, and perhaps the Flynn effect should have us questioning more the meaning of IQ tests and less what this means about human intellectual development. But (almost) regardless of what an IQ test actually measures, the fact that scores in tests assessing fluid abilities have improved steadily over the last century tells us something about young children's brains. They are plastic and able to adapt to a very different physical environment from the ones their ancestors evolved in.

Reversing the Effects of Early Deprivation

When I was an undergraduate student taking courses in child psychology, the received wisdom was that children who were deprived of a mother's love for the first 12, or perhaps 18, months of life were destined to a life of mental retardation and psychopathology. Maybe it wasn't a mother's love, per se, but a general lack of physical and social stimulation that was responsible for the negative effects. Regardless of the cause, in all but rare exceptions, early social and emotional deprivation had a life-long effect.

This viewpoint was consistent with popular theory of the time that stressed the importance of early experience on later behavior and was documented by both animal and human research. One of the most compelling examples came from the work of University of Wisconsin primatologist Harry Harlow with rhesus monkeys. Harlow raised infant monkeys without mothers. Some were provided either a cloth or wire surrogate mother that they could cling to and that would "feed" them (a bottle could be inserted into the chest of these motionless mothers). Initially, Harlow found that infant monkeys raised on the cloth mothers behaved normally, in that they clung to their mothers and ran to them for succor when they were frightened. The monkeys raised on the wire mothers gained no sense of security from their mothers and were pathological in all ways. Monkeys raised without mothers at all, so-called *isolates*, were even worse. These monkeys displayed socially and sexually bizarre behavior when introduced to a laboratory troop of monkeys, and if the isolation lasted for the first 6 months, they never fully recovered. And, as it turned out, the monkeys raised with cloth mothers were never fully normal either. On a television program broadcast to the nation in 1959, Harlow stated that if monkeys had not learned to love by 6 months, they may never learn to love at all. When asked about humans, he put the age at 12 months.[30]

Harlow's claim for humans was bolstered by the experiences of children raised in stultifying institutions, mainly in the early part of the last century, in which infants were housed in overcrowded, under-staffed orphanages or foundling homes and lacked both social and physical stimulation. The negative effects of such child rearing were apparent by 3 or 4 months of age and became progressively worse over infancy. For example, Sally Provence and Rose Lipton described 2- and 3-month-old institutionalized infants as feeling "something like sawdust dolls; they moved, they bent easily at the proper joints, but they felt stiff or wooden." And things only got worse over the first 2 years. Developmental psychologist Wayne Dennis followed the outcomes of children reared in the Crèche, a charity-run institution for illegitimate children, in Beirut, Lebanon. Like many institutions of its time, infants spent much of their day in barren cribs, often with sheets covering the sides. (This was done for sanitary reasons, and one expressed purpose for minimal adult contact was to reduce chances that the babies would be exposed to germs.) Caretakers were often graduates of the Crèche and showed a general non-responsiveness to the infants. Signs of severe mental retardation were apparent within the first year of life, with the IQs of the 16 children in Denis's study ranging between 50 and 80. This contrasted with children who had left the Crèche for adoptive homes before their second birthdays, who regained normal intellectual functioning and had early childhood IQs of about 100.[31]

Most psychologists and neuroscientists today still believe that early experience is critical in shaping the human mind and behavior. But more recent work has also clearly shown that the effects of early experience are not cast in stone but in more flexible material. When the course of an animal's or a child's life takes a turn, for either the better or worse, patterns of development can be drastically altered. This plasticity of behavior and intelligence is attributed, in large part, to the slow growth of the brain.

Perhaps one of the clearest demonstrations of a radical environmental change modifying the effects of long-term social deprivation came from the lab of Harry Harlow, the same one whose earlier work suggested the limitations of plasticity. Harlow and Stephen Suomi provided "therapy" for monkeys that had been raised in social isolation for 6 months.[32] Each isolate was placed in a cage for one hour a day, five days a week, for 26 weeks, with a "therapist" monkey, who was 3 months old at the beginning of the experiment. This age was chosen because 3-month-old monkeys are physically active but socially immature. An older, more experienced monkey would know that the isolate's behavior was abnormal and treat it accordingly, either ignoring the animal or acting aggressively toward it. (Think how you would act if you entered a doctor's waiting room and found a person balled up in the corner, clasping himself and rocking back and forth. You hopefully wouldn't start hitting him, but you also probably wouldn't say "hello.") The younger "therapist" monkeys, however, did not realize that the withdrawn, often fearful behavior of the isolates was strange. They directed their actions toward the isolates, initially by climbing on and over them, trying to elicit some social behavior from their recalcitrant cage mates.

You can imagine how difficult it is to ignore a small monkey climbing all over you. Thus, the first therapeutic thing that the younger monkeys did was to break down the isolates' self-directed behavior. Then, over the weeks of the experiment, the therapists and isolates developed social behaviors together. The therapist monkeys spent most of their days in a monkey colony where they developed normal social behavior. They in turn "taught" the isolates how to be social during their one-hour sessions. The result was that at 12 months, the isolates were introduced into a monkey colony and behaved normally. What was once thought to be a permanent disability was reversed when the conditions of the environment appropriately matched the needs of the socially deprived animal. In this case, the best cure was not a more sophisticated animal, but a socially naive one who would not recognize and react to the abnormal behavior the isolate brought into the situation.

Although such therapy has also been shown to be effective with monkeys experiencing up to 12 months of deprivation, there are age limits to plasticity. The isolate monkeys had developed pathological behavior patterns – pathological when viewed from the perspective of normal monkey behavior, but not so bizarre for an animal who has never seen a fellow member of its species or whose only physical contact with another living being was itself. These patterns, however, were not so firmly established that they could not be reversed under appropriate situations. Had the brain of the isolate monkey been more sophisticated – been able to automatize responses to repeated environmental events – the likelihood of reversibility would have been much less. Infants' brains are inefficient and prevent them from learning too much early in life that may interfere with later learning. This becomes especially apparent when early life experiences produce pathological behavior.

And what about once-institutionalized children? They didn't all become basket cases. Many showed signs of recovery from their early deprivation. But recovery was limited. For example, Wayne Denis, in his study of children of the Crèche, reported that children adopted after their second birthdays showed some intellectual gains, although they typically lagged several years behind age-level on subsequent IQ tests. Other investigators reported that institutionalized children who were placed in foster or adoptive homes showed some recovery of what would be considered "normal behavior." Provence and Lipton described the behavior of a small group of once-institutionalized children who had been placed in foster homes, most between 18 and 24 months of age. They remarked on the impressive resiliency of these children, while still noting that some problems persisted. These children did not relate well to other toddlers and did not form strong attachments either to their foster parents or to other children. They described their emotional behavior as "increasingly impoverished and predominantly bland...One gained the impression on watching them that they had largely given up on their efforts to initiate a contact with the adult..."[33] They continued to get better over the preschool years, and to a casual observer may look quite normal. But closer examination revealed problems with forming and maintaining relations, impulse control, and flexible problem solving. They were loners, rarely looking to others, including their mothers, for help or reassurance.[iv]

These institutionalization studies provide evidence both of the long-term effects of early social deprivation, but also of the possibility of change. Other studies have been even more promising, showing that, under the proper conditions, the insults children experience early in life can be overcome.

One of the most dramatic examples of reversibility of the effect of early social deprivation is found in the work of psychologist Harold Skeels.[34] A group of infants living in an overcrowded and understaffed Depression-era orphanage were showing signs of retardation due to

---

[iv] I recall a child who joined our small-town school in eighth grade. Johnny had come from a foster home and was placed as an adoptee with a family in town. He made friends, but seemed to lose them just as fast. He had a temper, and the littlest thing would set him off, often leading to fights, sometimes with older and bigger boys. And despite his bravado, I remember him crying when he lost these fights, something 13-year-old boys in the company of other boys try not to do. He'd ride around town on his bicycle, joining groups of boys playing baseball, for example, but never quite fitting in. I remember feeling uncomfortable around him and not knowing why. Johnny didn't return to school the next year. The story was that his adoptive parents "sent him back," to where I never knew, and no one in town, as far as I knew, ever heard from Johnny again.

their stimulus-deprived conditions. These children (average age, 19 months) were removed from the orphanage and placed with women in a home for mentally retarded adults where they received loving attention. In almost every case, a child formed a close attachment to one particular person, and this attachment served as the basis for social relationships with other women and staff members on the ward. The change in intelligence and general social behavior was remarkable, with most children functioning at normal levels by age 4 and being placed in foster or adoptive homes. A 20-year follow-up showed that this small group had developed normally, attaining an average level of education, economic success, and social adjustment. Most were married and had children. The severe effects of social deprivation had been reversed at the hands of loving, mentally retarded women. A comparison group that remained in the institution over their preschool years did not fare nearly as well, attaining, on average, a third-grade education, and many remaining institutionalized or making only a marginal living.

The Skeels study is somewhat analogous to the "therapist monkey" study discussed earlier. In the Skeels study, mentally retarded women may have provided the children with stimulation that they might not have had at the hands of more mature caretakers. Chances are, the characteristics of the orphanage children were not those that would seem "normal" to most adults. Most well-meaning adults who interact with a child expect some response in return. Children who are nonresponsive and generally lethargic tend not to receive continued attention from adults, particularly adults from stressed environments. It is difficult to shower attention on children who do not respond, and this might be especially true of an overburdened institution staff. But because of the limited mental capacity of the retarded women (and probably unlimited time to spend), their attention may have been repeatedly directed to the children, even in the absence of "normal" social responses from their young wards. Following months of loving stimulation, the children may have become more responsive, much as the isolate monkeys did. As with the monkeys, the pattern of the children's behavior could be reversed because of their limited mental abilities. If their brains processed information more readily and stored experiences more permanently, a reversal of such deleterious behavior patterns would be much less likely.

Don't get the wrong impression. Highly responsive adults of normal intelligence can also serve as effective "therapists" for once-deprived children. One of the consequences of war is malnourished and traumatized youngsters, and many compassionate adults seek these children for adoption, hoping to provide them with a chance for a better life.

In the 1970s, war in Southeast Asia produced many such orphans, and many American parents took in these sickly children, nearly all of whom showed clear signs of intellectual and social-emotional retardation. In several studies following the progress of such children, the turn-around was outstanding. For example, in one study of 25 adopted Asian refugee infants, all of whom had experienced physical and psychological deprivation, the reversibility of their early negative experience was nearly complete. By 4 years of age they tested far above the national average on tests of intellectual and social competence. Within two years of being placed in the homes of highly motivated middle- and upper-middle-class families, these once impoverished and malnourished children displayed no residual signs of their earlier deprivation.[35]

The more scientifically minded readers may be questioning how much we can trust the interpretations of these institutional and adoption studies. They all have methodological problems. For example, children are not randomly assigned to be institutionalized or not, and perhaps only the brighter and healthier children get adopted into "good" homes. The lack of experimental rigor is a problem with all "natural experiments" that take advantage of situations in the real world to evaluate the psychological consequence of conditions that could never ethically be repeated in the laboratory. Researchers do what they can, and interpretations must be made based on the "preponderance of the evidence," as in a court trial. And most of these studies are old, which shouldn't be a problem in and of itself, but it would be nice to have relatively "new" data to confirm the old.

And unfortunately, we do. I say "unfortunately" because one would hope the stultifying institutions that produce such deprivation were a thing of the past. But not so. Some of you may recall the fall of the Berlin wall in 1989 and with it shortly afterwards the fall of communism in Eastern Europe. One formerly communist country was Romania, with its dictatorial leader Nicolae Ceausescu. As Western eyes saw Romania close-up for the first time in decades, one heartwrenching discovery was institutions for infants and young children that were at least as horrendous as any that existed during the Great Depression. And the descriptions of the children could have been taken from the files of Rene Spitz, the pioneering psychiatrist who documented the emotional distress of motherless babies reared in orphanages in the first half of the 20th century. The good news was that many of these children were adopted and that researchers followed the development of some of these children, providing us with a contemporary picture of the degree to which children can recover from early maltreatment.

An important part of these studies was an examination of children's intellectual progress as a function of when they were removed from the Romanian orphanages. Some were placed in adoptive homes within their first 6 months of life, whereas others experienced institution life for up to 3 years before being adopted. What are the consequences of prolonged, versus brief, life in an environment that is psychologically stultifying? In one study by Thomas O'Connor of London's Institute of Psychiatry and his colleagues, Romanian children adopted into British (UK) homes were given IQ tests at 6 years of age. Some children had been adopted within their first 6 months of life, others between 7 and 24 months, and others between 24 and 42 months. They also looked at a sample of UK infants adopted shortly after birth. The IQ scores of the early-adopted Romanian children (114) were high and comparable to those of the UK-adopted children (117). The IQ scores decreased some for children adopted between 7 and 24 months, but were still average (99), and scores were lower still for children adopted after their second birthdays (90). Yet, even this later group was within the normal range of intelligence, scoring just 10 points below the population average.[36]

Studies such as this provide a finer-grained analysis of the reversibility of the effects of early deprivation. They demonstrate remarkable resiliency on the part of deprived children, but also reveal the limits of plasticity. It should not be surprising that children who spent 2 or 3 years in conditions with minimal human contact do not develop normally. Then again, these children were only 6 years old when tested and had only been in an "enriched" environment for several years. Maybe they'll show even greater improvement after spending a few more years in their adopted homes. Their brains are still developing, afforded by their slow growth, and I would not be surprised to find that many of these children, upon reaching adolescence, are indistinguishable from other kids in their neighborhood. In fact, a study by Michel Duyme from the University of Paris and his colleagues (1999) documented that low-IQ children adopted between the age of 4 and 6 years of age do display subsequent IQ gains by adolescence. These gains, however, were greater in more advantaged (an average of 19.5 points) than less advantaged (an average of 7.7 points) homes.

Extreme Cases: Wild and Feral Children

Romulus and Remus, the fraternal founders of Rome, were raised by wolves, or so the story goes, and so was Mowgli, the protagonist in Rudyard Kipling's *The Jungle Book*. There are dozens of tales of children allegedly being raised by animals, ranging from wolves (the most common) to monkeys (the second-place winner), to bears, dogs, goats, apes, gazelles, and even ostriches. These stories data back to the 3rd century in Italy, through the Middle Ages, and continue to this day. Some cases even come with pictures. (For a listing of cases, go to www.feralchildren.com.) In some instances, such as Axel Rivas, the Chilean Dog Boy, or Ivan Mishukov, the Russian Dog Boy, a child may have left the company of humans at a relatively advanced age to live with animals. Alex, for instance, escaped from a children's home when he was 8 and is said to have lived with a group of stray dogs and slept in a cave outside of a port town in Chile. Ivan was 4 when he left home and preferred to live on the streets of Reutova, west of Moscow, in the company of dogs. In these cases, it hardly seems reasonable to say that dogs raised these children, or even that the children were devoid of human contact.

Other accounts, such as Saturday Mthiyane, a South African boy who roamed with a troop of monkeys, have greater credibility. The case of Saturday Mthiyane (named after the day of the week he was found and the school he attended) is reasonably well documented, and a local newspaper followed up on the child 10 years after his discovery to find that at an estimated age of 15 he had learned to walk, but still did not talk, and refused cooked food, preferring raw vegetables and fruits. Or consider the cases of Amala and Kamala, two girls perhaps 3 and 5 years of age (there is discrepancy about their ages) when they were found in a wolf's den, along with two wolf cubs, by the missionary Joseph Singh, in India in 1920. The girls had no language, walked on hands and feet, refused to wear clothes, and would eat only raw meat. Amala died before any significant rehabilitation could take place, but Kamala learned to walk, was toilet trained, mastered a small vocabulary, and eventually was able to speak in short, broken sentences. But after more nearly 10 years in "captivity," Kamala still had the mind of a three-and-a-half-year-old (according to prominent developmental psychologist Arnold Gesell). She died of typhoid in 1929.

Whether these children were truly raised by animals or merely lived in the company of animals, one may never know. I recommend a healthy dose of skepticism at the possibility that children can indeed be raised by animals from infancy or shortly thereafter and remain alive. But the evidence seems clear that at least some of these children were indeed living "in the wild" and had survived for a matter of years without any evidence of contact with other people. Once discovered, these *feral children* have sometimes gone through extensive education, attempting to humanize a child who has apparently resorted to animal ways. As the examples of Saturday Mthiyane and Amala and Kamala reveal, reversal of years of living outside of human contact takes its toll and there is little sign of reversibility of language, intellectual, or emotional normalcy.

The best documented case of a feral child is that of Victor, the Wild Boy of Aveyron. In 1800 Victor was living in the woods in southern France and was captured and placed in the care of the State. He was about 12 years of age, could not speak, and had numerous scars, suggesting that he had been living in the woods for some time. Physician Jean-Marc Gaspard Itard took Victor in and began an intensive program to civilize the boy. He had limited success. After 5 years, Victor was able to speak and read a few words, displayed affection for his caretakers, and could carry out simple tasks. Some expert opinion of the time, as well as the opinion of many readers of Itard's account today, believes Victor was mentally retarded or autistic. Cause and effect, of course, cannot be determined in most cases of feral children.

Other cases involve children being locked in rooms or basements by deranged parents. One of the better documented cases is that of Kasper Hauser, found wandering the streets of Nuremberg, Germany in 1828. Kasper had been confined to a small cell and had minimal social interaction. Food and water had been placed in his cell while he slept. At 16, when discovered, Kasper had only a few words and behaved like a small child. Unlike feral children, Kasper eventually learned to talk and even to read and write. It is likely that Kasper had learned to talk before being confined.[37]

A more recent account of a confined child is that of Genie, who was kept in her room, chained to her bed or a potty chair, from about 18 months until her discovery at age 13 years. Genie showed signs of severe mental retardation and had no language. Through educational intervention, she displayed substantial social and problem-solving skills, as well as many vocabulary terms; but she never fully developed language, lacking the grammatical structure that makes language unique.[38]

What do these extraordinary cases of survival in the wild or confinement, when they can be verified, tell us about plasticity and human nature? Clearly, plasticity is limited. Children who are abandoned by their parents (as most feral children must surely have been) show a remarkable ability to stay alive, with or without the help of animals. But in situations where children did not possess language before being abandoned, they failed to acquire it after being reunited with people, and even intensive education had limited success in rehabilitating such children. What do these accounts tell us about human nature? There can be much debate here, but I think the bottom line is that human nature develops within human culture. Our species did not evolve for lives with wolves or monkeys or in isolation, but with our own kind. The fact that children can survive under such bizarre conditions is a testament to human resiliency. The fact that they cannot easily resort to human ways reflects the extreme limits of human plasticity.

Righting Early Wrongs

How pliable are we humans? At what age is plasticity lost? Unfortunately, we are not able to answer these questions definitively. We do know that plasticity is reduced with age and that we are most malleable as infants. Early development tends to follow a similar path for most children under most circumstances. In the words of developmental psychologist Robert McCall, early development is highly *canalized*, following a species-typical course "under a wide range of diverse environments and exhibits strong self-righting tendencies following exposure to severely atypical environments."[39] That is, infants are not immune to the negative consequences of their maladaptive environments, but, at least in first 2 years of life, there is a strong tendency to return to a course of normalcy when more beneficial environments are experienced. This plasticity is reduced, beginning as early as 24 to 36 months of age. But it is not lost, and it is the slow growth of the human brain that, in large part, affords this degree of social, emotional, and intellectual flexibility.

Babies suffering from malnutrition, reared in stultifying institutions or war-torn lands, do show signs of their abuse and neglect. They have learned to be unresponsive to social attention and to shut out a hostile world. But our slow development can be kind to such deprived and abused children. Given proper stimulation, children can learn new ways of responding. Their brains certainly experienced the horrendous events of their early lives. But young brains are not like tape recorders; they do not record everything for posterity. Young brains, because of their immaturity, can be rewired – recorded over if you will. Were children born with more mature brains, or if development proceeded more rapidly than it does, the mental, social, and emotional flexibility of young children would be lost. This behavioral and cognitive flexibility is perhaps our species' greatest adaptive advantage and it is afforded by the prolonged period of mental (and thus brain) inefficiency.

82

Developmental Plasticity and Evolution

If plasticity is so important to development, does it also play an important role in evolution? That depends on whom you ask. In the middle of the 20th century, biologists integrated Darwin's concept of natural selection with the field of genetics, producing the *Modern Synthesis*, or *neo-Darwinism*. At the crux of neo-Darwinism is the idea that inheritance is genetic, and that evolutionary-inducing changes occur principally by mutations to genes in the sex cells, or gametes (ova and sperm). What happens to the individual during its lifetime (developing strong muscles as a result of hard work, for example) cannot change the genes in the gametes, and thus cannot be passed on to one's offspring. From this perspective, development is an epiphenomenon with regard to evolution. What happens during the life of an individual has great consequence for survival, but otherwise has no consequences for evolution. Thus, developmental plasticity is irrelevant to discussions of evolution.

But there have always been people who have argued that development does matter in evolution, and more recently that developmental plasticity may be the engine that generates variation upon which natural selection works. The argument goes something like this. Natural selection works by favoring individuals who fit better with local environments over less-well-fit individuals. At the extreme, the better-fit individuals live and the less-fit individuals die. In less extreme situations, the better-fit individuals have more offspring than the less-fit individuals, altering the gene frequency in the population. But where does the variation to produce better- and less-fit individuals come from? It could be mutations, of course, but another source is developmental plasticity. Changes in environments (particularly early environments, including prenatal) may produce an organism that is different from the norm. If this difference results in an organism that is better fit than ones not able to alter their body or behavior to this new environment, it will be at an advantage and out-reproduce lesser-fit members of the group.

As an example, consider the moth *Nemoria arizonaria*. Depending on the type of food the caterpillar of this moth eats in the first 3 days of life, it develops one of two different forms. If it hatches in the spring, it feeds on oak catkins and develops an appearance similar to the oak's spring flowers. If it hatches in the summer, it feeds on oak leaves and develops an appearance that resembles oak twigs (the flowers are long-gone by summer). Each form (or morphology) helps the animal blend in, camouflaging it from bird predators. What evolved is an animal that now has two choices, both surely under genetic control, each of which produces adaptive (that is, good fitting) responses to the local environment.[40] For this to evolve, an ancient ancestor of *Nemoria arizonaria* must have had the developmental plasticity to vary its morphology to changes in response to local situations. Some of those variations produced forms that "fit" the environment (in this case, hid them from hungry birds), and these were favored by natural selection and thus increased in frequency. Others surely produced less than desirable outcomes, and natural selection eliminated those individuals from the population. So natural selection continues to play a vital role here, but *it was developmental plasticity that generated the options upon which natural selection worked.*

This is fine for caterpillars, but might it have any relevance for human evolution? Some think so, believing, for example, that developmental plasticity may have been particularly important in the evolution of language or advanced forms of social learning.[41] For instance, chimpanzees, although they are wonderful social learners, seem not to be able to observe someone execute a series of actions and then after a delay of minutes, hours, or days, imitate those actions. This is called *deferred imitation*, and some speculate that it requires a symbolic memory system (explicit, or declarative, memory) to perform. Nine-month-old human babies display this type of imitation under some circumstances, and 2-year-old children are very good at it. Several researchers have shown that chimpanzees reared by humans as if they were children (called *enculturation*) do display deferred imitation, indicating a high degree of cognitive plasticity in these animals. My colleagues and I have speculated that this may have been one factor in the evolution of human intelligence. An ancestor of modern humans and chimpanzees may have been sensitive to differences in parenting behavior and developed the cognitive capacity for deferred imitation, and thus enhanced social learning. This provided an advantage to such individuals living in a complex social group, and thus was favored by natural selection. It's a theory that's probably impossible to prove, but it is one that fits with much data from developmental biology and new ideas about the possible role of developmental plasticity in evolution.[42]

When Slow is Fast Enough

The lament of the preteen child at the beginning of this chapter reflects a truism of our species. It's a long road to adulthood, and apparently always has been since *Homo sapiens* first graced the Earth. Our long journey to adulthood defines our species as much as our big brains and unique intelligence do. In fact, the evolution of big brains and intelligence was made possible by an extended period of immaturity, existing as they did in animals living in socially complex groups. Most critically, our slow-developing brains and extended childhoods gave us the time to learn the complexities of human culture. Slow growth also permits children to make adjustments to changing environments – to modify their behavior in response to possibly nonresponsive or even detrimental environments, and to recover from the effects of early deprivation or misfortune.

Our slow growth gives us not only a juvenile body for extended years, but also juvenile behavior and thought patterns well into our teens. Juvenile features such as play, curiosity, and a love of novelty result in an exploring and fun-seeking character, which, in many ways, is unique to humans, at least among adults of a species. These youthful behavioral characteristics are the side effects of slow physical growth, and they play a vital role in psychological development.

4

Adapting to the Niche of Childhood

It has been tacitly assumed by most students of normal and aberrant development that differences between adults and infants reflect deficiencies in the infant, and therefore, represent handicaps which must be overcome if development is to proceed normally.

Gerald Turkewitz & Patricia Kenny[1]

◆   ◆   ◆   ◆

I was in the first grade at the time. We were at recess when a fellow student began to inquire about my family. "Do you have any brothers or sisters?" Glenn asked.

"Yah, I got three brothers," I said. "Who's the oldest?" he asked. "I am," I told him.

Glenn gave me a look of mild disgust. "You are not," he said. "You can't be. You're only in the first grade! First graders are never the oldest!"

Glenn was bigger than I was, so I didn't let the argument get too far out of hand, but I was displeased and confused that anyone should question my assertion that I was the eldest of four brothers. As I later found out, Glenn also had a brother. His brother, however, was a big brother – a third grader – and as far as Glenn was concerned, all first graders, if they had siblings at all, had to have older siblings. I assume that Glenn's brother had made the difference in their status clear to him, and that being a first grader was considered about as low as one could go. The notion that a first grader could have the status of older brother was simply not believable: it violated too substantially his knowledge of how the world worked.

As someone who teaches college classes in child development, I collect stories of young children's immature cognition. They tend to strike a familiar and amusing chord with students (and boost teacher evaluations), and they perhaps give us adults a feeling of superiority –

boy, how silly young children can be. The Swiss psychologist Jean Piaget formulated a theory of cognitive development in which children eventually attained *formal operational thought*, the ability to apply abstract mental operations (logical thought processes) to interpret the world (in adolescence), but only after first mastering *concrete operations* (logical thought on concrete, that is, not abstract, content) in middle childhood. Before this, during the preschool years, children's thinking was said to be *preoperational* – it was symbolic (they could use language, for example), but it was intuitive and without logic. Piaget described the preschool child by what he or she could not do. This cognitive-deficit approach led Piaget and subsequent generations of child psychologists to amass tales of immature thinking of preschool children, and many such tales brought a smile to the logical adult. Preschool children's thinking served as comic relief in the study of cognitive development.

But perhaps some of the nonadaptive aspects of preoperational thinking also have a hidden adaptive side. Maybe there's a positive side to some aspects of immature thinking. Maybe being young and foolish has some compensatory value.

As I emphasized in previous chapters, one important reason for humans' prolonged immaturity is the extended time available for practicing adult roles and learning the complex ways of society. Once agriculture was developed and the wheel invented, it belonged to the culture and was available to future generations through cultural transmission, allowing the next generation to get a jump start, so to speak, and eventually contribute their own inventions. While other species advance via the genes of their members, passing on the biological traits best suited for their environment, we advance by teaching the new generation all the knowledge our generation was given plus our additions to that knowledge.[i] The method of transmitting cultural knowledge requires a long childhood – a cultural apprenticeship.

But there may be benefits to slow growth other than just providing children more time to learn the ways of the world. Young children's imperfect understanding and their immature cognitions may actually provide them with some advantages. Being too smart too young may not always be too good.

---

[i]   In fact, the power and speed of cultural evolution has caused some, such as the Nobel Prize winning biologist Sir John Eccles (1989), to propose that, for humans, biological evolution by natural selection has ended.

The demands of infancy and childhood are different than the demands of later life. Our prolonged period of immaturity was necessitated by constraints on brain growth and the complexity of tasks, particularly in the social realm, that we must master to be successful. The emergence of childhood brought with it new niches that members of our species had to navigate. Some aspects of infants' and children's perceptual, cognitive, and social abilities were shaped by natural selection to fit these new niches – to adapt children to the ecology of childhood, increasing the chances that they'd make it to adulthood. In Chapter 1 I referred to such characteristics as *ontogenetic adaptations*. They serve to adapt children to their current environment, not necessarily to a future one. Some of these characteristics, by definition, are reflections of an immature brain and mind, and they limit what a child can do or know. But there is a flip side to immaturity, and that is the focus of this chapter.

I begin by discussing some of the benefits of sensory limitations in infants. Taking too much information into a still-developing brain too early can have negative consequences for later development and learning. I next look at children's self-centered, or egocentric, view of the world and how it may, in some circumstances, actually provide a boost to learning. Such egocentric views are not limited to children, but are also seen in adolescence and are reflected in high levels of risk-taking behavior. Although such risk-taking can be dangerous, it can also provide substantial benefits for those teenagers who survive the experience. I then examine language learning and how young children's limited information-processing abilities may actually facilitate learning a first and second language. The final section turns the table, asking if children's immature thinking is viewed positively by adults, possibly affording them increased protection, care, or at least greater license for misbehavior.

The Benefits of Limitations

Newborns of many species are notable for their immaturity. Mice and rats, for example, are born bald and blind. Human infants fare a bit better initially, with all of their senses working to a limited degree at birth. But just barely. And whereas mouse and rat pups will fully develop all of their sensory abilities within days of births, it will be several months before the human infant's senses are at full (or near) capacity. Actually, given how long it takes before children's intellectual and social skills are fully operable, their basic perceptual abilities develop quite quickly. But this is only in a relative sense.

To some degree, this level of sensory immaturity is a by-product of being born too early. As I noted in a previous chapter, as humans evolved larger and larger brains, birth had to occur earlier relative to other primates (earlier not in absolute time but in relation to the size of the brain at birth); otherwise, the newborn's skull would not be able to pass through the birth canal. So naturally the brain and associated abilities are immature. But many of these limitations are not simply by-products of a too-early birth, but adaptations to insure that brains get hooked-up properly. And although they may be exaggerated in slow-developing humans, they are not limited to us, but are characteristic of other animals as well.

The basic argument, first articulated by developmental psychobiologists Gerald Turkewitz and Patricia Kenny, is that sensory limitations of many young animals reduce the amount of information infants have to deal with, which facilitates their constructing a simplified and comprehensible world. The various sensory systems develop in a constant order for all vertebrates, with audition, for instance, developing before vision. This means that early-developing senses do not have to "compete" for neurons with later-developing senses. The idea of competition for neurons has been termed *neural Darwinism* by Nobel laureate Gerald Edelman. Edelman proposed that groups of neurons compete with one another to recruit undedicated neurons, and that neural activity, which can be the result of sensory stimulation, determines, in part, which neurons become organized with which other neurons. Limited sensory functioning (poorly working eyes, for instance) reduces sensory input and thus serves to decrease competition between developing senses. From this perspective, immature sensory systems are not handicaps that must be overcome, but are adaptive and necessary for proper sensory development and sensory learning.[2]

Brains mature as a function of genetic and other endogenous (within-the-body) processes, but also as a function of external stimulation. For the most part, perceptual experiences are coordinated with maturation of sensory organs, and as a result competition between the senses is minimized and the senses come "on line" in a species-typical order.

But what happens when perceptual experience is altered, when infants get too much stimulation too early, or not enough? This question has been studied experimentally using precocial birds, such as ducks and quail, who are able to walk and form close attachments to their mothers shortly after birth. It has long been known that many precocial birds form an attachment to the first moving and quacking thing they see and hear hours after birth. The Austrian Nobel laureate Konrad Lorenz referred to this as *imprinting*.[3] This can be demonstrated under controlled conditions by placing a chick in the center of a circular container and playing the maternal call of the chick's species from a speaker on one side of the container and the call of another species on the opposite side. Quite reliably, the chick (be it duck or quail) will approach the speaker playing the call of its mother. This was touted as an example of instinctive behavior, some adaptive response that occurs without the benefit of prior experience. But later research demonstrated that some experience was necessary – not experience after hatching, but experience while still in the egg. University of North Carolina developmental psychobiologist Gilbert Gottlieb showed that ducks will only approach the maternal call if they hear their species' call in the last few days before hatching. What they hear can be the call of their mother, the peeps of their broodmates still in the egg, or even their own peeping. But without some prehatching auditory experience, they do not show this "instinctive" behavior.[4]

Gottlieb demonstrated the importance of prehatching sensory stimulation on imprinting by *depriving* some birds of species-typical experiences. What would happen if birds received *extra* sensory stimulation, particularly stimulation that they wouldn't normally get until after hatching? Florida International University developmental psychobiologist Robert Lickliter asked this question by removing part of the shell from the eggs of bobwhite quail and showing them pattern light two to three days before hatching. Bobwhite quail embryos normally experience some diffuse light coming through their eggshells days before hatching, but they would not normally "see" patterns until after hatching. Two to three days after hatching the bobwhite quail chicks were placed in the middle of a container, and the maternal call of a bobwhite quail was played from one speaker and the maternal call of a chicken was played from another speaker. Control birds, those who had the tops of their shells removed but did *not* experience pattern light, invariably approached the "right" speaker (29 of 32 animals), the one playing the maternal call of their own species. Not so for the chicks that received the extra visual stimulation. Twenty-five of 44 chicks (56%) showed either no response or no preference, and some (7 of 44, 16%) actually approached the chicken call. In other words, extra visual stimulation hindered important auditory functioning. I should note that Lickliter's birds did show accelerated visual development, although this was at the expense of the development of the auditory system.[5]

Other research showed that extra visual stimulation interferes with later auditory *learning* (being able to discriminate their own mother's call from that of another female quail), that certain types of auditory stimulation in bobwhite quail interfere with subsequent visual development, that extra vestibular (that is, rocking) stimulation interferes with auditory development in ducks, and that extra visual stimulation can interfere with the sense of smell (olfaction) in rats.[6] With respect to newborn rats, which are functionally deaf and blind, developmental psychobiologist Norman Spear wrote: "If this animal could be made to see and hear, it seems at least as likely that severely maladaptive behavior would result due to distraction from the more conventional events (e.g., odors) upon which its survival depends."[7]

These findings, and others like them, fit nicely with Turkewitz and Kenny's argument that the differential rate of development of the various sensory systems reduces competition between the developing senses. Normally, neural development and sensory experience are coordinated. But when animals experience sensory stimulation earlier or in greater intensity than "expected," the choreographed dance between gene-influenced neural development and perceptual experience is disrupted, and so is the pattern of development.

Perhaps the greatest benefit of doing research with animals is that we can investigate issues that cannot be investigated with experimental rigor in humans. One cannot systematically enrich or deprive human fetuses with the expectation that some aspect of their development will be hindered. But there is at least one naturally occurring situation analogous to Lickliter's quails, and that is the experience of many premature infants. I say "naturally" occurring, but it is only relatively recently that infants born much before their due date have survived in large numbers. Incubators for premature infants date back only to the early part of the 20th century. Before this time, the likelihood that an infant born even one or two months before full term would survive was small. With incubators, and later antibiotics, the "age of viability" was brought down to 27 weeks, three months preterm. In the past 20 years infants born as early as 24 weeks post-conception now have a good chance of surviving. Survival, however, requires what, not many years ago, would have been considered heroic efforts. Premature infants are essentially fetuses who are poked with needles, handled, and exposed to sensory stimulation that most of their full-term peers never experience. At the least, they receive sensory input far earlier and in excess to what a *Homo sapiens* fetus could normally expect.

What are the consequences of such stimulation? Not surprisingly, many premature infants have subsequent learning difficulties, sometimes general, such as mental retardation, and sometimes specific, such as reading or math disabilities. Such effects may have nothing to do with excessive and early sensory stimulation, however. They may instead be attributed to the early birth and subsequent development that should have occurred in a protective, biological environment evolved to support maturation, occurring instead in clinical, technological context that does its best to mimic life in a womb. That some of the deleterious cognitive effects of prematurity are attributable, in part, to species-atypical patterns of stimulation can be inferred from the fact that these cognitive disabilities are sometimes accompanied by cognitive exceptionalities. According to Harvard neonatologist Heidelise Als, some of the same children who display learning problems in the classroom may score in the gifted range on some IQ subtests. That is, just as Robert Lickliter's bobwhite quail displayed enhanced visual abilities along with their auditory deficits, so too do premature infants; as they grow up, they sometimes display unevenness in intellectual aptitudes. Lickliter himself makes this analogy, as does Als who writes that the premature sensory stimulation these infants received may have "differentially accentuated development of certain brain systems ready to take advantage of the extrauterine challenge while inhibiting other brain systems that expected intrauterine inputs for several more months." Als concluded that "Social contexts evolved in the course of human phylogeny are surprisingly fine-tuned in specificity to provide good-enough environments for the human cortex to unfold, initially intrauterinely, then extrauterinely…With the advances in medical technology, that is, material culture, even very immature nervous systems exist and develop outside the womb. However, the social contexts of traditional special care nurseries bring with them less than adequate support for immature nervous systems…leading to maladaptations and disabilities, yet also to accelerations and extraordinary abilities."[8]

See Things My Way

Most adults seem to appreciate that young children see the world a bit differently than they do. Although they sometimes find such differences in perspective frustrating and troublesome, other times they find them quite amusing, as reflected, for example, in the words emblazoned on the front of a toddler-size t-shirt, "I'm 2: Welcome to my world!" There's a recognition here that the world-view of the 2-year-old is very different from that of the adult, and there's very little the adult can do to make the 2-year-old see things differently but to wait. They'll grow out of it, but only gradually.

Piaget described preschool children in particular as *egocentric*. By this Piaget did not mean that young children have narcissistic personalities, but rather that they see things from their own personal perspective and assume that other people see things the same way as they do. They cannot easily take a perspective (visual, social, emotional, or intellectual) other than their own. Piaget proposed that young children's egocentricity permeates their entire being, and they have a difficult time perceiving the world as someone else does.

Many readers will be familiar with the egocentricity of preschoolers. The story that began this chapter reflects a 6-year-old's difficulty appreciating that first graders *can* be the oldest in some families. As another example, when a neighbor child asked about my parents' age, I told him I didn't know, but I believed that my mother was older than my father. This 7-year-old peer informed me that I must be wrong: "Daddies are *always* older than mommies. It's the law." It turned out that his father was 15 years older than his mother, and he believed that this must be the case for all families. A telephone conversation with a 4-year-old can be interesting, but in the absence of face-to-face visual cues, much important information is often lost. For example, the voice on the other end of the phone asks "What are you wearing today, Kelly?" and in response Kelly says "This," while looking down and pointing at her dress. Allen, the son of a high school math instructor, asks another 7-year-old "What does your daddy teach?" – assuming that everyone's daddy must teach something. He knows there are other jobs in the world; in fact, he's going to be a fireman when he grows up. Nonetheless, daddies teach.

Better Learning through Egocentricity

Despite numerous observations (child psychologists have more stories than you'd ever want to hear) attesting to the phenomenon, more recent research indicates that Piaget overstated his case; preschool children are not as impervious to the emotions, desires, and knowledge of others as Piaget believed them to be and are often quite inconsistent in their perspective taking.[9] For example, at 5, my daughter Heidi one evening in her bath placed her head under the running water and excitedly called me in to hear the new sound. "Listen to this, Daddy," she said as she lowered her head under the faucet again while I watched. In a different context, however, this same child showed a keen ability to take the perspective of another. One evening, sometime before the bath episode, she and I were beginning a pre-bedtime card game and I was exhorting her to hurry because, I said, the game is more fun when you play it fast. Her response to that was quick. "No sir, Daddy," she said. "You only want to go fast so we can finish and you can put me to bed!" I had been caught. This child, who thought I could hear the rushing water when *her* head was under the faucet, in this instance, saw my perspective quite clearly. So young children are not as hopelessly self-centered as we once believed. Nonetheless, despite the contradictions, Piaget's observations ring true. Preschool children are far more self-centered in their thinking than older children.

Egocentricity is a classic example of immature thinking, and it seems unquestionable that such a cognitive disposition would have serious drawbacks. Maturity means getting rid of self-centered thinking. But is egocentricity all bad? When looked at from the child's perspective, what could be more adaptive for a small, defenseless, and cognitively limited creature than relating all experiences to one's self? This self-centered perspective is likely important for survival.

For starters, people of all ages tend to learn and remember things better when they reference the information to themselves, something that children are naturally prone to do. In research with both children and adults, people remember more target information (usually sets of words) when they are asked to relate the information to themselves. For example, in 1980 psychologist Charles Lord showed adults a series of adjectives and asked them to determine whether each word was either like them, their fathers, or a famous person (Walter Cronkite, a news anchorman, who at the time was the best-known person in America). People who related the adjectives to themselves remembered more of the words overall, indicating that self-referencing enhances learning.[10]

If self-referencing enhances memory in adults, perhaps young children's natural bias to reference everything to themselves will give them a leg up when it comes to learning and remembering. I don't mean to imply that young children will learn or remember *better* than adults in most situations. In fact, their general learning abilities (to say nothing about their self-concept) are much less well developed than adults', so preschool children's learning and memory are much poorer than are those of older children or adults. It is *because* of their generally poor information-processing abilities that self-referencing becomes so valuable. A memory study by Darlene Mood illustrated this nicely. Preschool children were given sets of sentences to remember. Some sentences described the children and their personal experiences, whereas others described animals or non-personal relations with other people. Children remembered sentences containing personal references better than the other sentences, suggesting that their natural egocentrism provides them with a cognitive benefit that allows them to practice and refine comprehension skills that they would not have had the opportunity to do otherwise. From this perspective, egocentrism is not simply a cognitive deficit, but provides some information-processing benefits to young children.[11]

An egocentric benefit can be seen in situations in which children must determine whether they or someone else performed an action. *Source monitoring* refers to the ability to pinpoint the origins of our actions or the source of our knowledge. For example, when remembering an event, such as a car accident, did you see the accident yourself, hear about it on the radio, read about it in the paper, or did someone tell you about it? We all make source-monitoring errors occasionally, thinking we saw something that we actually read about, for example, but children are especially susceptible to them, at least certain types of them. And the types of errors they make may actually help them remember information better. For example, developmental psychologists Hilary Ratner, Mary Ann Foley, and their colleagues asked preschool children to create a collage with an adult. The child and the adult took turns putting pieces on the collage. After the collage was done, the children were unexpectedly asked who had put each piece on the collage, they or the adult. As you might expect, when children made errors, they were more likely to say that they had put a piece on the collage when in fact the adult had ("I did it" errors). They rarely erred in the opposite direction ("You did it" errors). This is another example of an egocentric bias (when in doubt, take personal credit for an action). Perhaps, Foley and Ratner reasoned, this self-referencing may lead to better memory for the actions. They tested this in another study in which 5-year-old children took turns with an adult placing furniture in a dollhouse. When later asked who had placed each item in the dollhouse, children made more "I did it" errors than "You did it" errors, but also showed better memory for the location of the furniture than children who did not collaborate with adults. So collaboration enhanced children's performance, but probably not in a way one might have expected. Rather, we have the counterintuitive situation of children's immature cognition (in this case their self-centered perspective) causing them to confuse their actions with those of their partner, which in turn actually produced better learning. This is consistent with the argument that immature aspects of young children's cognition are actually well adapted for their stage in development and may actually foster, as opposed to hinder, learning in some contexts.[12]

From Talking to Yourself to Playing with Others

Play is a characteristic of young animals. (I will have more to say about the role of play in childhood in Chapter 6.) But the topic of play intersects with egocentricity at least at one juncture. It seems that, in some contexts, young children's tendencies to talk to themselves, something Piaget called *egocentric speech* but others have termed *private speech*, helps them progress from solitary to more social forms of play.

It is not uncommon to see 2- and 3-year-old children standing or sitting around together, each engaged in similar playful activities. But a closer examination indicates that children are not actually playing with one another; rather they are playing side-by-side, so what one child says or does rarely affects the other. This has been termed *parallel play*. One thing you'll notice if you hang around groups of preschool children for any length of time is that they will often talk aloud while playing – not necessarily to one another, but describing or directing their own actions. One child might say, for example, "I'm gonna fly my plane and drop bombs on the road. Boom!" while another child rambles on how about he's going to build a road with this bulldozer and take all the dirt away. Piaget referred to such talk as *collective monologues*; the children talk "with" one another, but not really "to" one another. Children engage in more private speech when they are with other children, so the social setting does stimulate speech. It's just that it is speech for oneself and is not contingent on what other children do or say. The play cannot be described as cooperative or social, but perhaps as semi-social.[13]

Is such play merely a reflection of children's immature cognition, or might it have some adaptive features as well? Psychologists Roger Bakeman and John Brownlee observed 2.5- to 3.5-year-old children while they played over a three-week period. They identified five types of play activity varying in complexity: *unoccupied* (alone and not playing); *solitary play* (playing alone); *together* (with another child but not playing); *parallel play* (playing beside, but not with, another child); and *group play* (playing with another child or children).[14] Of particular interest was how children made transitions from one form of play to another. The transitions were not random. Children frequently made the switch from parallel play to group play, or from parallel play to "together," which in turn led to group play. What's happening here? One hypothesis is that children may engage in parallel play as an unconscious strategy for joining a group.

Perhaps the term "strategy" is a bit overblown here, but perhaps not. These children are perfectly capable of communicating with other people – they do so with their parents all the time. Their social skills are greatly limited, however, and they really have no deliberate plan for making friends or engaging in cooperative social behavior. But their egocentric language is well suited for getting conversations started. By hovering outside of a group of playing children and engaging in similar activities while talking to themselves, children may gradually work their way into group play. One cognitive handicap may help them overcome a social handicap.

Self-talk as Self-guidance

Piaget wasn't the only theorist to have an opinion about children's egocentric speech. The Soviet psychologist Lev Vygotsky, writing in the 1920s and 1930s, had a different perspective. Rather than seeing children's self-talk as a mere reflection of an egocentric worldview, Vygotsky believed that it played a role in intellectual development. Vygotsky believed that one important role of language is to guide problem-solving behavior. We essentially "tell ourselves" what to do when solving a problem. Egocentric speech, or what Vygotsky referred to as *private speech*, is essentially speech intended to guide behavior. Vygotsky referred to private speech as a *cognitive self-guidance system* that, with age and experience, eventually goes "underground" as covert verbal thought, or what Vygotsky called *inner speech*.[15]

Most adults use inner speech to guide their behavior. We talk to ourselves "in our heads," not needing to make overt the language we use to help solve some problem. Even adults, however, fall back to talking out loud, especially when the problem is a new one. I recall dancing a polka with my mother some years ago, and counting "one, two, three; one, two, three" aloud as I danced. It helped me, a novice dancer, keep on beat. But it apparently disturbed the covert counting of another dancer, who politely asked me to keep my counting to myself.

Preschool children are just learning to gain control of their own behavior, and as a result, need all the support they can get. That support comes in the form of private speech. Vygotsky noted, and others have since confirmed, that much of the private speech of young children occurs during problem-solving situations. A 4-year-old child putting a puzzle together may say to herself, "This one is blue in this corner, so I need to match it with another blue piece. I gotta find another blue piece with an edge to go here," and so on. The language does more than simply describe what the child is doing (although some private speech may do just that), but actually directs behavior. More recent research by developmental psychologists Laura Berk, Adam Winsler, and their colleagues have found that school-age children also use private speech to help them solve a host of school-type tasks, such as addition and subtraction problems. Young children who talk to themselves while solving such problems tend to be the brighter kids, apparently realizing before their peers that there is something they can do to make their job easier, even if that something is viewed as immature from adult standards. In contrast, children who are still using private speech to solve math problems at 10 years of age tend to be less bright than other children. They still need the support that self-talk provides them, whereas their intellectually more advanced peers are now using covert speech to guide their behavior.[16]

Both Vygotsky and Piaget agreed that private (or egocentric) speech characterizes young children and is thus a sign of immaturity, but they disagreed on the role that this immature form of functioning may play. It seems clear now that children's self-talk can have some advantages. Most people who have given the issue serious thought believe that Vygotsky had more of the story right than Piaget. Private speech, while perhaps reflecting a general egocentric worldview as Piaget proposed, also helps children gain control over their own problem-solving behavior. Children's self-talk is a window to their thinking. This is why asking a new reader to "read to yourself, in your head," may be futile. Young children need to make overt what an older child or an adult can make covert. Private speech is not just a sign of an immature mind, but a mechanism in achieving a mature one.

Risk Taking in Adolescence

Being self-centered is not a feature unique to preschoolers, of course. In fact, a special type of self-centered thought can be observed in adolescence. It's a long way from the egocentric perspective of the preschool child, who believes if she can hear the water rushing into her ears so can her father, to the adolescent, whose self-centeredness seems qualitatively quite different and frequently more problematic. Teenagers are often so caught up with their own issues – with defining who they are with respect to their family, friends, and the larger society, and who they will become in looming adulthood – that they seem to be in a world of their own. There is no lack of theories about adolescence, and several psychologists have extended Piaget's ideas about egocentricity to explain some aspects of teenage behavior. Such egocentricity can lead to risk taking, which can have some obvious negative consequences, but may also have some adaptive value for those youngsters who survive adolescence.

Tufts University developmental psychologist David Elkind suggested that two features express adolescents' egocentricity. First, they believe that they are constantly "on stage," playing to an *imaginary audience*. They think that other people are as interested in and as observant of them as they are of themselves. This results in a type of self-consciousness that, in some ways, is as extreme as that of the preschooler. Elkind referred to the second feature as the *personal fable*, a belief in one's uniqueness and invulnerability. Adolescents see themselves as invincible and that bad things only happen to other people. It goes without saying that such an attitude can result in high-risk and dangerous behavior, based on the dual belief of their invincibility ("I can drive 90 miles an hour on the highway. It's the slow-moving old farts who are the real problem"; "Other girls get pregnant, not me"; "I can drive fine after three or four beers"), and their mistaken belief that others are watching and are as concerned about their behavior as they are themselves. This can make *not* engaging in some risky behavior in a social setting difficult. (I recall a teenage boy swallowing three goldfish at a showing of the "Rocky Horror Picture Show" because he "didn't want to look like a jerk" by not doing it.[17])

At the same time, this attitude surely results in teenagers separating themselves from the safe haven of their parents and setting out to make their own lives. They may believe, for example, that, "Starting one's own business is a piece of cake," or "Going to school fulltime while working 40 hours a week is nothing to worry about," or "I can get a good deal by trading the family cow for a bag of magic beans." Although there are obviously some negative consequences to such risk-taking behavior, it results in adolescents experimenting with new ideas and tasks, some of which will be important for adult life.

This argument is not too dissimilar from those made by evolutionary theorists such as Richard Alexander and John Crook, who each proposed that hunting skills may have first developed in our species as a result of the risk-taking and exploratory dispositions of young males. The only way they could get access to females was by attaining something the older males wouldn't take risks for themselves – namely meat. By "bringing home the bacon," the young males had something to entice females with (the quickest way to a woman's heart is through her stomach?), or to share with the dominant male, who might reciprocate by sharing his harem.[18]

It would be disingenuous of me to suggest that risk taking in adolescence can be explained primarily by teenagers' unique brand of egocentricity. It clearly plays a role in their judgment of risk, but egocentricity itself cannot explain why teenagers, especially boys, so frequently engage in risky behavior. There is an emerging consensus among evolutionary psychologists that adolescent boys' risk taking is done mainly to impress girls, gain status among their peers, and intimidate male rivals.[19] This is consistent with Robert Triver's parental investment theory discussed in Chapter 1. Males, as the less-investing sex (less investing with respect to parenting responsibilities), compete with one another over access to females, the latter "choosing" males. This makes males more competitive for status and puts the onus on them to make a good impression with members of the opposite sex. Rising testosterone levels at puberty increase boys' self-confidence and reduce their fears. Teenagers also tend to be exceptionally healthy and resilient, making some of the risky behaviors they engage in less dangerous than they appear to adults. Adolescents have also not been prepared by evolution for many of the risky behaviors they engage in. Drug use, reckless driving, and gun play are all evolutionarily novel and thus don't trigger evolved aversions. Thus, although a cognitively immature perspective of one's abilities and judgment of risk clearly contributes to heightened risk-taking in adolescence, one must look to other theories to explain their prevalence.

Learning Language

We generally think that learning ability improves with age. We delay the instruction of complicated material until adolescence or beyond, believing that young children do not have the cognitive abilities, and likely the perseverance or motivation, to master such esoterica as calculus, chemistry, mechanical engineering, existential philosophy, or neuropsychology. And we're generally right. The neural immaturity that affords plasticity across childhood also limits information-processing and learning abilities.

But there are some exceptions to this general trend, the most obvious being language acquisition, a feat that anyone who has tried to learn a second language as an adult can attest to. Children's brains seem especially adapted to acquire language. Young children are better at learning a first and second language than are older children and adults. Even when an adult does manage to get a handle on a second language, there's always the accent. Children can seemingly acquire not only the semantics (meaning) and syntax (rules of grammar) of a second language easily, but also the pronunciation. In fact, school systems should take advantage of children's special aptitudes for language learning and begin teaching foreign tongues as early in the curriculum as possible. Some schools are doing this, but others are sticking with the same approach I encountered as a student, not offering foreign-language instruction until middle school or later.

The explanation for the age differences in ease of language acquisition focuses on the slow maturation of the brain. With age, the nervous system loses its flexibility, so that by puberty, the neural organization of the brain with respect to language is, for all practical purposes, fixed, making learning a language difficult. In a similar vein, a number of researchers have speculated that the advent of abstract thinking skills in adolescence interferes with implicit (unconscious) learning strategies, making language acquisition from this time and beyond difficult. In fact, rather than lamenting adults' difficulties with new languages, we should be impressed with preadolescent children's ability to acquire them. Slow growth extends the time when multiple forms of this uniquely human communication and representation system can be mastered.

That children are especially adapted for learning language is reflected in University of Hawaii linguist Derek Bickerton's observations of how a cohort of children will invent a real language from the nonlanguage communication systems that adults around them use. Throughout history, different groups of people, each with their own language, have come together, often to work. How do people communicate with one another without a common language? Gestures help, and the language of the "bosses," the plantation owners, for example, becomes the core of a communication system. The result is something called a *pidgin* – several languages combined at a rudimentary level used to convey necessary information within the group (the "workers") and between group members and their "hosts." A pidgin is not a true language. Word order is often highly variable and there is little in the way of a grammatical system. It is similar to the way tourists in a foreign country speak. They know a handful of words, may not know how to make nouns plural, often use only the present tense, and sprinkle their prose with words from their own, and perhaps other, languages. (This is the way *I* speak German or Spanish, anyway.) But pidgins can quickly transform into true languages in the hands (or mouths) of children. Based on his own studies and historical evidence, Bickerton documented how the children of pidgin speakers transform the language they hear and turn it into a true language – called a *creole* – often in a single generation.[20]

Compelling recent evidence of this process comes from studies of deaf children who invented Nicaraguan Sign Language. Before the 1970s, there were no schools for the deaf in Nicaragua, so there was no deaf culture and no recognized sign language. With the opening of a school for the deaf in Managua, deaf children were taught to read Spanish and to read lips. They were not taught to sign. Children brought with them the gestures they used at home to communicate with friends and family, and used these signs to communicate with other deaf children. From these interactions a true sign language emerged. Over the course of three cohorts of students, children created a true sign language. Nicaraguan Sign Language was systematically modified from one cohort of children to the next, with children aged 10 years and younger generating most of the changes. In other words, sequences of children created a new sign language from the incomplete forms used by their predecessors.[21]

Bickerton speculated that the transition we see in children from pidgins to creoles might be similar to what occurred in human evolution. Early language, such as that possibly used by our *Homo erectus* ancestors, may have been much like pidgins. While we're speculating, how did ancient humans convert pidgins, or *proto-languages*, to true languages? Physician and science writer Lewis Thomas proposed the idea that the *capacity* or *potential* for language had evolved as a result of brain expansion, but no one had yet thought of using it. Adults communicated with grunts, gestures, and individual words to express ideas, perhaps stringing words and gestures together to form something like a pidgin. Children learned these words from their parents; but in large, continuous, playgroups with other children they discovered how to put them together into sentences. That is, through play and the process of discovery learning, children invented grammar, and thus language. Language is the child's gift to the man.[22]

Although this must remain as speculation, it is a hypothesis that has much appeal. Given what we know about both human and nonhuman-animal development, it seems likely that it will be children who explore and "play with" new ideas, in a "purposeless" way, leading to new discoveries. Language is not likely to be the intentional invention of a committee of adults, but more likely the emerging product of groups of playful youth who create and use language for "no apparent reason."

What should be clear is that for language to evolve it must have been associated with changes during *childhood*, not during adulthood. Most theories of the evolution of language focus on what adaptive problems it solved or advantages it provided to *adults* of a community; but it should be clear that there must have been some substantial advantages to children as well, for here is where mutations related to language acquisitions must have had their effect. Developmental psycholinguist John Locke and anthropologist Barry Bogin recognized this and proposed that the ability of young children to communicate with their parents, particularly during (what we call now) the preschool years when children are no longer nursing but are still dependent on their parents for survival, was one such advantage. Another came in adolescence and was more related to courtship of the opposite sex and to competition between members of the same sex. Locke and Bogin's hypotheses are speculative, of course, but are based on the wealth of evidence we have on language development, how language is used by people around the globe today, communication systems in other species, and fossil evidence. Although we can't say for certain that their ideas are correct, we can be confident that they're right about natural selection being related to the evolution of language operating on *children*, and that it was something about children's immature cognitive system that made the acquisition of language possible.[23]

This research, and many other studies illustrating a sensitive period for language acquisition, attests to the fact that children are well adapted to this particular niche of childhood. But language has always been viewed as special, and it may seem a bit of a stretch to use children's particular proficiency in acquiring language as an example of the adaptive value of cognitive immaturity. A more compelling argument for the role of cognitive immaturity on language could be made if there were a general cognitive limitation that actually facilitates language acquisition, in addition to explanations that attribute young children's facility with learning to talk with the loss of neurological flexibility over time. There is some evidence, albeit indirect, for this position.

Psycholinguist Elissa Newport has speculated that young children's limitations in encoding complex stimuli may make some aspects of language learning easier. According to Newport, "If children perceive and store only component parts of the complex linguistic stimuli to which they are exposed, while adults more readily perceive and remember the whole complex stimulus, children may be in a better position to locate the components."[24] Specifically, children should have an easier time learning aspects of language that involve analysis of particular components, such as learning the prefixes, suffixes, and word endings that denote important syntactic rules and categories (such as plurals, gender, and tense markings). Adults, on the other hand, should have an advantage in learning aspects of language that require integration and/or complex wholes, such as whole-word learning. Newport's *less-is-more hypothesis* holds that children's limited information-processing abilities reduce the complexity of what they must master, resulting in easier initial acquisition. This is similar to the arguments made by Turkewitz and Kenny discussed earlier in this chapter, who proposed that perceptual limitations in infancy are adaptive in that they allow one sensory system to develop (hearing, for example) without having to compete for neural resources with another, usually later-developing system (vision, for example).

With success and time, maturationally paced abilities gradually increase, as does language learning. Newport notes that children's early language learning starts out slowly, more slowly actually than adults learning a second language. This is because children process only parts of complex stimuli, starting with usually single syllables. This is true not only in spontaneous speech but also in imitation. As a result, children extract only limited pieces of the speech stream. But the simplified language children deal with makes the job of learning language easier. In comparison, adults begin learning a second language faster than children do, because they more readily perceive and remember the whole complex stimulus. But the advantage is short lived. They are then faced with the problem of making sense of this larger corpus of language they have acquired in a rote-like fashion.

Newport tested her hypothesis using a computer simulation that essentially limited how much the computer program could keep in memory at any one time. This is comparable to varying the size of children's short-term memories, or how much they can keep in mind at any one time. Just as children's short-term memories increase with age, so did how much the computer simulation could process over repeated trials. Basically, Newport found that restricting "memory" resulted in early losses (for example, whole words were often lost), but that word endings, such as those that denote plurals and verb tense, were more apt to be retained. There was also an improvement in signal-to-noise ratio (that is, the ratio of relevant linguistic information to irrelevant background information). In general, the restrictions on how much the computer program could process, analogous to young children's limited short-term-memory store, made language learning easier than when restrictions were lifted, analogous to the short-term-memory store of adults. Psychologist Jeffrey Elman, using a very different type of computer simulation, reached a similar conclusion, and used the metaphor *the importance of starting small* to describe his findings. In support of the computer simulations, experimental research has shown that adults learn an artificial grammar faster when presented with smaller units of the language.[25]

Not only are children's brains limited in how much language information they can process, but adults seem to realize this and simplify their speech when talking to infants and young children. Adults use what has been called *child-directed speech* (or *infant-directed speech* when addressed to babies) in talking to children. Such talk will be highly familiar to anyone who has interacted with infants or young children, or seen others interacting with them. Adults (and older children, for that matter) keep their speech short and simple. There is often much repetition in child-directed speech and it tends to be more grammatical than adult-directed speech. It is also universal (or nearly so), although some cultures engage in it more (or use more exaggerated forms of it) than others. There is often a sing-songy character to such speech, and infants, in particular, are more attentive when spoken to in infant-directed speech than adult-directed speech. Much as the computer simulations of Newport and Elman, as children get more proficient in using language, the language adults direct to them gets more complicated.

The coupling of children's limited information-processing abilities and the simplified language they receive provides them with a reduced body of linguistic data from which to extract the sounds, grammar, and semantic rules of their mother tongue. Language acquisition seems to be a conspiracy between children's developing brains and adults whose speech to children seems to match the brain's processing abilities.[26]

How Do Adults View Children's Immature Thinking?

In Chapter 1 I mentioned briefly Konrad Lorenz's observation that adults find infantile facial features endearing and cute. In research since Lorenz's initial observations, adults consistently view children with immature facial features as cuter, more in need of "parental" caregiving and protection, and less responsible for misdeeds they commit than more mature-looking children. This preference for "babyness" is first seen in girls between the ages of 12 and 14 years, and two years later for boys, suggesting that it may have evolved to prepare adolescents for parenthood. There is a caveat to this effect, however. In one study, parents recommend less severe punishment for baby-faced 4-year-olds who committed some misdeed than for mature-faced 4-year-olds; the reverse was true, however, for 11-year-olds. When perceived intentionality of the act was held constant, baby-faced 11-year-olds were punished *more severely* than mature-faced 11-year-olds. In other words, when an older child commits a misdeed "on purpose," looking young for his or her age becomes a detriment, not an advantage.[27]

Are there similar benefits, and perhaps detriments, for children's immature thinking? On the one hand, young children's interpretation of the world can be very amusing. Art Linkletter, a pioneer of early television, had a segment on his weekly show called "Kids Say the Darndest Things," where he interviewed young children with the explicit intent of getting them to "say the darndest things," which they did to the amusement of Mr Linkletter and his audience, and often to the chagrin of their parents. On the other hand, the immature thinking of young children can sometimes be exasperating. One problem with immature thought is that it's not very effective in getting a job done.

My colleague Carlos Hernández Blasi from James I University in Castellón, Spain, students Justin Rosenberg, Hye Eun Shin, and I asked groups of college students to determine which of two hypothetical children, one professing immature thinking and one more mature thinking, was more intelligent, more cute, and more sneaky.[ii] We told some participants to imagine the children were 3 years old, whereas others were to imagine the children were 9 years old. We thought that the adults would think kindly toward the younger, immature-thinking children, rating them as more cute and less sneaky, although also less intelligent than the more mature children, but that they wouldn't be as kindly toward the older, immature-thinking children.

[ii] We actually asked participants to make judgments on 11 different items, which, through statistical analyses, were grouped into three categories: cute (C), intelligence (I), and sneaky (S). The 11 items were: Endearing (C), Intelligent (I), Nice (C), Cute (C), Friendly (C), Sneaky (S), Likely to lie (S), Smart (I), Protective of (C), Aggravated with (S), Impatient with (S).

That's not how the results turned out, however. The age of the child made no difference in the college students' ratings. What did make a difference was the type of immature thinking children displayed. Some of the examples of immature thinking fell into a category we called *intuitive*, which reflects thinking that still persists in adults, even though it is suppressed, and schooled knowledge and rules of logic make it clearly incorrect.[28] For example, attributing life characteristics to inanimate objects reflects intuitive thinking, as reflected in the following scenario:

At breakfast on a cloudy day, Carla's mother asked her, "Why do you think the sun's not out today?" Carla replied, "Because it's mad."

Adults know that the sun isn't mad and that attributing emotion to the sun is nonsensical. Nonetheless, we can easily identify with attributing human, or life, characteristics to inanimate objects, and when we see children do it, we find it endearing. We believe that such intuitive thinking stems from people's tendencies (perhaps unique to humans) to attribute events to the *intention* of some agent, usually (and appropriately) other people, but also to natural forces (The weather must be out to get me. Every time I wash my car, it's sure to rain), or even inanimate objects (The old guitar didn't want to sit in the closet, but wanted to be played).[iii]

Other types of thinking fell into a category we called *non-intuitive*, defined as patterns of thought that adults tend not to make past childhood. Our general knowledge, logic, reasoning, and cognitive abilities, combined with experience, override such immature cognition. These included a tendency to overestimate one's abilities ("I can remember all 20 pictures real easy"), an inability to inhibit behavior ("I couldn't wait as long as the teacher said to, so I peeked"), and an inability to reverse thought, as reflected in the following example:

[iii] I recall as a not-too-young elementary school student having mixed feelings about getting a new baseball glove, not wanting to "hurt the feelings" of my old, trusty glove, or being careful to use all the ink in a favorite pen, so not to "disappoint" the unused ink. The ink had a "purpose" and to discard it without letting it fulfill its purpose somehow seemed wrong (perhaps this was just an aspect of my frugal Yankee upbringing). I knew very well that baseball gloves and ink were inanimate and had no thoughts or emotions, and I remember, even then, believing how silly such thinking was. But I couldn't avoid my intuitions of attributing intentions and emotions to some of the inanimate objects that I was particularly fond of.

Alexis came home from school one day and told her mom, "Mommy, today at school, we learned that 2 plus 3 equals 5." Alexis's mother then said, "That's good, then how much is 3 plus 2?" Alexis said, "I dunno ! I never learned that!"

In brief, immature thinking appears to enhance adults' positive feelings and reduce their negative feelings toward children, but only for those scenarios that reflect intuitive cognitive errors. So some aspects of children's immature thinking seem not only to provide children with benefits in terms of information processing, but also in terms of how adults perceive, and presumably, behave, toward them.[29]

Adapting to Childhood

Both Newport's metaphor "less is more" and Elman's "the importance of starting small" are good ones for this entire chapter. Sometimes, given how much one has to learn, it makes sense starting out small, gradually building up complexity. Although this may seem like a sensible strategy, what's counterintuitive about it is that real limitations in how infants and young children perceive or understand the world are beneficial toward this end. The underdeveloped sensory systems of infants allow their brains to get one perceptual system organized before starting on another. Children's egocentric perspective causes them to reference many experiences to themselves, enhancing their learning at a time when their intellectual skills are quite limited. And in addition to what may be special "language organs" children possess that make acquiring language possible, their limited information-processing abilities, coupled with adults' simplified language when talking to them, make the job of learning language easier. Cognitive immaturity has an upside. The brain has evolved to develop on a schedule that matches the demands of children's environments. It really couldn't have gone much differently, or our ancestors would not have survived the niche of childhood and we would not be here today.

5

The Advantages of Thinking You're Better than You Are

The child carries the seed of the future, and nature's primary interest in children is that they reach puberty safely and produce the next generation of children. Nature has buffered our children not only physically – prepubescent children have the lowest death rate from all causes – but psychologically as well, by endowing them with hope, abundant and irrational.

Martin E. P. Seligman, *Learned Optimism*

Children are natural optimists, for the future appears to them to be suffused with promises that will surely be fulfilled with growth. That is why children are so impatient to grow up.

Ashley Montague, *Growing Young*

◆　　◆　　◆　　◆

I remember it well even 50 years later. The first-grade class was getting fidgety. There were a few minutes left before the bell rang, so the teacher decided to fill the time with some entertainment. "Can anyone sing a song for us?" she asked, and several children gave renditions of their favorite tunes. "Can anyone dance?" she asked. I felt that this was my time to shine. "I can tap dance!" I answered. I walked to the front of the room and proceeded to shuffle my feet, trying my best to imitate the dancers I had seen on TV. Well, the result *was* entertainment, but strictly comedy. My classmates roared with laughter and even the teacher was unable to hide her amusement. Fortunately the bell rang, and the children lined up to go home, so my stint in the spotlight was short lived.

My false belief in my artistic talent was not unusual – young children believe that they are more competent than they really are. They believe that they are smarter, stronger, faster, and generally more talented than an objective evaluation of their behavior would suggest. What is a bit different about my experience is that I found out quite rudely that the belief I held in my tap-dancing skill didn't correspond to reality. I had seen dancers on television many times, had practiced in the privacy of my room, carefully watching my feet go through the same movements as the TV dancers. If it hadn't been for that fateful day in first grade, I might *still* believe I possess superior dancing ability (although adolescent dating experiences would have likely persuaded me otherwise).

Sooner or later, we all come to grips with our own limitations, and so it should be. Life would be a strange and dangerous place if we adults had the same over-confidence in our skills as the average 6-year-old does in his or her own abilities. It is not adaptive for adults to believe they can fly planes, operate heavy equipment, or climb mountains without training, but these are all beliefs that many young children hold. But unlike adults, children receive adaptive benefits from these beliefs. The overblown confidence young children have in themselves contributes to their future success. Believing one is competent, even when one is not, frequently results in competent behavior – maybe not immediately, but in the long run. Young children, who have so few true talents because of their immaturity and lack of experience, need to feel competent in what they attempt. It seems that our species has evolved so that young children's poor physical and cognitive abilities are paired with poor *metacognitive* abilities; counterintuitively, this double deficit may be a plus in the long run.

I begin this chapter with an examination of *metacognition*, the knowledge people have of their own cognition. Young children typically have poor metacognition, consistently overestimating their abilities. They usually display unrealistic optimism for their future, but can develop a pessimistic attitude from adults who interact with them. I next examine the possible reasons for this optimism. Among the candidates are children's limited cognitive abilities, how they (and adults around them) define success and failure, how they view effort and ability, and their expectations for success. Next, I leave the cognitive realm and investigate children's appraisals of their social standing. Children don't only overestimate their intellectual abilities, but also their position in social hierarchies, believing that they are of higher status than others believe them to be. I then look at the benefits of young children's poor self-knowledge; children who overestimate their abilities develop a positive sense of *self-efficacy* and persist at difficult tasks, eventually mastering problems that a more metacognitively in-touch child may have quit. But they are also more prone to injuries and accidents, an obvious negative side effect of believing one is more skilled than one really is.

The Development of Metacognition – Knowing What We Know

Metacognition refers to the knowledge people have about the workings of their own minds – their mental strong and weak points, the skills they possess – as well as their ability to evaluate and monitor their own behavior. This was a major area of research in cognitive psychology in the 1970s and 1980s – with both adults and children – and continues today.[1]

Issues of metacognition – knowing what we know – deal implicitly with self-awareness, or consciousness. To what extent are we aware of the processes underlying our thinking? And what difference does it make to our mental lives? Does having a high degree of awareness of our cognitive functioning affect how we think? Or is metacognition, and consciousness in general, merely an epiphenomenon, the inconsequential product of unconscious cognitive activity? The problems involved in defining human consciousness and in formulating a theory of consciousness free from the "ghost in the machine" are difficult ones. Yet consciousness cannot be ignored, and most cognitive developmentalists today believe that age changes in metacognition play an important role in children's intellectual development. I go a bit further here and argue that children's poor metacognitive skills are actually adaptive.

For every form of cognition one can think of, there is a corresponding form of metacognition. So, for example, the processes of attention, memory, reading, communication, and imitation all have associated "metas." Typically, high levels of cognition are associated with high levels of metacognition, but this is not necessarily the case. People of all ages, but particularly children, often show cognitive abilities that are not consistent with their level of self-awareness.

For example, in a series of experiments my wife Barbara and I performed in the early 1980s, first-, third-, and fifth-grade children were asked to recall, in any order they liked, the names of the children in their current school class.[2] Because this was the end of the school year, we expected that most children would have little difficulty with this task, and we were right. Even the first-grade children remembered greater than 70% of the names correctly. And nearly all of the children showed some systematic way of remembering the names. For example, children would start recalling the names of their classmates in the row nearest the door and continue until arriving at the last child in the row nearest the window. Such attempts were rarely perfect. For instance, a child may remember CHRIStopher and then jump two rows to recall CHRIStine, before returning to a more organized approach. Different children used different schemes – some used seating arrangement, some reading groups, some friends – but most children used at least a semi-systematic approach to recalling the names of their classmates.

When later complimented on their high levels of performance and asked how they had recalled so many of the names, a majority of the younger children were at a loss. Most first-grade children shrugged their shoulders or said things such as "I used my brain," or "I just *know* them." Others provided us with "real" answers, such as "I remembered them alphabetically. Mrs Johnson calls the roll every morning and I remembered them that way." In many cases, these "real" answers were unrelated to what they actually did. Most children were out of touch with their memory functioning, performing well in this case, despite not knowing exactly how they had done it. Their metamemory was lagging behind their memory. Children did no better when we presented them with a forced-choice task, telling them "Some kids your age remember children by where they sit, some use reading groups, some name the boys and then the girls, or some kids name the black kids and then the white kids. Which one did you use?" Although most first- through fifth-grade children did indeed use, to some significant extent, one of these four techniques for recalling the names of children in their class, the majority failed to pick the strategy that corresponded to what they did when remembering their classmates' names. Their recognition of strategy use was no better than when they were asked to explain what they had done. Children who described accurately the strategies they had used in recalling their classmates' names *did* remember a few more names than children who were unable to describe their strategies, but memory for the latter children was still exceptionally high. Good metacognitive knowledge (or *metamemory knowledge* in the present case) may enhance task performance, but it obviously is not necessary for it.

Admittedly, this is an atypical example. What is more customarily the case is that both cognition (memory, attention, reading) and metacognition (metamemory, meta-attention, metareading) improve with age. However, as our studies with children's recall of their classmates' names indicate, the relationship is not a straightforward one.

Rather, the relationship between cognition and metacognition is a *bidirectional* one, with changes in one factor influencing changes in the other.[3]

Predicting and Evaluating Performance

A particularly important aspect of metacognition for our purposes is prediction. How well do children evaluate how well they will perform on a particular task? How "in touch" are they with their cognitive and physical abilities? On the other side of the coin is post-task evaluation, how well children think they had performed some task. Prediction and evaluation are important factors in both cognitive and social development. Social psychologist Albert Bandura[4] concluded that the confidence people have in their competence in a particular domain influences what tasks they choose to perform and how long they persist at those tasks. (I'll discuss Bandura's ideas at greater length later in this chapter.) Thus, a child's degree of confidence will influence which tasks he or she attempts and how long one persists at a task before quitting. This, in turn, will determine to a significant extent what is learned.

Basically, young children are the Pollyannas of the world when it comes to estimating their own abilities. As the parent of any preschool child can tell you, they have an overly optimistic perspective of their own physical and mental abilities and are only minimally influenced by experiences of "failure." Preschoolers seem to truly believe that they are able to drive racing cars, use power tools, and find their way to Grandma's house all by themselves; it is only their stubborn and restricting parents who prevent them from displaying these impressive skills. These children have not fully learned the distinction between knowing about something and actually being able to do it. They don't understand the difference between identifying a set of actions ("Look, that's tap dancing!") and producing those actions themselves (shuffle, stumble, shuffle).

One example of preschool children's overestimation of their cognitive skills comes from a pioneering study by developmental psychologists Steven Yussen and Victor Levy. They showed nursery school children, third graders, and adults sets of 10 pictures and asked them to predict how many pictures they could remember in the order they had seen them. Most older children and adults estimated that they would be able to remember five to seven pictures, and they were generally right, although adults overestimated considerably less (overestimation = 6%) than the third graders (overestimation = 40%). In contrast, most of the 4- and 5-year-olds predicted that they would remember far more than they actually did, with half predicting that they would remember all 10 pictures. But when tested, they remembered only three or four, far short of their predictions. In fact, the degree of overestimation for these young children was 152%! Were they discouraged by their poor performances? Not really. "I'm sure I could remember all 10 if we did it again," was a claim made by many of the preschoolers. They had *seen* all the pictures, they *knew* what all the pictures were, and of course, thought they could remember all of them perfectly.[5]

Although the children in the Yussen and Levy experiment were better able to judge afterwards how well they had done on the task than they were able to predict ahead of time, this is not always the case. Young children often do not have the knowledge to fully judge their performance after a task is completed, or they use a very lax standard when it comes to judging their own proficiency. An anecdote will illustrate young children's frequent overestimation of their abilities. Five-year-old Nicholas sat at the computer at his grandparents' house and wanted to "write." After being shown a few fundamentals, he was left to his "writing." (This was before the days when most 5-year-olds were more computer-literate than their parents.) After a short while, he appeared, paper in hand, and gave it to his grandmother. "Here, *you* can read, Grandma," he said, "tell me what I wrote!" He knew he couldn't read, but he still thought he could write. When she told him it looked a lot like *The Three Billy Goats Gruff*, he was very happy and went back to the den to type another story (which turned out to look a lot like *Peter Pan*). Later, Nicholas showed one of his stories to his grandfather, who had been informed that there was another writer in the family. "Isn't that nice," his grandfather said. "It looks a lot like *The Three Billy Goats Gruff.*" Nicholas frowned and said, "You're just being silly, Papa, it's *Peter Pan!*"

Researchers examining children's achievement motivation have also noted differences between children's predictions and performances. In research dating to the 1960s, before the coining of "metacognition," young children had been shown to overestimate how well they will perform on a variety of tasks, ranging from balancing balls on a moving platform to putting Xs into squares. These studies make it clear that young children often ignore evidence of failure, refusing to believe that their performance is as poor as it is. Of course, these children are not incapable of accurately evaluating their own behavior. When children are given very explicit and salient feedback, they are better able to make accurate assessments of their own performance. One shouldn't think of preschoolers as little people walking around who are totally detached from reality. They *can* make relatively accurate assessments of their performance under many circumstances; they do, however, have a more difficult time doing this than older children, and they don't seem particularly motivated to make accurate assessments of their less-than-perfect achievements.[6]

In fact, research clearly indicates that children as young as 2 years of age are aware of adults' expectations and know when they have not met them, at least when simple tasks with definite criteria of success are used. For example, in one study, preschool children were given simple puzzles to solve (some of which had oversized pieces making success impossible). Many children, some as young as 2 years of age, responded to failure on these tasks by turning their head or body away from the experimenter and otherwise generally avoiding social contact. They seemingly realized that their performance was not as it should have been and anticipated some negative response from the adult. Likewise, when young children succeeded on these tasks, they sought adult approval. Thus, even very young children are sometimes aware of their successes and failures and are responsive to reactions (or anticipated reactions) from others to their performances.[7]

UCLA psychologist Deborah Stipek and her colleagues have done extensive research looking at how children view themselves in terms of "smartness" and how they judge their academic abilities.[8] Stipek reports that young children's assessments of their school-related ability are quite high. Most children in the first grade and younger think of themselves as being "one of the smartest kids in my class." It is only at the second and third grades when children begin to have a more realistic estimate of their own academic standing. Beginning about this time, children's assessments of their own school abilities are similar to those of their teachers and peers. Also worth mentioning is the fact that young children's overestimations are usually reserved for themselves; they are more accurate when it comes to evaluating the "smartness" of other children.

Children are not the only ones to overestimate their abilities or knowledge, of course. Adults do it all the time, especially with respect to their understanding of mechanical devices (how a crossbow works) or of physical or biological phenomena (what causes earthquakes, how the heart works). But when adults are required to provide detailed explanations of how something actually works, or if they are provided with an expert's description of a phenomenon, they quickly readjust downward their judgment of their own knowledge, realizing that they didn't know quite as much as they thought they had. Leon Rozenbilt and Frank Keil referred to this as the *illusion of explanatory depth*.[9]

What about children? We know they tend to overestimate what they know, but will they also re-evaluate how knowledgeable they are when they have to explain how something works or when given an expert's description? Yale psychologists Candice Mills and Frank Keil[10] asked kindergarten, second-, and third-grade children to rate how well they understood the workings of several mechanical devices: a toaster, a gumball machine, a water faucet handle, a stapler, a toilet, or a music box. They were to give themselves 5 stars if they really knew a lot about how a device worked and 1 star if they didn't understand the workings of the device at all. Not surprisingly, the younger children initially gave themselves more stars than did the older children. They were then asked to explain how a device worked, and later were given an explanation by an expert. Each time they re-rated their understanding of the device. Fourth-grade children, and to a lesser extend second-grade children, showed the same pattern of the illusion of explanatory depth as adults do. They lowered their ratings after generating an explanation themselves and after hearing an expert's description. For example, 71% of the second graders and 79% of the fourth graders gave lower ratings of their knowledge about a device after providing an explanation for how it worked than they had initially. Not so the kindergarten children. Although a third of these youngsters did lower their ratings of self-knowledge after explaining how a device worked, nearly as many (25%) increased their ratings. And their average ratings actually *increased* after hearing an expert's description. The higher ratings were not due to these children actually knowing more about how the devices worked. Based on their explanations, they actually knew a good deal less than the older children.

Mills and Keil speculated that the illusion of explanatory depth might be adaptive, both for children and adults. Because one cannot have complete knowledge of how things work, believing you understand something better than you do keeps people satisfied with their "skeletal theories about the world." One does not have to truly understand how a radio or toaster works to use them, and it does one little good to spend time pondering these things (unless one is a scientist or engineer). But this adaptive bias develops, with children much younger than 5 years old seeming not to benefit from feedback, but maintaining their generally overly optimistic sense of what they know about the world.

Some years ago, Jane Gaultney, Brandi Green, and I reported evidence of children's overestimation of their performance in a study of *meta-imitation*, an awareness of one's own imitative abilities.[11] In one study, we asked parents to keep diaries of their children's imitative attempts. Nineteen mothers and two fathers watched their children over a two-week period and made assessments of their children's attempts at imitating models. To get an idea of age changes in children's meta-imitation, we divided the children into a younger (average age = 3 years, 7 months) and older (average age = 5 years, 2 months) group. Parents asked children how well they thought they would be able to imitate the behavior in question (prediction). They wrote a description of children's imitative attempts, and, after children had attempted to imitate a model, they asked them how well they thought they had done (post-task evaluation, or postdiction). We then compared the children's predictions and postdictions with their parents' accounts of actual performance and rated each as either an overestimation (stating that they could imitate more accurately than they actually had), accurate, or an underestimation (stating that they could imitate less accurately than they actually had).

Not surprisingly, both the younger and older children's predictions of their imitative abilities were rated as overestimations greater than 50% of the time. These children told their parents that they would do a fine job of imitating activities, when it was obvious, even to their own parents, that they were not. Children were a bit more accurate in their post-task evaluations, but even here, they overestimated approximately 40% of the time. What is particularly striking is that underestimations were rare, accounting for only about 5% of the predictions and 2.5% of the children's post-task evaluations.

Some examples of children's predictions, attempts at imitations, and post-task evaluations may be helpful. Many children tried to imitate some adult tasks, such as washing dishes or putting on make-up. One mother wrote that she was awakened one morning by a crash from the bathroom where she found her 5-year-old son standing over the broken pieces of his cereal bowl. He explained that he was washing his bowl, just like his mother does, but it was slippery and fell out of his hands. He insisted that he was quite capable of washing his own bowl, and that the slip that morning was just an accident. Another mother wrote about her 3.5-year-old daughter. The girl was watching her mother put on make-up and asked to be allowed to do the same. She said that she could put on lipstick just like mommy and proceeded to demonstrate. Her mother reported that she got more on her face and hands than on her lips, but her daughter was pleased with her efforts, saying, "Look mommy, just like you."

Parents also reported to us that occasionally their children tried to imitate TV characters dancing or performing other physical feats, such as karate. Almost unanimously, the parents said that their children's attempts were little more than jumping up and down or relatively uncoordinated kicking. Yet that was not the way the children saw things, often professing pride in how well they mimicked the actions.

We reported two other investigations, each confirming that pre-school children rarely underestimate their abilities to imitate, and are sometimes better at evaluating after-the-fact than predicting their imitative attempts, with older children (5-year-olds) usually being more accurate than younger children (3-year-olds). For example, in one study, 3-, 4-, and 5-year-old children were shown videotapes of adults performing behaviors varying in difficulty (for instance, juggling one, two, or three balls) and were asked to predict how well they thought they could do each task. After having a chance to actually attempt the task, children were asked to rate how well they thought they had done it. Children's estimates of their performances were compared with assessments made by adult observers. Our findings showed that all groups of children overestimated their imitative abilities, predicting ahead of time that they would be able to do a better job and believing afterward that they had done better than they actually did. Expected age differences were found, with 3-year-olds overestimating more than the 4- and 5-year-olds. In general, even the oldest children tested in our studies (5-year-olds) were out of touch with their imitative skills, thinking that because they observed the behavior and presumably understood it, they could also reproduce it ("I see therefore I know").

It would certainly seem that being able to accurately predict and evaluate one's abilities and performance would be an intellectual plus. Generally, individuals who know about their strong and weak points are likely to be more successful in solving problems than individuals who do not have these metacognitive skills. But being out of touch with one's physical and mental abilities has its benefits for young children, who are at the low end of the mental ability scale. Having poor metacognitive skills results in children believing that they are capable of more than they really are. This encourages exploration of new territories and reduces fear of failure in young learners. If our budding young writer, Nicholas, had realized that his first literary attempt actually looked more like a laser printer demo, he might still be suffering from writer's block.

When Failure Cannot Be Denied: Belief in the Future

But even the most optimistic child has to realize his or her limitations. Anyone who has tried to teach a 5-year-old how to ride a bike knows that children experience failure. Young children may believe they're more talented than they are, but they're not stupid. They know that they cannot out-run their older sister, tie their shoes, or skateboard down their driveways without falling. They know this because they've tried repeatedly and failed. Nonetheless, they believe that they *will one day* be able to do all these things, and many more. In fact, they have an overly optimistic perspective in the ability to change, specifically to improve one's behavior, psychological characteristics, and even one's physical limitations with time. This is fitting, for there are many things that children cannot do well in the present that they will be able to do in the future (riding a bike, for example). But this belief in change also extends to characteristics that older children and adults believe are relatively stable over time, including physical characteristics (a short stature), as well as psychological ones (propensity toward aggression, or fearfulness).

Developmental psychologist Kristi Lockhart and her colleagues[12] investigated what they termed *protective optimism* by assessing how children of different ages and adults viewed the likelihood that different physical and psychological traits were likely to change over time. Children were told stories about children who, both at age 5 and at age 10, had certain negative traits. Some of those traits were described as biological in nature, such as being extremely short, missing a finger, or having poor eyesight. Others were described as psychological, such as being unusually mean, very messy, or fearful. Still others were described as hybrid traits (combining aspects of both biological and psychological features), such as being very aggressive, having attention problems, or being ugly. Both 5- and 6-year-old children and 8- and 9-year-old children were more likely than adults to believe that these negative traits would change in a positive direction by the time the protagonists in the stories reached 21 years of age. But the effect was particularly large for the youngest children. Although the 8- and 9-year-olds believed that many of these negative characteristics would change so that these children would grow up to be "average" (like everybody else), nearly half of the 5- to 6-year-olds believed that traits would change to the opposite, more positive pole. This included not just the psychological and hybrid traits, but also the biological ones, such as a change in physical stature, growing a new finger, or having good eyesight. When other children were asked similar questions about positive traits (for example, being tall, attractive, friendly), 5- and 6-year-olds, like older children and adults, generally believed these good traits were likely to persist over time. It's the negative ones that become more positive, not vice versa.

Young children also believed that people have a good deal of individual control in changing traits, of all kinds. They realized that one may have less control when it comes to changing a physical trait, such as growing back a missing a finger, than a psychological trait, such as being mean; but they were nonetheless more apt than older children and adults to believe that people have great control over changing their physical and psychological selves.

What is "protective" about this optimism? As I've discussed before, children's lack of awareness of their physical and intellectual limitations permits them to try new tasks, and persist at older ones, without taking too seriously the negative feedback they get. But what about when negative feedback is unavoidable? Children do fall off their bikes, do (sometimes) cry at little provocation, and cannot reach the glasses in the cupboard without standing on a chair. But these things will change with time, and young children realize this. They are not easily discouraged by their shortcomings, because these, they believe, will change for the better over time. And why shouldn't they believe this? Children's positive view of change is an accurate reflection of their own experiences. Abilities change quickly in early childhood. Children learn to tie their shoes, to swim, and to balance on the fence in front of the house. Adults encourage them, telling them that their less-than-perfect performance is "pretty good," and that they will improve with age. Also, young children tend to view adults as universally capable, and they may believe that with time and adulthood they, too, will be able to accomplish anything they set their minds to (even growing another finger). Just growing up will take care of most of children's shortcomings, and the rest can be handled by practice and a desire to change. (I recall one 6-year-old telling me that he would stop picking his nose when he turned 7. He realized that this behavior was far from grown-up; but he was only 6. By 7 he'd be old enough to stop picking his nose in public. My recollection is that there was no magical change in nose-picking behavior on this child's seventh birthday, but by the time he was seven and a half, I don't recall seeing him with his finger up his nose.)

Without a belief that they will become more competent in all aspects of their functioning, childhood could be a depressing time, indeed. But as it turns out, children rarely feel helpless, but have optimism "abundant and irrational" for their future.

The Roots of Pessimism and Depression

Does such optimism in their behavior and the future inoculate children from depression? Young children can be sad, but do they ever get depressed? Children do become depressed, but the absolute rate is low. Yet, rates of depression are increasing in adulthood, in adolescence, and even during the preteen years, and with it, a generally pessimistic view of the world. How do optimistic preschoolers and young elementary school children turn into pessimistic, and often depressed, teenagers? Martin E. P. Seligman of the University of Pennsylvania has spent a distinguished career studying optimism and pessimism in adults, children, and even rats. He has documented that pessimism in both children and adults is associated with negative outcomes. Compared to more optimistic people, pessimists are more likely to do poorly in school, on the job, and on the playing fields than their talent would suggest; they get depressed more often; and they have poorer physical health.

What are the roots of pessimism? Seligman identifies four sources: genetics; parental pessimism; pessimistic criticism from parents, teachers, and coaches; and mastery and helplessness experiences.

Pessimistic parents tend to have pessimistic children. This is the case even when parents do not rear their own children (for example, in the case of adoption), suggesting that the trait of optimism/pessimism is heritable (that is, that some significant portion of individual differences among people in optimism/pessimism can be attributed to genetics).

Children can learn a pessimistic explanatory style from observing their parents. Pessimistic people tend to blame their failures on a pervasive and permanent lack of ability ("I'm not very good at math"), whereas they see their successes as due to some temporary conditions ("I tried very hard this time"). When bad things happen, they tend to view them as reflecting global characteristics ("I stink at sports"; "Nobody likes me") as opposed to specific situations ("I'm not very good at basketball"; "Michelle doesn't like me"). Children learn these attitudes without the need of specific instruction, simply by observation.

Children also learn a pessimistic explanatory style from the way parents, teachers, and coaches criticize them. All children fail and need feedback. The way that feedback is given can promote a worldview of optimism or pessimism. Is failure attributed to a specific context ("You didn't do well on your spelling test last week") and to lack of effort ("I just don't think that you're putting the time into studying your spelling that you should"), or is it attributed to a global characteristic and a general lack of ability ("You're not very smart")?

Finally, pessimism may be linked to specific experiences of feeling helpless – of being out of control of important events in one's life. For instance, the death of a parent, the bullying by classmates, or the humiliation of public rejection by members of the opposite sex can promote a pessimistic view of the world and make children feel that they have no control over important parts of their lives.

The bad news, according to Seligman, is that modern society has become increasingly pessimistic and cynical, and the "self-esteem" movement in American schools has produced children who feel good about themselves often without the accomplishments to justify their warm, fuzzy emotions. This is a flimsy edifice on which to build a personality and can lead to depression when, up the road, bad things happen. The good news is that optimism can be taught, or at least encouraged, by parents and teachers. In his book *The Optimistic Child*, Seligman presents the results of research studies that have fostered optimism and combated depression in adolescents and provides a program for raising an optimistic child.

Optimism is not a cure-all. Being optimistic in itself will not make one talented in any domain, and an unrealistic perspective of one's abilities will likely lead to failure and possibly ridicule. But a realistic sense of optimism is associated with a host of mental health (and physical health) benefits. Children start life as unrealistic optimists but gradually gain a more realistic view of the world, as they must. But their optimism need not turn to pessimism. Parents, teachers, and anyone who deals with children can foster optimism in youngsters with the goal of producing an optimistic adult.[13]

What is the Origin of Optimism in Young Children?

Young children's optimism in their own ability is impressive and perhaps refreshing compared to the more accurate, and thus necessarily less positive perspective older children and adults have of their own skills. I have suggested that such optimism may be adaptive, and I will examine the possible advantages of such optimism later in this chapter. But first we need to examine the origins of such optimism. Why can't (or don't) young children see themselves and their abilities more as others see them?

Cognitive inability. An obvious explanation for young children's overly positive assessments of their own skills might be that they just can't do any better. They have real cognitive limitations that prevent them from accurately assessing their own skills. This position holds that young children are *unable* to make accurate assessments and cannot use feedback from previous performance to alter their estimations of future performance. They lack the basic intellectual abilities to discriminate between competent and incompetent behavior. They just can't do it.

This explanation, at its extreme anyway, cannot be true. First of all, recall that young children are able to provide more realistic estimations of *other* children's abilities; they reserve their overly optimistic assessments for *their own* behavior. Moreover, when young children are given very salient and explicit feedback about their performance, they will adjust their estimates downward toward reality. This is a frequently found phenomenon in cognitive development. Young children have the basic competencies, but tend to display those competencies only under optimal situations. For example, young children can be trained to use learning or memory strategies that they typically do not use spontaneously (such as rehearsing sets of words on a memory task), and they benefit from using the strategies. However, once training is over and they are allowed to perform on their own, they frequently return to their earlier, nonstrategic ways. There is some suggestion that using an advanced strategy is so mentally effortful that children prefer to approach the task without it. Something similar may be happening with respect to children's estimates of their own skills. Young children may be able to make accurate assessments of their own behavior, but the mental processes involved in doing this are not well developed and not easily executed. It's as if the process of making accurate self-estimations is too mentally effortful. In such cases, they apply their "fall back" strategy, which is to assume that everything is fine.[14]

Defining success and failure. Another reason for young children's poor estimation of their own behavior has to do with how they define success and failure. Young children seem to enjoy performing a task for its own sake and are less concerned about achieving a specific goal. Simply performing a task, therefore, may constitute a success in the child's eyes, whereas the adult would rate the act a success or failure on the basis of the outcome. Moreover, adults provide young children with considerable latitude when it comes to defining success or failure and to changing the goal of the task when the original objective proves too far from reach. Deborah Stipek suggested such latitude allows preschool children "to avoid situations in which they are required to violate an adult's prescription. Consequently, most toddlers and preschool-age children probably experience positive feelings of mastery and little anxiety about failing to meet adult expectations in most real-life achievement situations."[15]

Effort versus ability. Evidence from a variety of sources indicates that young children do not differentiate effort (trying hard) from ability (having talent) when it comes to performing some tasks. The message that most preschool children are likely to get from their teachers and parents is that trying hard is as important as doing well. A parallel finding is that young children generally hold what has been termed an *incremental* theory of their own intelligence, believing that they can become smarter with effort. Their experience supports this theory – many tasks young children attempt are done poorly initially, but their performance improves with practice. Thus, despite previous failures, children may believe, based on past performance and comments from adults, that they will do better "next time," a way of thinking that accounts for their failure to adjust their estimations of past or future performance as a result of feedback. This can account for their more accurate assessment of other children's ability. They don't know how hard the other children are trying and therefore consider only the observable performance.[16]

Wishes versus expectations. Stipek has proposed an explanation of young children's overestimations based on Piaget's idea of "wishful thinking." According to this concept, preschool children often do not make a distinction between their wishes and their expectations. They believe that their desires are efficacious in and of themselves, and they therefore judge future performances by how well they *want* them to be. For example, University of Würzburg developmental psychologist Wolfgang Schneider found that the desired outcomes and expectations of 4- and 6-year-old children were identical for tasks involving jumping, throwing a ball, or remembering things. Their *wished* performance was their *predicted* performance. And, not surprisingly, for all tasks, children's predictions (and wishes) were in excess of their actual performance. Although wishful thinking can explain why children are more accurate judging other children's abilities than their own, it can't be the entire answer. It runs into some of the same problems that the "cognitive limitations" explanation does. With salient feedback, children can learn to make more realistic expectations.[17]

There seems to be no single reason for young children's consistent overestimation of their competencies. Rather, there appears to be a variety of factors that contribute to children's overly optimistic evaluations of their own abilities: cognitive limitations, with children performing in a sophisticated manner only under optimal conditions; different definitions of success and failure; an emphasis on the role of effort; and wishful thinking. This combination of factors results in a self-enhancement bias in young children, which, although on the surface seems to be a hindrance to intelligent functioning, may actually provide them with some cognitive benefits.

Overestimating One's Social Status

To this point, I've been discussing children's overestimation of their cognitive or problem-solving abilities. Intelligence and problem-solving ability, although highly valued in all cultures, often take a back seat to one's social standing. As I've emphasized in previous chapters, we are a social species and how children maneuver their way through the social network influences greatly their status and possibly even their future reproductive efforts.

I should say at the outset that status seeking and dominance hierarchies ("pecking orders") are not limited to adolescents and adults but are found even in preschool children. High-status, or dominant, children (and adults) have greater access to resources, be they food and mates in adults, or toys in the case of preschool children. Although many factors influence a child's position in a dominance hierarchy, physical strength and "toughness," particularly among boys, strongly predict a child's rank. This is true at all ages, from preschool through adolescence.[18] In many cultures, high-status adolescent boys have many sexual opportunities; these are the boys whom girls prefer and "choose." In contrast, many low-status teenage boys are shut out of the adolescent mating game. Most teenage girls can find a sexual partner if they want one, but high-status girls are able to select more desirable (that is, higher status) boys as partners than lower-status girls. (I should note that in contemporary society, men with high levels of testosterone, associated with strength and toughness, tend to die younger, be more prone to criminality, and have less-stable marriages than men with lower testosterone levels. Men with lower levels of testosterone also tend to spend more time with their wives than men with higher levels.[19] Thus, the virile men that young women find so attractive tend to be at a slight disadvantage later in life in comparison to less virile men, who seem to make better husbands.)

Given the importance of social status, it should not be surprising that children tend to overestimate their place in social hierarchies. For example, children over a broad age range, from 3 years through early adolescence, tend to rate themselves as stronger and tougher and generally higher in a dominance hierarchy than teachers or their peers rate them. This effect is sometimes greater for boys than for girls, but not always.[20]

Some Benefits of
Less-Than-Perfect Metacognition

It is admittedly counterintuitive to propose that young children's overly optimistic opinions of their abilities are an asset and not a liability. Yet, I believe this is so. Having limited metacognitive skills results in children believing that they are capable of more than they really are. This encourages exploration of new territories and reduces fear of failure in young learners.

I See, therefore I Can Do

This may be a nice hypothesis, but is there any evidence for it? Some. As you may recall, in one of the meta-imitation studies I described earlier, 3-, 4-, and 5-year-old children watched a videotape of a man skillfully juggling one, two, or three balls.[21] They also watched a videotape of a man accurately tossing a ball into a basket from 1.5, 3, and 7 feet away. Children predicted how well they thought they could perform these tasks "just like" the man had. They then attempted the tasks and were asked how well they thought they had done. As part of the study, children were given a verbal IQ test, and the relationship between this IQ measure and degree of overestimation was obtained. The relationship between degree of overestimation and IQ varied with age. As expected, 5-year-old children who overestimated less (that is, were more accurate) had higher IQ scores. In other words, good metacognition was associated with good prediction and post-task evaluation, consistent with findings from school-age children. This pattern was not found, however, for the younger children. Rather, brighter 3- and 4-year-olds actually overestimated *more* than the less bright children of the same age.[i]

Our interpretation of these results is that immature metacognition allows young children to imitate a broad range of behaviors without the knowledge that their attempts are inadequate. Without this negative feedback, bright young children will continue to try their hand at many behaviors, from dancing to authorship to juggling, permitting

---

[i] For statistically minded readers, the correlations between degree of overestimation (prediction) and verbal IQ scores were .19, .20, and −.21 for the 3-, 4-, and 5-year-olds, respectively; the correlations between degree of over evaluation (post-diction) and verbal IQ scores were .15, .46*, and −.39* for the 3-, 4-, and 5-year-olds, respectively (* denotes significance, $p < .05$).

them to practice and improve their skills at a time when trial-and-error learning is so important. As their motor skills improve, so do their metacognitive skills, which later in development are associated with more advanced thinking abilities.

We must be somewhat cautious in our interpretation of these findings. For one thing, they do not mean that young children with good metacognition will grow up to be older children with poor cognitive abilities, or vice versa. Although I know of no studies that have examined the stability of children's metacognition from early to late childhood,[ii] it is well established that bright young children (as measured by IQ scores) usually maintain their intellectual advantage in later childhood. In fact, the correlations between IQ and meta-imitation in our study, while statistically significant, were relatively low. What is important, however, is their direction. The typical, positive relationship between metacognition and intelligence was not observed until age 5, suggesting that the rules are different for young children, who, in general, overestimated their imitative abilities, with accurate children having no intellectual edge over inaccurate children, at least through the age of 4. In fact, the reverse was true.[22]

Poor Metacognition and Strategy Development

The topic of the development of children's learning and memory strategies may bring a yawn to many readers, but it's a topic to which I devoted most of my research energies for much of my career. And, because it is central to children gaining control of their own problem-solving behavior, it's a topic of considerable interest to cognitive developmental psychologists. Strategies are usually thought of as deliberate, goal-directed mental processes designed to improve problem solving. Children (and adults) learn to use strategies to help them solve arithmetic problems, to remember important information, and comprehend stories they hear or read, among other things. One robust

---

[ii] The Munich Longitudinal Study on the Genesis of Individual Competencies (LOGIC) has collected metamemory judgments from children at least once per year between the first grade (average age 7 years, 4 months) and the beginning of the fourth grade (average age, 9 years, 9 months). The correlation between the earliest and last measurement points was .20, which approached statistical significance ($p = .058$). Thus, long-term correlations of metamemory are of low to moderate levels between the early and later elementary school years. (Data from Wolfgang Schneider, personal communication.)

and not too surprising finding is that children become more strategic with age, with corresponding improvements in task performance. Also, proficiency of strategy use and the corresponding benefits on task performance are associated with metacognition. School-age children who know what strategies they have available to use, which tasks require which strategies, and how effective they are at implementing a strategy, typically perform better on cognitive tasks and score higher on IQ tests than less metacognitively enlightened children.[23]

People use strategies because it improves their task performance – helps them remember more of a story or solve a problem more quickly. It was a bit unexpected, then, when developmental psychologist Patricia Miller and her colleagues observed a phase in strategy development when children spontaneously use a strategy but it does not help them in terms of task performance. Miller refers to this phenomenon as a *utilization deficiency.* For example, in work by Miller and her colleagues with preschoolers, children were shown a series of boxes with doors on top, arranged in two rows. On half of the doors were pictures of cages, signaling that those boxes contained pictures of animals. On the other half of the doors were pictures of a house, signaling that those boxes contained pictures of household objects. Children were then told to find and remember for later on all of the examples from just one of the categories, opening doors one at a time. The degree to which they searched boxes only from the relevant category (animals or household objects) was used as an indication of strategy use. Miller reported that many children searched boxes with the right pictures on the outside but failed to benefit in terms of remembering the target items.[24]

Work from my lab later found evidence for a similar utilization deficiency with 8- and 9-year-old children, indicating that this phenomenon is not limited to preschoolers. In our studies, children were given sets of pictures or words to recall that could be grouped into familiar categories. A strategy often used to enhance memory performance by older children in such situations is that of *organization,* in which children remember items from the same category together (for example, remembering all the ANIMAL words together and all the VEGETABLE words together). The 8- and 9-year-old children in these studies learned to use an organizational strategy, often implementing the strategy as well as a group of 14-year-olds. The difference, however, was that, like Miller's 3- and 4-year-old children, the strategy didn't help them. They used the strategy, but their levels of memory performance were no better than those of 8- and 9-year-old children who approached the tasks in nonstrategic ways.[25]

Why should children use an effort-consuming strategy to guide their behavior when it has no positive impact on their performance? One speculation is that utilization deficiencies may be related to children's poor metacognition and a belief that problem solving requires hard work. Perhaps children believe that performance will be enhanced by using a systematic approach to a problem but do not have the metacognitive knowledge to realize that this approach does not (as yet) yield benefits. Children may know, from informal instructions by adults or their own spontaneous problem solving, that doing "something" or "thinking" about how to solve a problem is generally better than doing "nothing" or "not thinking" about a problem. If this is the case, children may adopt a strategic approach to a problem when one is discovered, leading eventually to the efficient use of that and other strategies. Discussing children's possible motivations for using what he termed "faulty strategies," University of Michigan developmental psychologist Henry Wellman stated that "young children may simply come to prefer a strategic or intelligent approach to problem solving, regardless of immediate payoffs"...and that "faulty approaches are generated by coherent but mistaken notions of what will work."[26]

Thus, young children's poor metacognition may provide them an advantage; a child with better metacognitive skills may realize quickly that the extra effort being put into the task is not resulting in improved performance and thus resort to a less effortful and nonstrategic approach. In contrast, by being out of touch with the relationship between strategy use and task performance, utilizationally deficient children may persist using a strategy until it becomes sufficiently efficient to result in improved performance. In this case, children's immature cognition is adaptive, leading to eventual (though not immediate) benefits.

My colleague Hye Eun Shin from Sung Kyun Kwan University in South Korea, student Erinn Beck, and I have some preliminary evidence consistent with this hypothesis.[27] In a series of studies, children from kindergarten through grade 3 were given five trials with sets of pictures to study and later remember. Children were asked to predict how many pictures they thought they would be able to remember. Children who overestimated more on the first two trials (that is, whose prediction accuracy was poor) actually showed a greater benefit in recall on later trials than children who were more accurate in their initial predictions. This effect was particularly strong for the youngest children tested. Overprediction on early trials was also related to an increased use of strategies on later trials for some groups of children.

That is, as predicted, children who were out of touch with their memory abilities showed greater enhancement in how much they remembered and in the number of strategies they used than more accurate children.

The Perils of Overestimation

Although there may be some benefits to children overestimating their abilities, overestimating one's skills could lead to children attempting things that they shouldn't and getting hurt in the process. Little harm may come to a child who overestimates how many balls he can juggle at once, or who thinks she's the smartest kid in her first-grade class, but the same can't be said when a child is reaching for a limb on a tree, climbing a ladder, or crossing a busy street. University of Iowa developmental psychologist Jodie Plumert and her colleagues have investigated children's estimation of their physical skills and related them to their history of accidents.[28] In a series of studies, 6- and 8-year-old children were given a variety of physical tasks to perform. For example, one task involved ducking under a wooden bar attached to two posts (doing the limbo) and another involved reaching an object on a shelf. (Children were first tested for their abilities to perform such tasks; for instance, how high they could reach.) Children were then told that they would be playing a game. They would be asked to do things, such as reaching an object on a shelf, and they had to tell if they thought they could do them or not. If they thought they could, they would then try, and if they succeeded they'd get a point towards a prize. If they failed, however, they would lose a point. If they thought they couldn't do it, they would not perform the task, and they would neither gain nor lose points. There were four levels for each task: well below their ability; just at their ability; slightly beyond their ability; and well beyond their ability. For instance, a shelf would be placed at a height that was: 13% below a child's ability; at a height corresponding to a child's ability; at a height 8% higher (just beyond) than a child's ability; and at a height 13% higher than (well beyond) a child's ability.

The majority of children overestimated their ability to perform tasks both just beyond and well beyond their ability. A group of adults was also tested and they overestimated their ability to perform tasks just beyond their ability (but not as much as the children), but were accurate judging their ability to perform (or not to perform, actually) tasks well beyond their ability. So far, no surprises, for this is the same pattern that has been found for young children's estimation of their cognitive skills and academic achievement. The interesting finding is that 6-year-olds' estimation accuracy was related to the number of accidents that required medical attention children had had in their lifetimes. The more these children overestimated their physical abilities, the more trips to the emergency room they required. This effect was especially large in boys. By 8 years of age, however, the relation between estimation ability and accident proneness was no longer significant.[29]

So children as old as 8 are still very much out of touch with their physical abilities, and the consequences of such overestimation can be serious for 6-year-olds. And it will take some time before children's estimates of what they can do match those of adults. For example, 10-and 12-year-old children were less accurate than adults judging when it was safe to ride their bikes across a busy street. It took them longer to get moving, so the gap between cars that they judged to be adequate to attempt a crossing turned out to result in more close calls than when adults were doing the judging. (They didn't actually cross streets. Judgments were made on a "virtual" street.[30])

It's worth noting that not all young children overestimate their physical abilities. In one study, children who had been rated as preschoolers as having good inhibitory control and being low on the personality dimension of extraversion actually underestimated their abilities at age 6, counter to findings from most other research on the topic.[31] There was also a relation between extraversion, inhibitory control, and accidents requiring medical treatment: children high on extraversion and low on inhibitory control had more accidents by the age of 6 than more cautious children. Although this group of children may seem to be at an advantage during childhood in that they would be less prone to suffer serious accidents, David Schwebel and Jodie Plumert recognized that underestimating one's abilities could have a negative side. A child who underestimates his or her abilities may be reluctant to try new tasks, overcautious in playing with other children, and left on the playground sidelines. This may result in isolation, lowered self-esteem, teasing and ridicule by other children, and possibly rejection by peers.

Childhood, and development, by their very nature, involve reaching beyond one's current abilities. Development is not for the faint of heart. Children must have the motivation to change, to attempt new, and perhaps somewhat dangerous, tasks. Without such motivation, development would be short-circuited, with children engaging in easily performed and safe activities showing little change from one day to the next, and even from one year to another. As Plumert wrote,

"The developmental dilemma, therefore, is to continually aspire to trying new and difficult things but not to try things that might have dangerous consequences."[32] It may be a fine line to walk, and parents, of course, must monitor their children's behavior, encouraging some activities, discouraging others, and scaffolding still others.

Developing a Sense of Self-efficacy

Another important aspect of young children's overly optimistic view of their own abilities is the confidence it gives them. Children who believe they are competent (even if they are not) develop feelings of positive *self-efficacy*. Self-efficacy refers to people's beliefs about their having control over their own lives. Stanford psychologist Albert Bandura has noted that when self-efficacy is poor, people tend to behave ineffectually, regardless of their actual abilities.[33] In other words, when people feel that they have little control over their lives, they behave as if that indeed is the case, even when there is something they *can* do to exert some control. Young children's beliefs that they know more than they actually do, and are able to do more than they actually can, provide them with positive perceptions of their own skills and their own control. This positive sense of self-efficacy encourages children to attempt things that they would not otherwise try if they had a more realistic idea of their abilities. Deborah Stipek has stated that children's tendencies to overestimate their skills may provide them with basic confidence in their own competence. Rather than trying to make young children's judgments of their abilities more accurate, she advocates that we should "try harder to design educational environments which maintain their optimism and eagerness."[34]

Children do not totally lose their optimistic view of the world by the second or third grade. Although children become more realistic in evaluating their own abilities, they still tend to see the world through rose-colored glasses, at least in comparison to adults. Martin E. P. Seligman has done research over the past 35 years on optimism and pessimism and the consequences such perspectives have on behavior and development (see Seligman's *Learned Optimism* for an easily readable review of this research). Seligman reports that children maintain their generally optimistic perspective of the world into adolescence. In fact, when a child has scores on tests of optimism and pessimism typical for the average adult, it may be a sign of depression. In other words, a depressed child looks similar to a normal adult on these optimism/pessimism scales. Seligman believes that such a positive view of the world is not something limited to upper-middle-class children, who can afford to be optimistic about the future, but is characteristic of the species and was selected over the course of human evolution. As the quote at the beginning of this chapter reflects, natural selection has operated by endowing children with "hope, abundant and irrational."[35]

Optimism is something children start life with. With age and experience, their perspective on life becomes more realistic, as it must. It may be the job of adults to teach children the way of a world that is often cruel and unfair. But in teaching children these lessons, we should not try to break them of their optimism, even though their views may deviate from reality. Pessimists may never get disappointed, but they also put themselves in situations where they are less likely to experience success.

When We Deal with Children

What does this mean for our everyday interactions with children? One implication is that when children's attempts to perform adult tasks are met with criticism and punishment, nothing helpful is accomplished. Young children clearly do not understand ahead of time that these activities are beyond their ability, and once the activity is done, they often do not understand that the results are less than perfect. If anything, adults' negative responses only cause anxiety and general inactivity. When children are unaware of their limitations and are criticized for their abilities and their performances, they don't just learn what they can't do; they learn not to attempt things, period.

Although preschoolers have a difficult time anticipating their future performance, research by Stipek and her colleagues makes it clear that children as young as 2 years of age are sensitive to adult criticism. By age 3, children meet failure in the presence of an adult with frowns and pouts, with such behavior increasing substantially over the next half year. So although young children may have poor metacognition – may overestimate both their predictions and post-task evaluations of their own performance – they are not impervious to adult criticism, both real and anticipated.[36]

When children do perform tasks, adults should be conscious not to set the standards unreasonably high. Goals that are beyond children's reach may result in anxiety and concern about their competence, even in the absence of adult criticism. This does not mean, however, that adults should lavish praise on any and every project children attempt. Although being optimistic is a virtue, as is believing in one's own competence, praise that is indiscriminately given eventually loses its power. As children's abilities increase, so must expectations of their achievements. The point is not to ever let children experience failure. In fact, if all children receive at home is exuberance from their parents for every task they attempt, they will quickly learn from the "outside" how hollow such accolades are. The point, rather, is to foster self-esteem, self-confidence, and permit children to test their developing skills in a supportive, nonthreatening environment, with enough feedback and direction so that the eventual product is competent behavior.

Although optimism is an inherent feature of childhood, children also learn optimism or pessimism through regular interactions with and observations of their parents, particularly their mothers. In research by Seligman and his colleagues, the attributions of optimism and pessimism of mothers predicted how optimistic or pessimistic their children would be. There was no relation with attributions of fathers. So parents need not only watch what they say to children, but also what they say about themselves. Women who are optimistic tend to have children who are optimistic. Although children start life as believers in their own capacities and their ability to overcome adversity, they gradually become more realistic in their view of the world. Whether they maintain a generally optimistic perspective, which is conducive to good development – or develop a generally pessimistic outlook, which is conducive to poor development – depends not only on their experiences as preschoolers, but their experiences throughout childhood.

Know Thyself, But Not Too Well

"Know thyself" would seem to be good advice, especially when it comes to one's intellect. Adults who are cognizant of their intellectual strong and weak points can organize their lives accordingly, seeking out opportunities to make the best of what they do best and learning to compensate when their natural or acquired talents are less than ideal for a particular task. Such metacognitive skills, as most cognitive skills, improve with age. But intuitively it would seem that, at any age, people in touch with their mental skills would be at an advantage to people who are out of touch. This is likely true in most situations past the age of 9 or so, but it does not seem to be the case for young children. Young children's cognitive immaturity with respect to self-knowledge has some advantages. By not knowing what they don't know yet, children attempt tasks that are currently beyond their ken and their physical abilities. Yet, they are frequently unaware of their less-than-stellar performance. As a result, they continue to explore their world, feeling competent and confident, and along the way acquire some useful information that more "in touch" children may have missed because they would be cognizant of their failure ("If at first you don't succeed, quit – don't make a fool of yourself").

Adults do their part to perpetuate young children's feelings of success. Parents, teachers, and even strangers in the grocery store often confirm young children's feelings of accomplishment. Whether adults do this intentionally to bolster children's self-esteem or perceive the attempts of young children as "cute" and thus worthy of praise isn't always clear, but most adults are more than willing to lower standards of success for young children and applaud their attempts at performing "adult" tasks.

Young children expect success, and, as far as they're concerned, they usually achieve it. Such optimistic opinions of their own abilities are easily seen as something children will outgrow. In fact, children do outgrow their very positive and overly optimistic attitude about their own abilities, usually by the third or fourth grades. But their unrealistic optimism is actually something to be valued and protected. Children who believe they are skillful and in control are more apt to act that way. Rather than rudely awakening them to reality, adults can make the most of young children's optimism, encouraging them to practice new skills and praising them for their "successes." The bottom line is that children who *feel* successful in these early years will likely *be* successful in the long run.

6

Play: The Royal Road through Childhood

Animals can not be said to play because they are young and frolicsome, but rather they have a period of youth in order to play.
Karl Groos, *The Play of Animals*

Play is older than culture, has not been essentially changed by civilization, and has permeated from the beginning 'the great archetypal activities of human society.'
Johan Huizinga, *Homo ludens*

One of my favorite outdoor games as a child was called "Wolves and Pigs," which was a variant on tag. It started with one child being the wolf and running to catch the other children, the pigs. Once the first child was "caught," he or she too became a wolf and the two of them chased the other children until the last pig had been caught by one of the now many wolves. We played this on summer evenings until it became too dark to see, both boys and girls ranging in age from 6 or 7 to their early teens. I remember running in my parents' backyard, especially the quick turns and dodging I'd do to avoid being tagged. I particularly remember running in an arc to escape an oncoming wolf; my recollection is of making turns and being nearly parallel to the ground, held up by centrifugal force. I'm sure that neither my speed nor my violation of the laws of physics was as impressive as I recall them, but it's my memory and I'm sticking to it.

"Wolves and Pigs" is an example of vigorous exercise play, performed, by necessity, in the company of others. Children over the globe play similar games, and likely always have. We take play for granted, especially in children, and we discount it as unimportant in the big picture of things – something we should only do after we've taken care of more pressing, serious business. But play *is* serious business. As the pioneering Italian educator Maria Montessori said, "Play is the child's work." Some people, such as historian Johan Huizinga, have gone as far as using our playful nature as defining us as a species. Huizinga argued that the propensity for play is what makes humans special and what is responsible for the many accomplishments of our species, so different in quality than anything conceived or achieved in the rest of the animal world. He felt so strongly about this that he suggested the species be named for our playful ways: *Homo ludens*, or "playful man."[1]

But surely Professor Huizinga exaggerates. Play is not unique to humans, modern or otherwise. It is especially prevalent in mammals, and even in some reptiles. For most animals, play is the exclusive purview of the young. Older individuals of some species, such as chimpanzees, dolphins, and domesticated animals such as dogs and cats, also play, but much less than juveniles. And play in adulthood of many animals is often initiated by a youngster. Adult humans also play less than children, but, unlike most other species, adult *Homo ludens* remain playful throughout life. Adults may not romp around the house or have pretend tea parties with the frequency that children do, but we maintain our playful attitude and behaviors into old age, expressed in games, humor, and a little romping now and again. I'll have more to say about play in adulthood in the Epilogue.

Play is what children do. They do not build houses or make tools, and they do not compete for mates. Children are dependent on their parents, who take on the often-burdensome responsibility of feeding, sheltering, and protecting their offspring. Children in contemporary culture may seem especially likely to play, where the struggle for survival is not so arduous and the everyday perils not so great. But children's play is not a reward for technological advancement – a luxury for the culturally well-heeled. In fact, children in industrialized and schooled cultures likely have more demands placed on them than children in traditional cultures. Psychologist Yumi Gosso from the University of São Paolo in Brazil and her colleagues write that children from hunter-gatherer societies "neither hunt nor gather, they do not build houses and shelters, they do not cook or clean. In fact, the life of children, at least under 7 years of age, is mostly, if not solely, a playful life. From early morning to bedtime, they play, typically all together."[2] The lives of children in America, Great Britain, and other first-world countries are likely not as playful and carefree as those of some hunter-gatherer children. We restrict and regulate our children's activities more so than parents in traditional cultures, limiting what children do and with whom they do it. And a frequent activity for many children, watching television, is certainly entertainment, but most people would not classify it as play. Nevertheless, despite parental restrictions and not-so-playful alternative entertainment, preschool children in contemporary cultures spend much of their time playing.[i]

My first task in this chapter is to define play, which is not as easily done as one might think. Psychologists have studied children's play extensively and have developed a number of ways of classifying it. I spend the rest of the chapter examining the adaptive value of play. Play can have both immediate and deferred benefits, both in the social and cognitive realms. I take a close look at the relation between play and learning, first examining the connection between play and tool use, and then the possibility that some of the sex differences we see in play may be related to preparing boys and girls for the roles that they would have played in humans' ancient environments (and still play today in many parts of the world). I then look at the role of fantasy play in intellectual development (particularly the development of theory of mind), what children learn when playing games, and the connection between play and discovery learning. The bottom line is that play is not the purposeless activity that it is sometimes thought to be, but has been selected over the course of human (and mammalian) evolution to serve a significant role in social and intellectual development.

---

[i] I don't mean to imply that all of a preschool child's waking day is filled with non-serious activities. Young children take some parts of their lives very seriously. They are motivated to master culturally significant tasks, from the mundane, such as brushing their teeth, buttering their bread, and tying their shoes, to things that are truly out of their reach, such as tap dancing and writing books, and much in between. In his stage theory of psychosocial development, Erik Erikson described the 3- to 6-year-old as having to resolve conflicts revolving around *initiative versus guilt*. Children whose attempts at mastery are met with success and positive reactions from their parents will leave this stage with a sense of initiative, whereas those whose activities are met with criticism will leave the stage with a sense of guilt. But gaining initiative was not all serious business for Erikson. One way children gain control over important activities is through fantasy, or pretend, play. And I should note that the more carefree lifestyle of hunter-gatherer children is accompanied by more serious labor, which they engage in, typically along side a parent, earlier than children from schooled cultures.

What is Play?

Play is a lot like art: it's difficult to define but you know it when you see it (or maybe that's pornography). Children spontaneously and voluntarily play. Play is engaging and takes some effort. It is not a passive activity. Play is enjoyable, often accompanied by laughter or a "play face." Play is not serious, and is differentiated from work. And play is "purposeless." That is, during play one is not producing any product, gaining any resources, or seemingly doing anything to enhance the status of the individual players. In fact, one is expending often-considerable energy and not getting anything back for it (for example, food, shelter, or mates). But that's only on the surface. By definition play must *look* purposeless, but scientists who research play are nearly unanimous in the opinion that play does indeed have a purpose, likely many. The development and the patterns of play are so similar across cultures that many assume that it is an excellent candidate for a species-universal feature of humankind that has been influenced by natural selection and evolved to serve an adaptive function, much as language or infant–mother attachment have.[3]

There are different ways of classifying play, some based on the degree of social interaction involved, and others based more on the physical or cognitive components of the activity. Pioneering play researcher Mildred Parten published what was perhaps the first classification of play in a landmark 1932 study.[4] Although her categories of play can be seen as reflecting increasing social participation (and thus complexity), they do not necessarily reflect "stages" of play, with one being replaced by a more sophisticated type as children get older. This may happen to a significant degree, but a child can engage in any type of play depending on the situation.

The least complex form of play Parten called *onlooker behavior*, which involves children only watching or talking with other children while they play. *Solitary play* is simply a child playing alone, whereas *parallel play* involves playing alongside, but not with, another child. In parallel play, children may focus on their own play activities, seemingly ignoring what other children in their immediate surroundings are doing. Children may even share toys in their separate play, but maintain their independence. (I discussed in Chapter 4 how children could sometimes make the transition from solitary play to parallel play by talking to themselves.) More sophisticated is *associative play*, in which children share toys and talk to one another, but do not coordinate their play in any apparent way. And finally there is *cooperative play*, in which children truly "play together," often assigning different roles to one another (for example, doctor, nurse, patient) with specific goals in mind (playing hospital).

In contrast to Parten, Jean Piaget and University of Tel Aviv psychologist Sara Smilansky each described play based on the type of behavior displayed in the activity rather than the degree of social participation, and subsequent researchers have expanded on these categories.[5] The most frequent type of play early in life is *locomotor*, or *physical*, *play*, which includes *exercise play* (essentially vigorous movements in the context of play) and *rough-and-tumble play* (*R&T*). R&T involves games such as chase, wrestling, and play fighting. It increases in frequency over the preschool years, peaking at about 10% of observed behavior between 6 and 10 years of age, and declines in adolescence. R&T is common in most mammals, which also spend about 10% of their time and energy budgets in it. *Object-oriented play* includes the manipulation of objects, such as banging or throwing, taking objects apart and putting them back together again, and construction.[ii] Object-oriented play accounts for between 10% and 15% of preschool children's activities during school, similar to the amount of time chimpanzees (one of the few other animals to engage in object-oriented play) devote to it. *Fantasy play*, sometimes called *pretend play* or *symbolic play*, may be unique to humans (or maybe not, see Gómez & Martin-Andrade, 2005), and involves the game of pretending. Fantasy play has an "as-if" orientation toward objects, actions, and other children. It obviously requires a cognitive system capable of representing objects and people in a form other than what they really are. Like all other forms of play, it increases over the preschool years (infants, because of their limited intellectual abilities, are not capable of fantasy play), peaks around age 5 or 6, accounting for about 15% of children's time budgets, and then declines. Sex differences are often found in each type of play (which I'll discuss later), and similar age and gender patterns have been found for children from traditional cultures.[6]

Different cultures provide different opportunities for play, so the frequencies and styles of play vary among cultures. Anthropologist Douglas Fry provided the metaphor of "variations on a theme" for play. The theme of play and its development are universal, although variations of culturally specific elements will be incorporated into

---

[ii] Some theorists distinguish between exploration of objects, object play, constructive play, and tool use, see Pellegrini & Gustafson, 2005, whereas I've combined them into a single category here.

play.[7] Harvard developmental psychologist Paul Harris stated about play that "the stable timing of its onset in different cultures strongly suggests a neuropsychological timetable and a biological basis."[8] In other words, play is as much a part of the biological fabric of human childhood as is language or motor development, and not just some incidental thing that happens to accompany growing up.

The Adaptive Value of Play

Why should we infer that play has a "purpose," or more appropriately an *adaptive function*, that has been selected over the course of evolution? After all, given the extended period of youth and the general "uselessness" of children for accomplishing real tasks, what else are they supposed to do with their time? Play, in a sense, is what a slow-developing animal does by default. Perhaps play is merely the by-product of developing motor and cognitive systems; it is *symptomatic* of development, but has no real influence on survival or eventual adult success. Fantasy play, for instance, is a reflection of a child's blossoming symbolic abilities. Fantasy play doesn't *cause* children to become symbolic, but, as Piaget noted, is a symptom of their underlying cognitive abilities.

The alternative claim is equally simple. Play is biologically expensive, and biologists assume that any activity that costs so much in time, calories, and risks must also have substantial advantages. Play consumes about 10% of children's time and energy budgets. It takes children away from the protection of their parents and results in their engaging in activities that can produce harm, even death. Perhaps the most frequent reason for children's visits to hospital emergency rooms is accidents during play. In addition to its universality in *Homo sapiens*, play is also seen in other animals, often following similar patterns observed in children. All this suggests that play is more than a by-product of other aspects of human development (an *epiphenomenon*), but rather a real phenomenon of consequence itself.

Children's play, and likely the play of animals, is important in social and cognitive development. Children's early friendships are centered around play, and fantasy play, which can be done alone or with others, may have an important role in fostering intellectual development. Play is important in other species, as well. For example, animals that live in changeable environments versus those living in stable environments engage in more locomotor play, presumably as a way of learning about their surroundings.[9] Children's locomotor and physical play has also

144

been shown to be related to their spatial cognition, with more active children (oftentimes boys) having better developed spatial skills than less active children. For instance, developmental psychologists Jane Connor and Lisa Serbin noted that preschool boys engaged in more spatial play activities (for example, those involving throwing and eye–hand coordination) than girls, and also had higher levels of spatial cognition. They also found that the amount of boys' spatial activities was significantly related to measures of spatial thinking, suggesting that gender differences in play activity are partly responsible for boys' generally greater spatial skills. Why do boys engage in more spatial play than girls? It is likely related to the fact that boys are predisposed (both by genetics and prenatal hormone exposure) to be more active than girls, and that such increased activity levels lead them to have experiences different than less-active girls usually have.[10]

Other evidence for the importance of play comes from deprivation studies. When children (or animals) are deprived of play they often show a "rebound," engaging in play more vigorously and for longer periods of time. The assumption behind deprivation studies is that if play is developmentally important (that is, if it has positive consequences for children), it should rebound following enforced restriction.[11]

Play is not found in all animals, of course, and given the hypothesized functions of play, one would not expect it to be. Which animals should play? Play seems to help young animals learn about their physical environment and about conspecifics (members of their own species). The critical word here is *learn*. Although all animals with a nervous system learn, there is a premium on learning for big-brained, long-lived animals. It doesn't pay for short-lived animals to invest in a calorically expensive brain that enables flexible learning. They'd be dead long before they learned enough to "pay" for their high-cost brains. When behavioral flexibility is important to an animal it is likely that some mechanisms would evolve that promote learning the vagaries of a changeable environment. Play is one of those mechanisms, and it seems that prolonging the period of play would be adaptive. It is therefore fitting that species that place higher demands on their members later in life in terms of behavioral flexibility both need and benefit from an extended period of play and hence immaturity.

Is play of any benefit to modern children? Perhaps play is merely a remnant of our mammalian past, useful to young animals that lack culture and the symbolic abilities to understand their physical and social world in an abstract way, but of little consequence to modern humans. This is what Yumi Gosso and her colleagues believe to be the case for play fighting. Male animals that do not have experience at play fighting as juveniles do not learn how to fight and compete with other males as adults and are less successful in gaining and maintaining mates. Gosso and her colleagues believe that the benefits of skilled fighting likely declined in early human history, as social complexity increased and males had multiple ways of gaining access to females. Others would disagree, noting that the play fighting that boys do may have prepared them in the not-too-distant past for "dominance fighting" (fights among adult males that serve to establish one's position in a dominance hierarchy), as well as for primitive warfare. In traditional cultures, and certainly for our ancestors, some of the skills attained during play fighting – teamwork, defensive maneuvers, throwing projectiles – closely resemble behaviors involved in primitive warfare.[12] But even if the specific fighting skills are no longer important (and this is arguable), children still learn important lessons about competition, dominance relations, and fair play while play fighting.

In Chapter 1 I suggested that children have been prepared by evolution to be sensitive to certain stimuli or experiences, and that these come in two general forms. The first, *deferred adaptations*, anticipate adulthood, helping children acquire skills and knowledge that will be useful to them in the years ahead. The second, *ontogenetic adaptations*, provides some immediate benefits to children rather than preparing them for life in the future. Play likely has both immediate and deferred benefits, sometimes simultaneously. Play has been proposed to aid in the socialization process and to provide juvenile animals with the opportunity to develop motor skills, practice mastery and social behaviors, and learn by experimenting in a safe environment where the consequences of inept behavior are rarely serious.

The "play as preparation" position is perhaps the easiest to understand and was championed by many of the pioneers of child development, including Karl Groos, Jean Piaget, Lev Vygotsky, and Jerome Bruner.[13] From this perspective, play is seen as an imperfect version of adult behavior. For example, the play of boys is often qualitatively different from that of girls, perhaps preparing these juvenile males and females for the life they will live as adults, or would have lived in ancient environments (deferred benefits), a topic I will discuss in some detail below.

Much less investigated in the child development literature are the possible immediate benefits that play may afford, although this position also has a distinguished pedigree. G. Stanley Hall, the first person to hold a Professorship in Psychology in the United States and the father of child and developmental psychology on this side of the

Atlantic, believed that play was important in and of itself, and not as practice for adulthood. This was consistent with Hall's view of childhood as a time to explore and play, choosing their own activities and engaging in them without interference from adults.[14] Hall believed human evolution went through stages that are reflected in the play of contemporary children. For example, according to Hall, our adult ancestors were similar in intellect and behavior to modern 8- to 12-year-old children. Hall essentially believed that, through play, children were re-enacting human social history. By understanding children, we can understand what our ancestors were like. Consistent with this (outdated and discredited) idea, Hall advocated hunting and fishing for 8- to 12-year-old boys, activities their prehistoric ancestors would likely have engaged in.

What might be some of the immediate benefits of play? First, the social skills children learn, so important in preparing them for adult life, also serve to adapt them to the niche of childhood. Children form dominance hierarchies early, even during the preschool years, and such hierarchies serve not only to help children understand what adult life is going to be like, but how to navigate through the culture of childhood. High-status children have access to more resources (such as toys for young children), and the establishment of dominance hierarchies serves to reduce aggression and foster group harmony. Children also learn both to cooperate with one another and to compete for position within a social hierarchy, things that serve them well not only in the present but also in the future.[15] Play also serves to foster skeletal and muscle development and as a way of learning from one's environment, something that has both immediate and delayed consequences. Play also teaches children *how* to learn, how to generate solutions to novel problems, and provides a means for discovery. These skills are not only useful in adulthood, but also during childhood.

Children Playing, Children Learning

Children have much to learn on their way to adulthood, and, as I've suggested, play is an important vehicle in their education. Play may not be *necessary* for children to learn, but it may make learning more likely, easier, more enjoyable, and perhaps more flexible.

There is no single developmental path in mastering the ways of one's culture. There can't be, given the diversity of human lifestyles. But there are commonalities among cultures, and commonalities among children who grow up in these different environments.

Children around the world play, and enjoy themselves while they do, often gaining valuable knowledge in the process. Are there other ways besides play to gain knowledge? Of course. Some, such as direct instruction, are surely better suited to mastering certain skills, such as reading. Yet play is not the enemy of learning but a valuable ally. In this section I discuss some of the ways that children's play facilitates learning.

Play, Work, and Tool Use

The play of children from all cultures often involves imitation of adult roles, such as playing "house," "school," or "doctor." Such play is social (or cooperative to use Parten's term), involving taking the perspective of others (both the non-present adults whom they imitate and their peers playing other parts), and permits children to practice grown-up roles. Some fantasy play also involves tools and imitation of real adult work. This is much more apt to occur in traditional hunter-gatherer or horticultural societies, where children are more likely to observe adults at work on a daily basis, than in schooled cultures. In some traditional societies, children are given toy tools, often made by their parents, to use in play. For example, Parakanã fathers of the Amazon rain forests give their young boys miniature bows and arrows that they use in play, while mothers give their daughters small baskets. Parents do little or no teaching of hunting or gathering skills and there is no apparent pressure for children to behave in a sex-typed way; parents merely provide the traditional toys for their children, which children use in play with one another, much as they see their elders do.[16] California State University at Fullerton anthropologists John Bock and Sara Johnson observed the play of children of the Okavango Delta people of Botswana. Consistent with the "play as preparation for adult work" position, they noted that children spent significantly more time in play activities related to specific tasks associated with their subsistence economy than in other play activities.[17] Anthropologist David Lancy observed and interviewed Kpelle adults and children from Liberia. Most fantasy play for children between the ages of 4 and 11 years involved children re-enacting the chores and behaviors of adults in work-related situations, which was encouraged by adults. Children, usually boys, often made tools during play and occasionally built models of cars or houses, but rarely of people or animals.[18] In general, in cultures that lack industry, play tends to evolve into work as children grow into adults.

The pattern of play observed in traditional cultures suggests that there may be a relation between play and tool use. Humans are not the only tool-using (or even tool-making) species. Chimpanzees, dolphins, and several species of birds have been seen using, and sometimes even making, tools, such as termite fishing or nut cracking by chimpanzees. But none of these animals uses tools to the same degree as humans. Tool use plays a central role in human culture, and likely played an important role in our evolution. Tool use was one of the ways that anthropologists in years past defined *Homo sapiens*. (Recall the first-named member of the human line, *Homo habilis*, or handy man.) Do children learn about tools in their play? It seems unlikely that that play is *necessary* to learn to use tools, but does it make it easier or more likely?

Research with preschool children suggests that it might, mainly through object-oriented play. Such play should encourage children to learn that objects can be used in a variety of ways to solve a variety of problems. University of London developmental psychologist Peter Smith argued that object exploration and play may help prepare children to use tools "over and above what could be learnt through observation, imitation, and goal-directed practice."[19] Several research studies have found exactly this pattern using a simple lure-retrieval task. Children are shown an attractive toy that is out of their reach. In front of them is a set of objects, one of which is the right length and shape to reach and retrieve the toy. Children who are first given the opportunity to play with the objects are more likely to use the objects later as tools to retrieve the toy than children who did not play with them, and are just as good, or better, at the task as children who are given specific instructions.[20] In a related study from my lab with Jeffrey Gredlein, 3-year-olds played, not with the objects that would later be used in the lure-retrieval task, but with other sets of materials (toy animals, Lego®, a miniature set of tables and chairs). The amount of object-oriented play these children showed during the free-play periods predicted how well they performed the lure-retrieval task. Children who showed high amounts of object-oriented play were more likely to use the different objects as tools and were more apt to get the attractive toy.[21]

One interesting finding in many of these studies is that boys show higher levels of object-oriented play and greater subsequent tool use than girls. For example, in the study Jeff Gredlein and I did, boys displayed more object-oriented play, were more likely to use tools to solve the lure-retrieval problem, and the relation between play and tool use was statistically significant only for the boys. Girls were just as likely to use tools to retrieve the out-of-reach toy after they were given a simple hint, indicating that there is not an ability difference in tool use between preschool boys and girls. The difference is one of motivation, or the tendency of young children to think of using objects (tools) to solve problems. And the significant relation between object-oriented play and tool use in boys (but not in girls) suggests that there may be something special about young male psychology that orients them to objects. In fact, the sex difference in object-oriented play and tool use is consistent with hypotheses about gender roles in ancient environments in which the modern human mind evolved. According to evolutionary developmental psychologist David Geary, "From this perspective, the sex difference in manipulative and exploratory object-oriented play reflects an evolved bias in children's activities, so that boys, more so than girls, play in ways that elaborate the skeletal competencies associated with the engineering modules and later tool use."[22]

Learning to Behave like Adults

Sex differences are found in other types of play, which may also serve to prepare children for adult life, or at least for the life children over most of human history could have anticipated. Beginning in the preschool years, boys and girls around the world segregate into same-sex play groups, often despite attempts of adults to promote gender integration. Although there is no type of play that is the exclusive domain of boys or girls, the sexes do differ in how they play. For instance, as I noted earlier, boys (and other male mammals) engage in more rough-and-tumble play (R&T) than girls. R&T involves chasing and wrestling, and often looks like fighting, except it is done with a "play face" and children usually don't get hurt. One reason proposed for the sex-segregated play groups seen in childhood is that girls find the play of boys too rough and so form their own less-physical play groups. (I recall my father saying sarcastically to my three brothers and me on more than one occasion, "Okay boys, keep it up until somebody gets hurt," which often happened, followed by "I told you so." However, after the crying stopped, we boys usually resumed our "horsing around," the accidental infliction of pain forgiven and nearly forgotten.)

Some have argued that R&T is especially important for boys, serving as practice for hunting and fighting, at least in traditional environments. Boys' standing in the social hierarchy is more often based on physical skill and strength than is that of girls, and maneuvering through these pecking orders requires understanding the significance of the various social signals of your peers that are learned during mock combat. These skills are important at all stages of life, but may be particularly important for boys growing up in stable communities. The boys they play with as juveniles will become the men they cooperate and compete with as adults. This still reflects the pattern of children growing up in many parts of the world today, and surely reflected the lives of children for most of human history.

Girls can also play rough, but their play is more apt to focus on social roles, frequently parenting. For example, when girls engage in fantasy play they often take roles of mother, wife, or teacher. These are roles that nearly all women in years gone by would have served as adults (and roles most women in the world continue to serve today), and such play, usually in smaller, more intimate groups of children than for boys, serves to prepare girls for these adult roles. Boys also engage in pretend play, of course, but their themes are more apt to involve competition and dominance, such as the superheroes currently popular with young American boys, consistent with their more general style of play.[23] Boys (or their fathers) often chafe at being told that they are "playing with dolls" and will insist that their make-believe characters are "action figures." What the toys are called is really immaterial. Dolls or action figures, boys and girls tend to play with them differently, girls emphasizing relationships and boys emphasizing battles, competition, and dominance.

Neither girls nor boys may end up serving the adult roles that childhood play "prepares" them for, especially in modern societies. Boys might never be involved in a physical fight in their adult lives (and possibly not as children), and girls might not become mothers, or if they do they might perform the role in greater cooperation with their mates and in other ways that would be unrecognizable to their ancestors. Evolution is not forward looking. Children might be biased toward certain experiences, expressed through play, that, in our ancient past, were associated with adult behavior and success. We still possess those biases, and if childhood environments support them, children will play much as their ancestors played when they were children. Whether such play still prepares children for life in modern culture is an open question. To the extent that children learn how to relate to peers, how to cooperate and compete in socially acceptable ways, and to model some aspects of adult behavior, I believe that play continues to be adaptive. Children's evolved tendencies toward play are flexible, however. Play does not "prepare" children for tightly defined roles; it in no way destines boys or girls to specific, traditional roles. Play, rather, affords children opportunities to acquire social and physical skills that may be particular to their own society. Play takes advantage of the plasticity of the human mind/brain, permitting children, through enjoyable activities, to learn much of what they need to become successful adults in their culture.

Fantasy Play and Cognitive Development

Fantasy play is obviously based on children's abilities to use symbols. Although there is considerable debate among developmental psychologists as to the age when symbolic functioning is first available, most agree that children don't engage in fantasy play until usually after their second birthdays, and it gets more sophisticated as children's mental abilities develop. But does fantasy play also *enhance* cognitive development and learning? Let me answer this question at the outset. Fantasy play does not seem necessary for children to acquire important cognitive-developmental milestones, but it helps.

Much fantasy play is social, what Sara Smilansky referred to as sociodramatic play. In such play, children must take the perspective of others, negotiate roles, and especially *talk* about what they're thinking and planning to do. Some have proposed that fantasy play requires children to reflect upon language, insuring that they get their meaning across. This increased attention to language, seen more in the fantasy play of girls than of boys, may have important consequences for reading, and may account, in part, for the sex difference, favoring girls, seen in early reading.[24]

Other researchers have proposed that fantasy play might be especially important in the development of *theory of mind*, particularly an understanding that other people can hold false beliefs. Theory of mind refers to the understanding that one's behavior is based on what one knows, or believes, and what one wants, or desires, termed *belief–desire reasoning*. If *my* behavior is based on what I know and want, then it makes sense that other people's behavior is based on what *they* know and what *they* want. Moreover, these people can hold different beliefs and have different desires than I have, making predicting their behavior a bit difficult and resulting in possible conflicts of interests. This later piece of knowledge is slow to develop, with children much younger than 4 years of age typically failing to identify *false beliefs* in other people. For example, when children are shown a box of *M&Ms* and asked what they think is inside, they naturally say *M&Ms*. The box is then opened and instead of candy they see pencils. When asked what another child, outside of the room, will think is in the box, most

3-year-old children say "pencils," not realizing, apparently, that someone else can hold a false belief.

Understanding false belief requires understanding the mental state of another, something that is an essential feature of social fantasy play. A number of studies have looked at the relation between various measures of fantasy and performance on false-belief tasks, and most report positive relationships between the two. Young children who show higher levels of fantasy tend to perform better on theory-of-mind tasks. Not all of the relations are statistically significant, however (in fact, most are not), and few of them are large. In other words, the correlations are almost always in the predicted direction, but the effects are small. These findings led University of London developmental psychologist Peter Smith to conclude that pretend play does not have a strong causal role in developing theory of mind, but rather a facilitative one. Fantasy play is one route (albeit a likely important one) in which children practice social relations, and such practice enhances their social-cognitive abilities.[25]

Let the Games Begin!

Let's not forget games. Piaget believed that games represented a more advanced form of play that superseded fantasy play beginning around 6 years of age. Games involve agreed-upon rules, usually involving other children. The symbolic abilities required to understand the perspective of another in dramatic play are further honed when playing games. When children play games together, they are learning critical social skills and developing social intelligence that will serve them well both in childhood and adulthood. Unlike in school or in the home, there is no adult authority to proscribe a rule or mediate a disagreement when children play games together. Children must do this themselves, and this requires negotiation among equals. It is in contexts such as these that perspective taking, negotiation skills, and social intelligence develop. Games produce winners and losers, the need to compete and cooperate, and to maintain good relations even in the face of conflict or disappointment.

From this perspective, games, unlike R&T or symbolic play, seem to be serious endeavors. Children will practice their skills at games, take great pride in winning or performing well, and display disappointment or sadness when performing badly. Other children recognize gifted game players, especially athletic games, and afford high status to the talented. But games qualify as play nonetheless. They are joyfully joined voluntarily and their outcomes are viewed, in the bigger picture, as unimportant. Many a parent has tried to assuage a disappointed, frustrated, or even angry child by saying "it's only a game."

School-yard games are familiar to most readers, including games where many children participate, such as kickball, baseball, or tag, as well as games in which only a handful of children take part at any one time, such as hopscotch or "HORSE" (matching basketball shots, with each miss resulting in another letter until the loser has "HORSE").

Games are not limited to schooled societies, but, just as other forms of play, are found in traditional cultures as well. For example, Yumi Gosso and her colleagues describe the "hawk game," played by Canela Indian children of the Amazon rain forest. It reminds me of the game "Wolves and Pigs" I played as a child:

> One child plays a hawk and the others stand on a line that begins with the tallest child. Each child in the line strongly holds the one ahead. The "hawk" is released and screams *"Piu"* ("I am hungry"). The first child in line opens his or her legs, bends down so that his or her head is between the legs, and looks back, pointing his or her arm to the child behind and asking, *"Tu senan sini?"* ("Do you want this?"). All the children in line repeat this question. The "hawk" answers *"E pelé"* ("No") to all except the last one, to whom the "hawk" says *"Iná"* ("Yes") and begins to chase him or her. The group, without letting go of their physical contact, try to trap the "hawk." If the "hawk" catches the child, he or she will take him or her to his or her nest. The game continues until the "hawk" gets all the children, following the same order of the line.[26]

Older children and adults in hunter-gatherer cultures play various types of ball games, often competing between villages, that would be familiar to fans of hockey, soccer, or rugby. Board games, not too dissimilar from checkers, and games involving dice are also common among traditional people. As in industrialized societies, games with rules increase in frequency as children get older and fantasy play decreases.[27]

Children's participation in outdoor play seems to be declining in America, and as a result, so does the amount of exercise they get. (It is difficult to get solid empirical data documenting this, in part because large-scale data of children's frequency of outdoor play activities in years past were never collected.) Richard Louv, author of *Last Child Left in the Woods*, comments on this general trend and attributes some of it to adults declaring many outdoor areas "off limits" to children's play, in part for protection against injuries (and law suits) and in part for esthetic reasons (torn-up football fields or tree houses can be an eyesore for a community park). Modern parents are more reluctant than parents of past generations to let their young children roam free out-of-doors without adult supervision, based on their concern about safety and crimes against children. There are also other, more sedentary activities that children participate in today, such as watching TV and playing computer games, which are replacing more vigorous outdoor games. In part as a result of this switch from active, outdoor play to more sedentary, indoor play, obesity among children is at an all-time high.

In a recent study, parents from 10 locations around the county rated the safety of their neighborhoods. Of the children of parents who rated their neighborhoods as least safe, 17% were overweight at the age of 7. In contrast, of the children whose parents perceived their neighborhoods as most safe, only 4% were overweight. This trend held true for children from a wide range of socioeconomic levels, from lower to upper-middle class. Parents' concerns about their children's safety kept them inside, limiting their opportunities to exercise.[28]

When young children do play outdoors, research has shown that there are some real benefits. For example, University of Minnesota educational psychologist Anthony Pellegrini and his colleagues watched 77 first-grade children from two schools at outdoor recess over the course of the school year.[29] Boys generally engaged in more games and a greater variety of games than girls, especially games involving vigorous exercise, such as chase games. Girls, however, were involved in more verbal games than boys. Some of girls' games, such a jump rope, involved both motor activity and language. The researchers noted changes in the number and quality of game playing over time. Simple chase games declined over the year while more complicated ball games increased in frequency, as children's social-cognitive abilities and familiarity with their peers increased.

A particularly interesting finding in the study by Pellegrini and his colleagues was that children's facility at games early in the year, as judged by their peers and teachers, predicted aspects of social and academic competence later in the year. Children who were rated early on as good at games or as game leaders had higher levels of social skills and were better adjusted to school at the end of the academic year than children who were rated as less adept at games. This was especially true for boys.[iii] These findings are consistent with the idea

[iii] For those statistically minded readers, these end-of-year effects were significant after controlling for initial levels of social and school competence.

that outdoor play, at least among first graders, provides children with a context in which to develop social and coping skills and then generalize those skills to other contexts, in this case the classroom.

As I noted earlier, games can be more sedentary and "intellectual," as card games, from *Go Fish* and *Texas Hold 'em*, to *Pokémon* and *Yu-Gi-Oh*, or board games from *Chutes and Ladders* and *Hungry, Hungry Hippo* to backgammon and chess. These games can involve considerable cognitive and social skills. For example, most conventional card games require some understanding of probability, poker perhaps being the clearest example; and such games usually involve different strategies for making moves ("Do you have any 3s?" is more likely to yield a positive response in *Go Fish* if there are no 3s already laid down on the table than if a pair of 3s has already been declared). The social skills required in playing these games should also not be overlooked. Children must learn to take turns, know what they can talk to other players about during a game and what they should not ("Hey, I just picked up an 8. That's the card you wanted last time. OK, it's your turn"), and develop the social skills to maximize their success at winning games. Having a poker face is useful not just in cards but also in many social interactions.

Some of the card games that currently fascinate many American 7- to 12-year-old boys, such *Pokémon* and *Yu-Gi-Oh*, involve the memorization of many different cards and rules, and, seemingly, the application of complicated strategies. For instance, in *Yu-Gi-Oh* there are Monster cards that have various levels of attack and defense points. There are Egyptian God cards, spell cards, trap cards, and cards that modify the value of other cards. The game is sufficiently complicated that if one does not have the motivation to master it (as many people past their preteen years do not), it is difficult to acquire by "just watching." To be honest, I'm not certain whether my 7-year-old grandson actually knows all the rules and uses successful strategies or if he just makes things up as he goes along. But he is engaged in it, has learned a lot of details about the game, and always beats me when we play imaginary games where we make up the cards. (He permits me to make up my own fantasy names for characters, such as my "Magical Mystery Tour" card, which I tell him defeats his Egyptian God card – I still lose.) I'd be very interested to know if children who play these card games, or even more conventional card games such as whist, poker, or bridge, show any cognitive advantages, particularly in memory or in using learning strategies.

Children also play games with their parents, and these games can be opportunities for some subtle teaching in a playful context. For example, parents frequently play card or board games with their young children and often take the opportunity to teach them something about colors, shapes, letters, or numbers. Such tutorials, when done right, can promote learning of important technological skills, such as addition and subtraction, without the child being aware that any formal teaching is going on. Let me provide an example from some research my students and I did using a modified version of the board game *Chutes and Ladders*.[30] In this game, children move a token around the board, jumping ahead spaces when they land on a ladder and falling back spaces when they land on a slide, or chute. Moves are usually determined by twirling a spinner, which we replaced with a pair of dice. Five-year-old children and their parents took turns rolling the dice and making their moves. We asked parents to play the game with their children as they normally would at home.

Computing moves required determining the total on the two dice. One simple strategy that children sometimes used was counting the dots on the first die ("One, two, three, four"), moving their token the corresponding number, and then repeating it for the second die ("One, two"). This requires counting but no addition. A more sophisticated counting strategy that many children often used spontaneously is called *SUM*, in which children count the dots on both dice ("One, two, three, four...five, *six*") before moving. This is an addition strategy, but a rather laborious and unsophisticated one.

Although some parents were content to let children make their moves in these ways, most encouraged or taught some simple addition strategies to their children. For instance, on their moves, some parents would roll the dice, state each quantity ("Four and two") and provide the total ("That's six"), demonstrating that one can "just know" the sum of two numbers, a strategy called *fact retrieval*. Others would model what is termed the *MIN* strategy, stating the larger of the two numbers ("That's four") and then counting the smaller number ("five, six"). It is called MIN because it involves counting the minimal number of items. During the children's turn, many parents posed questions ("How many do you have?") or gave them some instructions in how to arrive at the right answer.

The techniques of some parents were quite successful. They started out giving their children a lot of support ("How many on this one? Good. Now how many on this one? Good. Now count them together and see how many you've got."), and gave fewer directions as their children started "getting it" on their own. They maintained the playful and game-like atmosphere, avoiding the impression that a lesson was taking place. This has been termed *scaffolding*, and is an important way in which children learn from parents and other more expert peers. Other parents were less supportive. Some provided no instruction, other than to correct children when they were wrong. Others did the computation for their children. Some insisted that children use a strategy, such as MIN, that they were not capable of using. For instance, one little boy would roll the dice and start counting the dots on each die, one at a time (that is, he used the SUM strategy). As the child counted, his mother would interrupt him and tell him to start counting from the larger addend (that is, to use the MIN strategy). When the child rolled a "five and four" and started counting the dots, his mother would interrupt him saying, "No, John, start counting from the five here," pointing at the five and saying, "You know this is five." John would start over counting all the dots on the dice, asking his mother to stop. This continued throughout the game with mom rolling the dice during her turn and stating the total of her dice ("Six and five are eleven"), which John ignored. The game was not fun for John, and although I'm sure his mother was well intended, he learned little about addition in the process.

There are also solitary games, such as solitaire, which I sometime play on my home computer when I should be writing, and these games can also influence children's learning. But solitaire is an old fogy's game and not a worthy example of the type of solitary games that contemporary children play. Many children today devote considerable time to video games, and there has been great debate about the merits and demerits of such activities. I discuss one aspect of video games later below, toward the end of the next section.

Play, Innovation, and Discovery Learning

Play, like genetic mutations, may also provide a source of creativity that may eventually help produce cultural (and perhaps evolutionary) diversity; and, because of the youthful tendency toward play and curiosity in animals, it is likely that new innovations will be introduced by the young rather than by adults. This was suggested by the philosopher of science Karl Popper, who proposed that curiosity and consciousness were characteristics of young organisms and that they were linked in our own species to delayed maturity:

> I want to formulate two hypotheses which are closely related and somewhat bold. The first...[is that] curiosity is the beginning of consciousness. The second is that, in the evolutionary story, young animals

become conscious before old animals. That is to say, consciousness may be connected with the exploratory period of evolution of animals… One actually has a kind of intuitive impression that old animals become less and less conscious: this is especially noticeable when compared with the behavior of young animals, which shows many more signs of consciousness. The distinctive evolution of consciousness in man may be linked with the delayed maturing and the somewhat delayed aging in man.[31]

A now-classic study of potato washing in Japanese macaque monkeys provides some tentative evidence for the idea that new innovations are more likely to come from juveniles than from adults. Japanese scientists had been observing a troop of monkeys and had provisioned them with food, including sweet potatoes. The monkeys lived near the sea and the potatoes frequently were covered with sand. One juvenile monkey learned to wash the potatoes before eating them, which removed the sand and also likely gave the potatoes a slightly salty taste. Other juvenile monkeys picked up the trick, and later so did a few adult females. Few adult males were ever observed to wash potatoes. Potato washing was then passed on from mothers to infants as part of the monkey "culture."[32]

Modern human culture is much more complicated than that of any monkey (or any species, for that matter), and I do not suppose that important innovations that eventually sweep through society will be discovered by children (at least not in post-industrial nations). But play can provide children with important insights and "discoveries" that may not be as easily acquired through formal instruction. Piaget emphasized the role of *discovery learning* in cognitive development. According to Piaget, "Children should be able to do their own experimenting and their own research. Teachers, of course, can guide them by providing appropriate materials, but the essential thing is that in order for a child to understand something, he must construct it for himself; he must reinvent it."[33] Piaget's reference to children doing their own "experimenting" could likely be restated as children "playing around with stuff."

Let me state explicitly that I believe Piaget overstated the role of discovery learning in cognitive development. It's important, but some things are better learned through instruction. Although some children will learn "on their own" how to decipher the secret code of letters on paper (or a computer screen), most will not. Children's unique cognitive abilities enable them to learn from teaching as well as from discovery. But information acquired through discovery is often of special significance to children. There is a satisfaction of "figuring out" a problem and a special motivation is associated with discovery learning.

Discovery learning is not in fashion in schools these days, but it nonetheless permeates the lives of many American children through computer video games. I'm not a game player myself, and am often befuddled by what it takes to get through level 1 of my 7-year-old grandson's Mario Brothers game. But despite many parents' chagrin at the time their children waste playing these games and what they're *not* doing with their time, there is some real discovery learning going on, and this may be one reason for their popularity. In his book *Everything Bad is Good for You*, science writer Steven Johnson examined what is involved in many video games, and it reminds me a lot of discovery learning. The rules of the game are only sketched out at the beginning. There are ways of getting past murderous monsters, gaining extra points or extra lives, and shortcuts through mazes that can only be discovered. Although non-gaming adults often look at child players and assume they are engaged in a mindless, and perhaps mind-numbing, pursuit, this is far from the truth. Most video games are hard work, require a high degree of motivation, an ability to tolerate frustration and perseveration in the face of failure, and mainly to discover how to play the game. Success feels very good.

This by itself may not be a good reason for a child's devotion to video games, but there seems also to be some cognitive advantages associated with game playing. Johnson cites research indicating that game players realize a variety of cognitive benefits, most related to visual processing. For example, Shawn Green and Daphne Bavelier at the University of Rochester contrasted groups of adult video game players with non-game players on a series of visual processing tasks. Game players were better able to locate targets within a field of visual distractors, were better able to keep in mind a greater number of visual items, and were faster at processing temporal visual information, all relative to non-game players.

Research with children has also shown a positive relation between playing some video games and spatial abilities. For example, UCLA psychologists Kaveri Subrahmanyam and Patricia Greenfield reported that children practicing the game *Marble Madness*, which involves guiding and intercepting objects, showed enhancements in spatial skills, and that this effect was particularly strong for novice players and for children who had relatively poor spatial skills before playing the game. Other research has shown that playing computer games can improve children's metal rotation abilities (rotating, in one's mind, objects as if to view them from a different perspective).[34] Also, video games are not always a solitary activity; in fact, they are often played with another child, making them both cooperative and competitive, and a context for socialization.

Not enough research has been done on the potential cognitive benefits of video games to get too excited about them. Their appeal to children may be due, in part, to the healthy dose of discovery learning that is involved in many of these games. Whether this is a blessing or a curse, I leave to others. I admit to finding it frustrating trying to have a simple conversation with a 7-year-old with his face just inches away from his Gameboy® (although I am sometimes thankful he has it on long car rides). And one cannot ignore the violent content of many of these games, which has been shown to be associated with aggressive behavior.[iv] In the bigger picture of things, video games are yet another example of our increasingly visual world, beginning with photography, and progressing through movies, television, VCRs, and now picture cell phones.

Play it Again, Kid

Play is the essence of childhood. Children do not need to be taught to play. Babies' initial exploration of objects turns into seeing what they can do with them, often accompanied by smiles or laughter when some unexpected outcome is achieved. Infants' early interactions with their parents become games of chase and peek-a-boo, and when infants and young children see other youngsters, they are immediately drawn to them and initiate play. The developmental psychologist Judith Harris proposed that children are actually socialized by their peers, not their parents.[35] Children do not aspire to emulate adults, but to become competent children. Their personalities are shaped by their interactions with other kids as much as, if not more than, by interactions with their parents. (Parents provide children with genes, of course, which Harris, and others, believes is a major contributor to children's personalities.)

[iv] Research examining the relation between playing violent video games and various aspects of children's aggressive behavior report a significant, though moderate, relation between the two. The findings from two meta-analyses (studies that look at the average effects from a large number of studies) report correlations reflecting effect sizes of .19 (Anderson & Bushman, 2001) and .15 (Sherry, 2001). These reflect only the short-term relations between playing violent video games and aggressive behavior. Little is known of any long-term effects.

Children live in a culture of play, a culture inhabited by other children with its own set of not-very-serious rules. They are aware of the culture of adults, and partake in that culture frequently, but act as if they are only visitors to this more serious world. Children's experience in play culture prepares them to become functioning members of the adult culture as their abilities improve. Children in societies such as ours become involved in the adult culture earlier than children from traditional societies. Schooling requires this. School is serious, although play doesn't disappear when children pass through the school doors.

Play is the natural expression of youth and the way in which children interact with their world. Play is a reflection of children's developing competencies, but in turn facilitates the development of those, and other, competencies. Play is the joyful conduit by which experience changes children's brains and minds. Children may not set out to learn, or discover, anything via play, but they do anyway. Learning can be more explicit, or intentional, as often happens in formal schooling, but parents and educators should not ignore how much children learn through play, usually without even being aware of it.

7

The Most Educable of Animals

We begin with the hypothesis that any subject can be taught effectively in some intellectually honest form to any child at any stage of development.

Jerome Bruner, *The Process of Education*

If, however, our concept of [early childhood education] is an accelerating experience where children are pushed to be little 'performers,' I think we may be creating anxious, stressed children ... Are we not inducing achievement anxiety in children being pushed? Are we saying to them their value lies only in their achievement? Are we depriving these children of the excitement of self-directed activities? ... Who, after all, is in a hurry – the children or the parents?

Irving Sigel[1]

♦   ♦   ♦   ♦

"At this point, I'm not certain that I'll be able to recommend Joshua be promoted next year," Mrs Gillespe said to the concerned mother at a parent-teacher conference. "His math is fine. In fact, he's one of the best in the class, and his reading is only a bit below grade level. But his handwriting is awful and he does not work independently very well. He needs to work on these things." Joshua had just finished his third month in first grade, and his poor penmanship and his inability to complete his "seatwork" without teacher direction marked him as a candidate for retention. Did I mention that he was only 6 years old and in first grade?

Joshua's parents worked with him at home over the course of the year and got him some after-school tutoring (they decided not to go with the $6,000 private "learning" center that would guarantee that he gets promoted to the second grade or their money back), and he was advanced to the second grade.

What was expected of Joshua and his classmates seemed to some to be really a bit beyond their years. Joshua could read some, albeit not well, and, as his teacher noted, he was very good at math. But this lefthander's penmanship was horrid, and he didn't have the discipline to do his seatwork without supervision. His mind, eyes, and entire body would sometime wander when he was supposed to be working "on his own." Such behavior, rather than reflecting a delinquent first grader, describes a normal 6-year-old. This is especially true for boys, who often lag behind girls in fine-motor coordination and general academic ability at this age.

First grade is also a time of substantial intellectual diversity. Many children can read reasonably well by 6, whereas others think that "elemeno" is a single letter of the alphabet. The match between Joshua and his teacher may also have been a problem. Other teachers may have not expected as much independence as Mrs Gillespe, and Joshua may have had a better attitude if he had been given more opportunity to exercise. (Joshua was thrilled with this second-grade teacher; the primary reason according to him after the first week of class was because she lets them go out on the playground at least once every day.)

Joshua's story is not unique. Elementary school is more challenging today than when I was a student. Reading instruction has been pushed back earlier and earlier, to kindergarten and even preschool. Yet, the cognitive abilities of 6-year-olds have not changed in the past 50 years, causing one to question whether educators in decades past were failing to take advantage of young children's learning abilities, or whether we may be pushing kids too hard too early today.

The pressures on American children to excel are greater than they were in the past, and, by some standards, we as a society are succeeding. More children are staying in school longer, and more are attending college than ever before. But are they learning more? Are today's high-school graduates more educated than their predecessors? Many would say no. Nearly a third of college freshmen require some remedial course work before starting "real" college courses; and international comparisons of educational attainment rarely place US children, at any age, among the top performers.[2] More commonly, American children fall in the middle of academic achievers among developed countries, often much below nations with considerably less wealth.[i]

---

[i] There are many reasons for America's less-than-stellar performance in international circles other than differences in curriculum. The United States has greater cultural and economic diversity than most other developed coun-

In the same period that early schooling has become more rigorous, academic achievement has remained relatively stable. For example, the National Assessment of Educational Progress is a federally mandated evaluation of reading and math achievement in American school children dating back to 1971.[3] Large samples of 9-, 13-, and 17-year-old children are tested on sets of items that have remained substantially unchanged, permitting a look at educational progress over the years. Results are presented in terms of scaled scores that range from 0 to 500. The youngest children have shown the greatest improvement over the years, with reading scores increasing from a scaled score 208 in 1971 to 219 in 2004, and math scores increasing from 219 in 1973 to 241 in 2004. Changes have been smaller for the 13- and 17-year-olds, especially for reading. Reading scaled scores changed from 255 in 1971 to 259 in 2004 for 13-year-olds, and were unchanged at 285 for 17-year-olds. Math scores changed from 266 in 1973 to 281 in 2004 for 13-year-olds and from 304 to 307 for 17-year-olds. These data do reflect improvements in reading and math over the past two decades, but these advantages are smallest (and not statistically significant for the 17-year-olds) for those who have been in school the longest.

It is not possible to interpret these long-term changes in any simple way, for there are many factors influencing secular changes in school performance. But the trend is one of general stability, especially for the oldest students, over a time period when early education became increasingly rigorous. Other research has found that some basic mathematical abilities have actually decreased over the decades in the United States. For example, David Geary and his colleagues reported that Chinese young adults outperformed American young adults on basic arithmetic tests. There was no difference, however, between the older Chinese and American adults. The pattern of results was

tries. For instance, although the per capita income of the United States is among the highest in the world, there is considerable variability in income – there are more very wealthy and more very poor people – than in European countries. Differences in socioeconomic status are in turn associated with where people live, the qualities of the schools children attend, the support schools receive from parents, education level of parents, parental attitudes toward the value of education, the type of intellectual support children receive in the home, medical (including prenatal) care, all known to be associated with school achievement. Attitudes toward education vary among nations, as does the amount of time parents spend supervising their children in their school work. Thus, international contrasts in educational attainment, though informative, are not easily interpreted.

attributed to the poorer performance of the younger Americans, suggesting that the Chinese-American difference in arithmetic ability is a relatively recent one.[4] This doesn't mean that early academic instruction isn't effective, but neither does it provide evidence that it has had long-term positive effects.

Americans also do not seem as concerned with their children's education as parents in other developed countries. We of course profess that we believe education is important, but that typically does not translate into demanding higher standards in schools, approving school bonds, raising teachers' salaries, or increasing the length of the school day or the school year. For example, in my home state of Florida voters approved a referendum that would limit the number of children in each class. That same referendum, however, did not allocate additional money for making the changes. Three years later, State legislators are attempting to rescind the voters' decision, complaining that they cannot achieve these goals without raising taxes, and that these same voters elected them on the promise *not* to raise taxes.

Americans also seem unconcerned about our children's ranking in international comparisons. For example, the United States is taking part in a global assessment of children's school achievement, the *Programme for International Student Assessment*, or PISA, and my guess is that few people reading this book have ever heard of it.[5] I was spending six months in Germany when the first PISA report was published, and my host, Wolfgang Schneider of the University of Würzburg, was the German representative to PISA. Germany did not fare well in the international comparisons, scoring below neighbor Austria and only slightly higher than the United States. Discussions of the PISA findings, particularly as they related to the German education system, were in the newspapers, on the radio and television, and a topic of conversation for professional and lay people alike. Professor Schneider was busy for several months, talking to the school principals and teachers, giving interviews to the press, and visiting the Ministers of Education of various German states as well as influential politicians at the federal level. The PISA findings were a big deal, and Germany's middle-of-the-road performance was a reason for concern. The only time I heard of the PISA results when I returned home was a radio story that related how concerned *the Germans* were about the results – nothing about how the United States fared in the comparisons, or, as I recall, even that the United States had participated in the study. In this century when economic competition is truly becoming worldwide (or as political columnist Thomas Friedman puts it, *The World is Flat*), Americans cannot afford to retain an insular perspective but must be concerned with how our children and their education stack up relative to others in the world.

My own opinion is that early schooling in America is too rigorous and later schooling isn't rigorous enough. This is especially true, I believe, during the preschool years, a time when children's cognitive abilities are well suited to understanding their surroundings, and learning is best achieved in more "playful" and "natural" settings.

This does not mean that I think preschool children should be untutored or left to their own devices. Preschoolers the world over have the same brains, which are not appreciably different from the brains preschoolers 40,000 years ago had in their skulls; but what they need to learn varies with the demands of their society, and ours is one that places great emphasis on literacy and numeracy. Our children learn the rudiments of reading, writing, and computation before entering school, or at least they should. They learn about the power of language and what writing and reading are "for." They acquire pre-literacy skills (referred to as *emergent literacy*), such as knowing that written words correspond to spoken words, that letters correspond to sounds, that written symbols "mean" something. They learn their letters and "conventions of print," such as reading is done from left to right (in English). They also learn something about mathematics, such as the number words through 20, and that numbers (and thus quantities) can be added and subtracted. Preschoolers often learn such valuable cultural knowledge through playful interaction with parents. Certainly letters or numbers are frequently "taught" to children, but not in the context of drill or formal instruction.

Young children need to be prepared for the demands of school, but they do not need to be "schooled" in the same way that older and more cognitively advanced children are. Formal education can wait until children have the intellectual wherewithal to master comfortably the technologies that would be so foreign to their ancient ancestors but are at the core of modern society.

This view, although quite common among developmental psychologists and some educators,[6] is at odds with the views of many middle-class American parents and some educators who believe that "earlier is better" and that the more education children get the better. In many ways it is difficult to argue against this position. If education is the key to success in modern society, then beginning formal education early should provide children with an advantage. We know, for example, that there is a positive relation between time spent in school and IQ, and other research has shown that one year of schooling has a greater impact on IQ and certain areas of academic achievement than does one year of age. We should be surprised if this were not the case, for what is school supposed to do if not make us smarter and provide us with the technological skills to succeed in society?[7]

Education in this context is viewed as formal learning, not the acquisition of knowledge through play or causal conversations with other children or adult family members. Early education need not be viewed in such a limited way. The position that children learn (that is, become educated) from day-to-day interactions with parents and other more expert individuals is the backbone of *sociocultural theory*, originally developed in the 1920s and 30s by the Soviet psychologist Lev Vygotsky. Vygotsky believed that teaching is most effective when done within the child's *zone of proximal development*, defined as the difference between a child's "actual developmental level as determined by independent problem solving" and his or her level of "potential development as determined through problem solving under adult guidance or in collaboration with more capable peers." University of California at Santa Cruz psychologist Barbara Rogoff expanded Vygotsky's ideas to include not just situations in which adults are attempting to instruct children, but children's learning during the more routine activities and communication of everyday life, a concept she termed *guided participation*. The general perspective of cognitive development emanating from a structured interaction between children and adults is nicely reflected in developmental psychologist Mary Gauvain's statement that "cognitive development is an active constructive process that involves beings who are evolutionarily predisposed to live and learn in social context with other 'like-minded' beings. They are like-minded in terms of both the neurological system available and the social requirements that are in place."[8]

My objection is not to early education. Human beings are the most educable species the Earth has ever seen, and the process starts early and never stops. My objection rather is to instructional techniques that ignore children's natural abilities and learning styles and to the idea that if something *can* be learned earlier than it typically is, it *should* be learned earlier. In a sense, I'm arguing against instruction that is done outside of Vygotsky's zone of proximal development (although I admit that such a zone is difficult to define precisely). Earlier is not always better, I believe. Despite recognition of this by many psychologists and educators, there is a trend toward increasingly rigorous "formal" education at all levels of early childhood, beginning before birth, during infancy, and through the preschool years.

My emphasis in this chapter is on children's learning and education, focusing mainly on the preschool years, but examining briefly learning and schooling in older children. I first take a brief historical look at how educators, psychologists, and the public have viewed the role of early experience on later intelligence. The main perspective has been, and continues to be, that experiences in the first few years of life shape a child's intellect and personality. Although there is surely some truth to this, intellectual or socioemotional functioning, once established, must be maintained by a supportive environment. In the next two sections I look at prenatal learning and learning in infancy, respectively. I examine devices and programs that have been designed to take advantages of fetuses' and infants' learning abilities and discuss why these may not always be such good ideas. I then look at developmentally appropriate practices in preschool education and contrast the outcomes of children who attend these child-centered programs with those who attend teacher-directed programs that stress formal educational practices. I then contrast the concepts of "acceleration" and "enrichment." In the next section I examine stress that elementary school children experience from curricula that emphasize "preparation" at the expense of fostering children's interests and talents, and the consequences of the "standards movement" on children's motivation for learning. I then look at an old solution to the problem of stress in schools, recess, and present research showing that recess promotes learning in elementary school children.

The Myth of "Earlier is Better"

The quest for smarter children through early education is not new, at least not in America, but its face has changed over the decades. When I was an undergraduate psychology student in the 1960s, the belief that the first four or five years of life were critical in establishing intellectual and social functioning held sway. This came from a variety of traditions in psychology. Still prominent was Sigmund Freud's theory that emphasized the critical role of parents (particularly mothers) on children's developing psyches during the early psychoanalytic stages of life (particularly the oral and anal stages, ranging from birth to about 3 years). Research from the behaviorist traditions of John Watson and B. F. Skinner emphasized the role of parents in shaping children's behavior through processes of reward and punishment that seemingly set the stage for all subsequent development. Patterns of emotional development were believed to be determined early and remain stable throughout life, based primarily on early infant-mother attachment as reflected in the research by Harry Harlow with monkeys and John Bowlby with abandoned children.

More recently the focus has changed from Id and Ego development to brain development. The 1990s was declared "The Decade of the Brain," and while much science emphasized the functioning of adult gray matter, children's developing brains were not ignored. In fact, knowledge about rapid brain development early in life put the spotlight on the "First Three Years" as a time when the brain is wired by experience and intelligence, and social/emotional competence is "set in neurons." In 1997 the White House held a conference on the topic, emphasizing the importance of children getting off to a good start and highlighting the new neuroscience research on the significance of early brain development. The press and general public were paying attention, and the past decade has seen a renewed emphasis on the role of early experience in development, but with a focus on the brain, and only indirectly on behavior.

Having the White House hold a conference and getting the media to take issues of child development seriously were important for the emerging field of developmental neuroscience. Brain development is influenced by experience and it is closely related to intellectual functioning. But then again, we've always known this, at least from the time we recognized that the brain is the seat of cognition. Seeing a multi-colored picture of the brain of a deprived child, reared in a stultifying Romanian orphanage, tells us quite emphatically that his neglect had serious consequences on how his brain is organized and how it works. But what did we think before we had the neuroimages of deprived children's brains? Seeing the pictures brings the message home to policy makers and the public at large, and this is generally good; but, in and of itself, it doesn't change what scientists understood about the source of intellectual deficits. The mind is based in the brain, whether we have fMRI images or not.

Many scientists stressed the importance of the first three years in sculpting the developing brain, and many educators and parents took these statements to mean that these are critical times in babies' and young children's lives and they should not be wasted. The problem is, there is no direct link between the developmental neuroscience research of the past decade and lessons for education.[9] Yes, children's brains grow rapidly and go through some quite remarkable transformations over this period. But other than making it clear that sensory, social, and intellectual deprivation are deleterious for brain development, no "brain curriculum" can be recommended with any authority. We know much about what it takes to rear an intellectually competent child, and this involves social, emotional, and cognitive support beginning in infancy and continuing through childhood. There is no compelling evidence that accelerated education will produce long-lasting effects in and of itself.

Yet, the data can *seem* quite compelling. Children who have high IQs during the preschool years or who are securely attached at 18 months of age tend to have high IQs and be securely attached in later childhood. And anyone would be a fool to believe that the early experience that contributed to these children's intellectual and emotional functioning did not also contribute to their later functioning. Behavior and cognition tend to be stable over time: young children who score high on some cognitive or socioemotional measure tend to score high on similar measures taken years later.

It would be a mistake, however, to make a direct cause-effect statement here. When intelligence or attachment, for example, is stable over time it is usually associated with stability in environments. Children who start life in intellectually supportive environments tend to stay in those environments. Parents who provide emotional warmth and intellectual stimulation to a 1- and 2-year-old usually are supportive and warm to a 5- and 6-year-old, and to the child when he or she is a teenager. What is supportive or enriching to children at these different ages changes, and so, too, does parents' behavior. What is stable is the supportive (or nonsupportive) attitude and actions of parents, and it is this that provides the stability of functioning in children. (Note that children's behavior itself is not stable. The bright 3-year-old thinks that age is determined by height, and that if she knows something, such as where a treat is hidden, so do other people. The bright 10-year-old she will become will believe none of this, but will still be among the smartest people in her group.)

You can't blame parents for wanting to enrich their children and getting them off to a competitive start, but it's wrong to think that accelerating early development will give children a permanent head start in life. Once intelligence is established it must be maintained. It is not the case that once you "got it," it's yours forever. Intelligence develops over the course of childhood, and although a bright 4-year-old usually turns out to be a bright 15-year-old, it is not solely because of the experiences that person had in his or her first four years. How children are treated early in life does affect their brains, and some children get more supportive and enriched environments than others. But an early advantage does not automatically translate into a later one, and it is questionable whether intellectually pushing infants and young children has any benefits at all. In fact, there may be some disadvantages associated with too-early academic acceleration.

Prenatal Learning

For advocates of the mantra "earlier is better," intellectual enrichment does not begin at birth, but before. Is there any reason to believe that prenatal "education" might even be possible? As it turns out, research over the past several decades has demonstrated what to many are surprising perceptual and learning abilities in fetuses. First, the brain grows rapidly during the prenatal months. Nearly all the neurons a person will ever have are produced by end of the fifth month after conception. Connections between neurons are being formed and we know that such connections are influenced by experience. Second, all of the senses are working before birth. Even vision may be operating at a very low level, with fetuses being able to perceive diffuse light filtered through their mothers' abdomens. We've known for some time that fetuses will startle to loud noise and will habituate (stop responding to repeated presentation of a stimulus) to certain repetitive sounds. Third and perhaps most impressive, there is evidence of prenatal auditory learning, but what precisely fetuses are learning isn't what most of us would classify as "formal education."

With respect to learning, the first question to ask is "how can one tell if a fetus has learned something?" For the most part, one has to wait until after the baby is born and then use some behavior newborns can control themselves to see if they show any evidence of being influenced by specific prenatal experience. This is demonstrated in research by developmental psychologists Anthony DeCasper and William Fifer, who placed pacifiers in the mouths of 1- to 3-day-old babies and fitted them with headphones. Then the researchers measured the infants' rates of sucking when no sound was coming through the headphones (the baseline period). They then played recordings of their mothers' voices or those of another woman over the headphones. Babies could change which voice they heard by varying their rate of sucking (increasing their rate for half the babies, decreasing their rate for the others). They found that babies changed their rates of sucking to hear their mothers' voices.[10]

First of all, it is quite impressive that newborns can demonstrate this kind of control over their own behavior. But equally important is the finding that these neonates showed a preference for hearing their mothers' voices so soon after birth. One interpretation is that it was not the day or two of postnatal experience that caused infants to show such a preference, but the weeks before birth when, as fetuses, they could hear their mothers talk. More recent research by Queen's University psychologist Barbara Kisilevsky and her colleagues makes it clear that this preference is based on prenatal experience. Kisilevsky and her colleagues measured changes in heart rate in 60 term fetuses (average gestational age, 38.4 weeks) to tape recordings of voices of their mothers and those of other women reading the same poem. Fetuses' heart rates increased when they heard their mothers' voices and decreased when they heard the voices of other women.[11]

Other researchers using techniques similar to those of DeCasper and Fifer have shown that newborns prefer to listen to the language spoken by their mothers over foreign languages. Developmental psychologist Jacques Mehler and his colleagues played tapes of women speaking either French or Russian to French babies shortly after birth. The babies increased their sucking rates when they heard their mother tongue. But, you may ask, who wouldn't prefer to listen to French than to Russian? To dismiss this claim, babies whose mothers spoke neither French nor Russian showed no change in sucking rate when played either the French or Russian tapes, illustrating that there was nothing intrinsically different in the French or Russian languages that was responsible for babies' responses. It was the prenatal experience of the babies to their French-speaking mothers that caused the difference.[12]

Perhaps the most impressive evidence of prenatal auditory learning comes from the work of Anthony DeCasper and Melanie Spence,[13] who asked pregnant women to read aloud one of three passages twice a day for the last six weeks of their pregnancies. The passages varied in rhythm and acoustic pattern, or *prosody*. One passage that some mothers read was Dr Seuss's *The Cat in the Hat*, which has a distinctive rhythmic pattern. Another was *The King, the Mice, and the Cheese*, which has a very different rhythmic pattern. Hours after birth the infants were fitted with pacifiers and headphones and heard one of two passages, including the one that their mothers had read. As in the earlier research, babies could change what they heard by changing their rate of sucking. The bottom line is that newborns were more likely to alter their sucking to hear the familiar passage than the unfamiliar one, even if their mothers did not read the passages. So it was not only the voice (or the language) that these infants had developed a preference for, but also the specific rhythmic pattern of the passage. Later research showed that it's not necessary to wait until infants are born to show prenatal learning. DeCasper and his colleagues used

173

changes in the heart rates of third-trimester fetuses to show that they had learned and preferred the passages their mothers had read to them.[14]

What is it that the fetuses are learning in these studies? They are learning something about language, definitely, but they are not learning the meaning of words or stories, or the grammar of their native tongue. They are learning about sound – the timbre of a voice and the prosody of language. This prenatal experience may make learning language a bit easier (or maybe not, there's no evidence either way), but they are not acquiring either content or structure at this early age. Playing tapes of the alphabet to fetuses will not give them a leg up when learning to read, and playing Mozart sonatas will not lead to greater intelligence or sophisticated sense of music appreciation. Fetuses do respond to music (they are activated by some types and relaxed by others) and may even develop a preference for a style of music as a result of prenatal experience. But such preferences are like the preference babies show for their mothers' voices, their native tongue, or the *Cat in the Hat*. It's the general acoustic pattern that infants are responsive to (which is, admittedly, impressive when you think about it) and not any content.

It is evidence such as this that some people use to argue that fetuses can learn, and thus we should not waste the months before birth but use this time to fill their brains with useful stuff. There have been numerous devices invented to help pregnant women communicate with and educate their unborn child, from the low-tech "pregaphone" that amplifies the mother's voice to her baby, to contraptions that flash lights at the mother's abdomen to (possibly) provide visual stimulation to her dark-dwelling fetus, audio recorders that play Mozart or the alphabet, and sonic sound generators. Brent Logan is the author of *Learning before Birth* and inventor of *BabyPlus*, a "fetal enrichment technology" that fits around a pregnant mother's belly and plays sounds to her fetus. Beginning two months post conception, *BabyPlus* plays rhythmic patterns to fetuses that resemble a mother's heartbeat, and these increase in complexity throughout pregnancy. The theory behind the device and practice is that prenatal brain stimulation can prevent the typical pattern of brain-cell death that occurs before birth, increasing the number of neurons and synapses a baby has when it first sees the world, setting the stage for better learning and greater intelligence.

Despite the numerous testimonials from satisfied customers on the *BabyPlus* website (www.babyplus.com) and research by Logan of precocious development for infants exposed to *BabyPlus*,[15] there seems to be no evidence from properly controlled studies that *BabyPlus* provides any long-term (or even short-term) intellectual benefit. Similarly, BébéSounds (www.bebesounds.com) offers a device pregnant women can wear around their abdomens that allows them to talk or play music (Mozart is recommended) to their fetuses. Similar to the claims of the manufacturers of *BabyPlus*, the purpose is to take advantage of rapid brain development and enhance the cognitive capacity of their yet-to-be-born children. Although there is some research evidence that babies exposed to violin sounds prior to birth showed some developmental advances in the first six months compared to control infants, the effects are small and get smaller with age;[16] and although I'm a fan of Mozart myself and don't doubt that music can have a soothing effect on children, there is no evidence that prenatal exposure to such music has any lasting effect on intellectual development.

I do not intend to be overly critical of parents who choose to use prenatal stimulation techniques to foster their babies' development, nor to the manufacturers of these products. I believe that parents who engage in such practices, and people who produce the gadgets for parents to use, do so for the best of reasons. Such parents want what's best for their children; they will likely provide intellectual stimulation in a warm supportive environment for their children, and their children will likely develop well. But it is a mistake to believe that the prenatal stimulation programs are responsible for any enhancement of a child's development. In fact, Mother Nature seems to do a decent job preparing fetuses and babies for learning what they need to know and when they need to know it. For example, as *BabyPlus* inventor Logan notes, there is a rapid loss of brain cells beginning prenatally and continuing through the first two years of life. This is a process known as *selective cell death*, in which some brain cells appear programmed to die, whereas others die due to lack of stimulation. (See discussion of early brain development in Chapter 3.) It may seem that keeping these neurons alive would afford a great advantage: the more brain cells one has, the more one can presumably learn. But selective cell death affords a pruning of the infant brain, and it is a necessary process of brain development. The human skull is only so large and can only house a finite number of brain cells. Neurons grow in size over development, become insulated with myelin to facilitate transmission of nervous impulses, and make connections with other neurons. All this takes space, and a brain that has not gone through the pruning process may not be better able to learn, but actually be hindered from learning. In fact, when selective cell death is limited, due to genetic abnormalities, the result is mental retardation. The distinguished University of Chicago developmental neuroscientist Peter Huttenlocher has gone so far to state that: "One has to consider the possibility that very ambitious early enrichment and teaching programs may lead to crowding effects and to an early decrease in the size and number of brain regions that are largely unspecified and that may be necessary for creativity in the adolescent and adult."[17]

We also saw in a previous chapter that the different parts of the brain develop at different times and that brain maturation is related to sensory stimulation. If fetuses receive "unexpected" sensory stimulation (for instance, quail receiving patterned light while still in the egg), they develop species-atypical patterns of abilities. Early stimulation of one sense can interfere with development of other senses. Granted, as in the studies by Robert Lickliter with bobwhite quail, deficiencies in one sensory system (audition) may be matched by accelerations in another (vision). But the underlying fact is that the nervous system has evolved to mature in concert with experience, and altering the pattern of experiences during a time of rapid brain development may have unintended consequences. Given the research to date, it appears that there are neither significant positive nor negative effects of contrived prenatal stimulation, but, should interventions be developed that produced meaningful effects, I would bet that they would be negative.

Early (Postnatal) Learning

Few people advocate doing much teaching in the womb. For the most part, attempts to "educate" fetuses are limited to exposing them to the voices of their parents, to music, and to heartbeat-like sounds intended to stimulate brain development. Although some have argued for more ambitious prenatal education, such as exposing children to the alphabet or a variety of languages, these are the exceptions. Part of the reason for this may be the limited access adults have to fetuses. We can't see them, we can't show them things, and, unlike Santa Claus, we don't even know when they are sleeping and when they are awake. This greatly limits how much "educating" we can do, and simple auditory and, perhaps, tactile stimulation is usually the limit of prenatal intervention. Not so once babies are born. Now we know babies' sleep and wake cycles and can direct auditory and, importantly, visual stimuli to them. We can coordinate what they see and hear, showing them pictures of common household objects while labeling

176

them, and pictures of artwork done by the great masters, who are also identified.

The Competent Infant

We know that young babies, even fetuses, can learn; there is no dispute about that. They can learn to associate sounds or images with outcomes. They can identify their mothers on the basis of smell by 10 days, and perhaps as soon on the basis of vision.[18] Shortly after birth, many infants are able to form visual memories, "remembering" which pattern they had repeatedly seen versus a new, or novel, one.[19] By 6 months, and certainly by 9 months, they are able to recall a simple action they had witnessed a day earlier and perform it, evidence of *deferred imitation*.[20] These abilities all improve with age, but many basic information processing and learning skills are present and used early in the first year of life.

It is only relatively recently that psychologists and other professionals who deal with infants have realized how smart babies are. When I taught my first child development course as a graduate student in the early 1970s, I told my class that all of an infant's senses were working at birth and that newborns can see – they can tell the difference between two visual patterns if they are discrepant enough. A middle-aged woman in the back of the class immediately spoke up and informed her young, wet-behind-the-ears instructor that he was wrong. She had had four children and her obstetrician and pediatrician had both told her, for each of her children, that babies are blind at birth. I knew I was right – I believed the empirical research published in peer-reviewed journals. But newborns and babies through much of the first year of life certainly didn't *appear* very smart to the casual observer, and it had only been in the previous decade that techniques for assessing what infants know had been developed. I may have been right, but public opinion and the opinion of many professionals at that time were on this woman's side.

But not for long. Research on infant perception and cognition was exploding, and psychologists, and eventually physicians, were beginning to see how much babies, beginning at birth, really knew. In 1973, Joseph Stone, Henrietta Smith, and Lois Murphy published *The Competent Infant*, a collection of scientific papers demonstrating that babies are not the mindless creatures we'd long thought them to be, but were intellectually and socially "competent." These were heady times for infant researchers, who had a new, some would say radical, model for how the mind develops; and educators, not wanting to be left behind, jumped on this "competency" bandwagon.

It was in this atmosphere that some people began to argue that infants should exercise these newly discovered intellectual capacities and begin formal education. For example, Glenn Doman, Director of the Institutes for the Achievement of Human Potential and author of *How to Teach Your Baby to Read*, *How to Teach Your Baby Math*, and *How to Give Your Baby Encyclopedic Knowledge*, argued (and still does) that it is easier to teach an infant anything than it is to teach an older child. Few scientists or educators would agree with Doman on this point, but he is not alone in advocating formal instruction, often using flash cards, beginning in the crib and continuing through childhood.

The latest twist in infant instruction is *lapware*, computer programs designed for infants and toddlers, as young as 6 months old, to be played with while sitting on mom or dad's lap. These programs are promoted as educational software, designed to teach babies a host of concepts, presumably faster or better than would be the case if computers were not involved. For example, the *ToddlerToons* website states that "ToddlerToons allows babies and toddlers to build language skills and to learn concepts such as cause and effect, big and little, up and down, happy and sad, colors and shapes, body parts, and more."

The perspective of "the competent infant" is still with us. In fact, infant researchers continue to discover often-amazing abilities in the youngest members of our species. Many think, however, that these abilities are not on par with those displayed by older children and may not reflect the level of intellectual competency that was once believed. The debate among theorists continues, but educators are not waiting for the academics to come to a consensus about what these demonstrations of infant abilities mean before applying the research.

The Potential Perils of Instruction in the Crib

The quote by pioneering developmental psychologist Jerome Bruner that began this chapter, "any subject can be taught effectively in some intellectually honest form to any child at any stage of development," has been misconstrued as supporting a Glenn Doman-type approach to early education. Although we can certainly quibble about Bruner's nearly 50-year-old pronouncement on early education, his intention was not to burden infants and children with pedagogy beyond their years. His contention was that young children are ready to learn much more than we think they can if information is presented to them in a way that suits their cognitive proclivities. Bruner was talking about *learning readiness*, about matching the task demands to children's intellectual abilities and building a curriculum based on children's changing ways of understanding the world and their previous accomplishments. It is somewhat ironic, then, that this much-quoted line has been used to justify formal learning beginning in infancy.

Assuming that early formal learning is possible for infants and young children (and it seems to be), is it wise? The answer to this question is a complicated one, involving how we view children and childhood, the role of children's intrinsic motivation to learn via formal, versus more informal, methods, and what goals a parent has for his or her children. One question we can ask without getting into philosophical debates is, "Is there any research demonstrating that early learning may actually interfere with later learning?" Recall from Chapter 4 that quail chicks and ducklings that received extra prenatal stimulation experienced interference with the development of late-maturing senses and displayed learning disabilities as a result. Is there any evidence for this with early *learning*, as opposed to perceptual, experiences? There has been relatively little research focused directly on this question, although relevant research does exist for at least three species: rats, monkeys, and humans.

Starting with rats, developmental psychobiologist Jerry Rudy and his colleagues trained rat pups to make mouthing activities to sounds (a form of classical conditioning). The rats started training at 10, 12, or 14 days of age, and testing continued until the pups were 16 days old. Despite having more experience on the task, animals that began training at 10 days of age performed worse on the conditioning task on days 14 and 15 than rats that started training at older ages. Developmental psychobiologists Norman Spear and Laura Hyatt from the State University of New York at Binghamton reported similar findings from several studies. Infant rats performed more poorly on learning tasks when they started training at earlier rather than later ages, causing the authors to conclude that "apparently, if experience with an episode to be learned later is given too early in life, learning of that episode in later ontogeny is impaired."[21]

Perhaps more compelling is research by famed primatologist Harry Harlow with rhesus monkeys. Infant monkeys were initially given simple shapes to discriminate (for example, pick the triangle and get a treat, pick the cube and get nothing). Although the task was a simple one, the objects varied on a number of dimensions, including color, form, size, and material. The monkeys solved 25 problems a day, five days a week for four weeks. Testing began when animals were 60, 90,

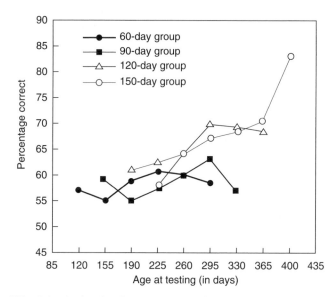

Figure 7.1 Discrimination learning set performance for monkeys as a function of age. The younger the monkeys were when they began training, the worse their eventual performance was (from Harlow, 1959). Reprinted with the kind permission of Richard F. Potter, Trustee, The Estate of Harry F. Harlow.

120, 150, or 366 days old. At 120 days of age, the monkeys were given *new* sets of more complicated learning trials (called learning-set problems, the specifics of which need not concern us), which continued for up to a year, totaling between 400 and 600 problems per monkey. I've presented the percentage correct performance on the learning-set problems for the monkeys in the various groups in Figure 7.1. As you can see, the performance of the more experienced monkeys, which started training at 60 and 90 days of age, never matched that of the monkeys that started training later. Like the rats in the earlier described experiments, starting early not only failed to provide any benefits, but it actually hindered performance. Harlow concluded that "there is a tendency to think of learning or training as intrinsically good and necessarily valuable to the organism. It is entirely possible, however, that training can either be helpful or harmful, depending upon the nature of the training and the organism's stage of development."[22]

It is, of course, difficult to do well-controlled experiments on these topics with human infants, but at least one study by the Czech developmental psychologist Hanus Papousek is directly relevant. Papousek trained infants to turn their heads to specific sounds – turn one way to the sound of a bell and the other way to the sound of a buzzer. One group of infants began training at birth, a second at 31 days of age, and a third at 44 days of age. The younger the infants were when they started training, the longer it took them to attain criterion (average number of trials, or attempts, to reach criterion: newborns = 814; 31 days = 278; 44 days = 224). This may not be too surprising, because the infants may have simply needed time to physically mature before they could "get" the task, thus the more trials necessary for the newborns to learn the problem. But neurological maturation wasn't the entire answer. In addition to looking at how many trials it took to reach criterion, Papousek also looked at how old the babies were when they finally solved the task. Those who started when they were newborns were, on average, 128 days old before they reached criterion; in contrast, those starting at 31 days of age reached criterion on day 71, and those starting at 44 days of age reached criterion on day 72. This is evidence that not all learning experiences are necessarily good for infants – that learning experiences will not only be useless for infants who lack the requisite cognitive abilities, but they sometimes may actually be detrimental to later learning and development. To quote Papousek, "beginning too early with difficult learning tasks, at a time when the organism is not able to master them, results in prolongation of the learning process."[23]

There is no dispute that infants can learn. To enhance learning infants need to be loved and provided linguistic, social, and intellectual stimulation to develop to their full potential. But this does not mean that a program of formal education, including flash cards, is the way to go. Infants learn through exploring their social and physical environments and having opportunities to investigate new objects, people, and events in supportive and safe contexts. There is no scientifically convincing evidence that early training and formal instruction in infancy has any long-term benefits, and there is some evidence that starting instruction too early may actually hinder later learning.

The alternative to formal infant education is not "leave the kid alone and she'll develop just fine." Intellectual development is an active process, with children initiating activity on the objects and people that surround them and modifying their ideas about the world as a result of the feedback they get from their actions. It behooves parents to provide infants with a stimulating environment for such development to occur. This is enrichment, which can be accomplished by being sensitive to infants' needs and abilities and not by implementing a "training regime."

Developmentally Appropriate Practices in Early Education

There has been a vocal group in early childhood education, led by the National Association for the Education of Young Children (NAEYC), advocating for what has been termed *developmentally appropriate practice*.[24] The NAEYC and their followers argue that young children learn differently than older children and that instructional techniques that may be appropriate when teaching older children are inappropriate when applied to preschoolers. Developmentally appropriate practice is based on Jean Piaget's theory of cognitive development. Piaget proposed that young children's thinking is qualitatively different from that of older children. Children are not simply smaller versions of adults, but qualitatively different thinkers with a unique way of understanding the world. For example, Piaget proposed that infants up to about 2 years of age know the world primarily by their direct sensations of it and their actions on it (*sensorimotor intelligence*). They do not possess symbolic, or mental, representation. With the advent of language and other symbolic abilities (for instance, deferred imitation, pretend play), children's thinking is drastically changed. They can represent events in the past and future, conceptualize things that are not immediately present, mentally rehearse their actions before executing them, and communicate their thoughts to other people. They are truly members of *Homo sapiens* (with an emphasis on the *sapiens* here), and intellectually different from any other species on the planet. In fact, intellectually speaking, a 3-year-old child is more like an adult than he or she is like a 1-year-old infant.

Despite the intellectual awakening that symbolic abilities bring, the preschooler is not the cognitive equal of the school-age child. The thinking of children during this *preoperational period*, though symbolic, is intuitive rather than logical. They interpret things in terms of how they *appear* or *should be*, rather how they logically must be. For example, 3- and 4-year-olds often judge a person's age by his or her height (taller people are older), and assume that a pizza cut into eight pieces has "more pizza" than one cut into four pieces. By 6 or 7 years, children have entered what Piaget called *concrete operations* and can now think logically, although only about concrete entities. It is not until adolescence and the advent of *formal operations* that children can think abstractly. Piaget's major point, and that of the NAEYC, is that children of different ages think and learn differently, and thus should be educated differently.

182

As I noted in Chapter 6, Piaget emphasized the active nature of the child in learning and development. Children should not be thought of as lumps of clay, waiting to be shaped by parents or teachers, nor as the products of their genes, destined by biology to understand the world in which they are born. Rather, children *construct* reality; they actively try to make sense of their surroundings based on what they already know, their stage of thinking, and the information in the environments. Knowledge is a *construction* and cannot be simply taught to children by well-meaning adults. In this respect, Piaget believed that the authority status of teachers actually hampered learning. Piaget wrote: "It is despite adult authority, and not because of it, that the child learns. And also it is to the extent that the intelligent teacher has known to efface him or herself, to become an equal and not a superior, to discuss and to examine, rather than to agree and constrain morally, that the traditional school has been able to render service."[25] Piaget emphasized the importance of *discovery learning*, discussed in Chapter 6, with children doing their own experimenting in order to gain an understanding of some phenomenon.

This is not the place for a critique of Piaget's theory. Most cognitive developmental psychologists today still hold Piaget in great reverence but believe that he was off the mark on many counts. Infants may have far greater representational abilities than Piaget had proposed, and young children's cognitive difficulties likely do not reflect their intellectual capacity, but rather their performance under less-than-optimal conditions. Although I believe that Piaget's descriptions of young children's learning are insightful, they are not the entire picture. Cognitive development is a multifaceted thing; some aspects of children's thinking do vary qualitatively, as Piaget described, but others vary in a more quantitative way. Children get a little better each year in the speed with which they solve problems and the number of ideas they can keep in mind at any one time, for instance.[26] And Piaget gave little attention to the social environment and its role in cognitive development (recall our brief discussion of the ideas of Vygotsky and the sociocultural approach to development earlier in this chapter). Nonetheless, I am in basic agreement with Piaget, and with the folks at NAEYC, that young children can best be educated using "developmentally appropriate" techniques that are different from those used with older children.

What would a developmentally appropriate curriculum for a preschool child look like? At its heart is the idea of discovery learning, or child-initiated activities, that may be facilitated by the teachers. This would be accomplished by providing children with a wide range of experiences; encouraging them to select their own activities; presenting problems and asking questions that actively engage them; providing support and guidance to children in skill acquisition as needed; and encouraging children to reflect on their experiences. Ideally, the curriculum would be integrated across areas, with children building on what they already know. This is contrasted with a more didactic, or teacher-directed curriculum, or what some unabashedly term a "developmentally inappropriate" curriculum. Here I will use the more neutral term *directed-instructional practices.*

A developmentally appropriate curriculum may make sense in theory, but it sounds almost like "let kids do whatever they want." How do teachers actually implement a developmentally appropriate curriculum? The proper contrast with an adult-directed curriculum is not an "anything goes" curriculum (if you could call an "anything goes" approach a curriculum). The NAEYC has published guidelines for implementing developmentally appropriate practice and they are far from "let kids do whatever they want."[27] In their guideline, the NAEYC addresses five interrelated dimensions of early childhood professional practice: creating a caring community of learners; teaching to enhance development and learning; constructing appropriate curricula; assessing children's learning and development; and establishing reciprocal relationships with families. They provide specific guidelines for each dimension. For example, within the dimension of "Teaching to enhance development and learning," they list seven guidelines. Teachers: (1) respect, value, and accept children and treat them with dignity at all times; (2) make it a priority to know each child well; (3) create an intellectually engaging, responsive environment to promote each child's learning and development; (4) make plans to enable children to attain key curriculum goals across various disciplines, such as language arts, mathematics, social studies, science, art, music, physical education, and health; (5) foster children's collaboration with peers on interesting, important enterprises; (6) facilitate the development of responsibility and self-regulation in children; and (7) develop, refine, and use a wide repertoire of teaching strategies to enhance children's learning and development.

Within each of these guidelines, they provide more specific guidance. For instance, for the guideline, "Teachers develop, refine, and use a wide repertoire of teaching strategies to enhance children's learning and development," nine more specific guidelines are provided:

1. To help children develop their initiative, teachers encourage them to choose and plan their own learning activities.

184

2. Teachers pose problems, ask questions, and make comments and suggestions that stimulate children's thinking and extend their learning.

3. Teachers extend the range of children's interests and the scope of their thought through presenting novel experiences and introducing stimulating ideas, problems, experiences, or hypotheses.

4. To sustain an individual child's effort or engagement in purposeful activities, teachers select from a range of strategies, including but not limited to modeling, demonstrating specific skills, and providing information, focused attention, physical proximity, verbal encouragement, reinforcement and other behavioral procedures, as well as additional structure and modification of equipment or schedules as needed.

5. Teachers coach and/or directly guide children in the acquisition of specific skills as needed.

6. Teachers calibrate the complexity and challenge of activities to suit children's level of skill and knowledge, increasing the challenge as children gain competence and understanding.

7. Teachers provide cues and other forms of "scaffolding" that enable the child to succeed in a task that is just beyond his or her ability to complete alone.

8. To strengthen children's sense of competence and confidence as learners, motivation to persist, and willingness to take risks, teachers provide experiences for children to be genuinely successful and to be challenged.

9. To enhance children's conceptual understanding, teachers use various strategies that encourage children to reflect on and "revisit" their learning experiences.

This is not the place to provide a detailed description of developmentally appropriate curricula, or how teachers are trained to create them, or even to evaluate the research behind such curricula. What's important to appreciate is that a "developmentally appropriate curriculum" does not mean "anything goes," but reflects a theory-based curriculum aimed at educating young children appropriate to their developmental level.

The trend toward more formal education for preschool children began in earnest in the 1980s. Beginning in the 1960s, as part of President Lyndon Johnson's *War on Poverty*, compensatory education programs for preschool children "at risk for mental retardation" were begun. These programs varied in style of instruction, but children in the more academically rigorous programs experienced some of the greatest gains.[28] The children in these programs came mainly from lower-socioeconomic homes, where intellectual stimulation appropriate for later schooling was lacking. The immediate success of these programs caused many educators to assume that more advantaged children could also benefit from formal preschool education, and middle-class parents soon demanded such programs.

But is a formal learning environment, characteristic of instruction in elementary school, appropriate for 3- and 4-year-old children? Does such academic acceleration benefit children in the long run, or might it actually be detrimental? Many early childhood educators and developmental psychologists thought the latter. Developmental psychologist David Elkind termed the accelerated instruction of young children *miseducation* and warned of a generation at risk.[29]

Despite the theory behind developmentally appropriate practice and the warnings against direct instruction with preschoolers, there was little scientific data for the skeptical consumer. This has been rectified to some extent in the past 15 years or so, with a number of studies investigating the pros and cons of different models of preschool education. However, our database remains meager, and so any conclusions on the benefits or deficits of developmentally appropriate versus directed-instructional programs must remain tentative.

First, the effects on academic performance are mixed. In some studies, children attending developmentally appropriate preschool or kindergarten programs show superior number and pre-reading skills at the end of the school year relative to children attending directed-instructional programs; other studies find better performance on some academic measures for children in directed-instructional programs; and still others find no appreciable differences.[30]

Other studies have looked at the effects of type of early schooling on *later* school achievement, and again the findings have been mixed, with some authors reporting no differences in academic scores one or two years following completion of preschool between children who attended developmentally appropriate and directed-instructional programs, whereas others report an advantage for children who attended the developmentally appropriate preschools.[31] For example, Rebecca Marcon of the University of North Florida followed for six years children who had attended either a developmentally appropriate or directed-instructional preschool. She reported that although there was no difference in academic performance between the two groups of children by the end of third grade, by the end of fourth grade children who had the developmentally appropriate preschool curriculum had higher grades than those who had attended the directed-instructional programs.

186

Although a benevolent reading of the research suggests that there are more benefits than detriments to academic abilities associated with developmentally appropriate practices, the results are admittedly not robust.[32] The benefits of a developmentally appropriate preschool program are clearer, however, when psychosocial and motivational factors are considered. Most studies have found that children attending developmentally appropriate programs experience less stress, like school better, are more creative, and have less test anxiety than children attending directed-instructional programs.[33] Let me provide a more detailed description of one of these studies.

UCLA educational psychologist Deborah Stipek and her colleagues compared children who attended developmentally appropriate and directed-instructional preschool and kindergarten programs for academic abilities as well as for several measures of psychosocial development.[34] The sample included children from poor and minority households, as well as children from middle-class families. By the end of the school year, children attending the directed-instructional program scored higher on knowledge of letters and reading achievement than children attending developmentally appropriate programs, although there was no difference between the two groups of children on tests of number knowledge. Score one for directed-instructional practices. In contrast, children in the developmentally appropriate programs rated themselves as having greater intellectual abilities, had higher expectations for success on school-like tasks, were less dependent on adults for permission and approval, expressed greater pride in accomplishment, chose more challenging math problems to perform, and said they worried less about school than children in the directed-instructional programs. In other words, any academic benefit gained from a teacher-directed program had its costs in terms of motivation. This perhaps explains the fact that the few studies that have examined the long-term effects of types of preschool programs found advantages for developmentally appropriate ones.

Psychologist Kathy Hirsh-Pasek and her colleagues came to a similar conclusion in a study that found no differences in academic performance between middle-class children attending developmentally appropriate and directed-instructional programs, but greater stress, less creativity, and more test anxiety associated with the didactic programs. They concluded that "enriched environments bring developmental advantages to young children: Within these environments, however, formal academic orientations do little good and may do some harm. Put more positively, well-adjusted, creative, and academically prepared children thrive in family and preschool environments that are carefully designed and thoughtfully planned, but that are more child-centered in their approach. Thus, it may be developmentally prudent to let children explore the world at their own pace rather than to impose our adult timetables and anxieties on them."[35]

There are many factors that influence children's learning. For example, although the focus here has been on curriculum, I have always thought that there is no such thing as a "teacher-proof" curriculum. Some teachers will bring out the best in children (almost) regardless of the curriculum, whereas other well-intentioned teachers will inevitably fail to do so under the best of circumstances. Just as there are developmental differences in how children learn, so too are there *individual* differences. In fact, given the variability we see in children, it's almost a bit surprising that the pattern of results is as consistent as it is.

The conclusion I draw from this research is that cognitive development during the preschool years can best be fostered outside of a formal, teacher-directed environment. The skills of young children are different from those of older children, and their learning and development might best take place in unstructured settings. Their skills may, in fact, be ideally suited for the learning they need to do at this time in their lives.[ii]

I want to make it clear that I am not opposed to some direct instruction for young children. Children have the ability to learn from instruction, and this is a critical mechanism for transmitting important cultural knowledge. It seems obvious that direct instruction should be a key instrument in all teachers' tool kits. It is only when direct instruction replaces more child-centered learning for young children that problems potentially arise.

Enrichment versus Acceleration

Young children have sometimes been described as sponges, soaking up knowledge effortlessly. If children can learn so much without any

---

[ii] Just as directed instruction has been applied, perhaps inappropriately, to preschoolers, so has another modern educational practice made its way to the preschool set: tutoring. My hometown newspaper, the *Palm Beach Post*, ran an article in September of 2005 describing a number of tutoring programs in the county designed to teach reading and math to 3-, 4-, and 5-year-old children. Kids are being prepped for kindergarten! The typical schedule is for children to come in for two half-hour sessions per week, one for math, one for reading. They also have 10 to 15 minutes of daily homework, supervised by their parents.

apparent effort, imagine how much more they could learn with adult supervision. But the consequence of such adult efforts all depends on the nature of that supervision.

It is difficult to argue against early education, and I am not doing so. Research has clearly shown that children can benefit from preschool education, and this is especially true for children from low-income homes, who may not receive the type of intellectual stimulation that is most conducive to later school success. The same can be said for enrichment programs beginning in infancy. But educational enrichment is not the same as acceleration. In 1987 developmental psychologist Irving Sigel defined acceleration "in developmental terms as placing intellectual and emotional demands on children – demands that seem over and above their cognitive and emotional level."[36] Perhaps this is a loaded definition. If children *can* accomplish certain academic feats, they are obviously not above their cognitive levels. But this does not mean that this is the most effective way to educate young children, or even that early acceleration will have positive long-term consequences.

This perspective has even been applied to the education of children with mental retardation. University of Pennsylvania Education Professor Joan Goodman, in her book *When Slow is Fast Enough*, suggested that attempts to accelerate the intellectual development of children with mental retardation, although understandably embraced by politicians, teachers, and parents, may be misguided. Goodman does not dismiss the gains that such programs can have on children's achievement, but she believes that the potential deleterious effects of these interventions are rarely considered. Too much instruction might suppress children's creativity, dampen spontaneity, or negatively impact their self-esteem as a result of failing to master an overly demanding curriculum. Instead of pushing these children as hard as possible, a better alternative may be to respect their pace of development by showing indulgence for their immaturity. Goodman writes that "slowing up will give these children, like other children, the opportunity for mastery and discovery, for fulfillment of their own drives while they meet expectations set by adults."[37]

Stress in the Schoolhouse

Formal schooling begins in first grade (that's why they call it "first"). My complaint about preschool education is that it often involves techniques more appropriate for older children, and by this I mean children in elementary school. The trend toward acceleration is not limited to preschoolers, however, but has made its way into the early school years as well, not always with positive results.

Formal schooling is a must in modern culture. But human children did not evolve to sit in classrooms with 20 or 30 agemates, listen to an unrelated adult tell them what to do, and learn to read, calculate, and search the web for information totally unrelated to their lives outside of school. Schooling is an "unnatural" experience, but one that children take to, and, over the centuries, has resulted in art, science, books, cell phones, computers, hospitals, and all the other conveniences of modern culture. We should not be surprised, however, that formal schooling is often difficult for children and that education can be best achieved when we take children's "natural" dispositions and abilities into consideration.[38]

Education, of course, is not new to our species. Children in all cultures throughout history have had to learn the complexities of their culture. And before you think that you, as a fully modern *Homo sapiens*, are far more advanced than your Pleistocene relative of 30,000 years ago, consider what they had to learn. Specialization is a modern invention (modern in that it is likely no more than 10,000 years old). Your ancestors had to learn to obtain and prepare food, make tools, fire, and clothes, avoid predators, defend themselves and their kin from other humans, and navigate vast terrains. How successful would a modern person be if transported to a Stone-Age community? Human intelligence was flexible in our ancestors and it is flexible today, but many of the things we need to learn have changed.

For one thing, learning is done "out of context," with children having to master tasks that have no relevance for their daily lives. In traditional societies, and surely for our ancestors, learning was accomplished by a child working in close interaction with a more skilled adult, often in apprenticeships. Children learned by watching and doing, with some language thrown in to make the goal of the task and its component parts more easily identifiable. Children learned to perform "real" tasks and often practiced such tasks in their play (see Chapter 6).[39] In contrast, modern technological skills are usually learned "for their own sake," not to solve any immediate real-world problem.[iii]

[iii] Apprenticeships have not disappeared in contemporary societies, and in fact are making a comeback, particularly in Europe. In 2000, the European Union approved *European Pathways*, a program to encourage apprenticeships in European Union countries, based on previous studies demonstrating that apprenticeships substantially improve employment prospects. See http://www2.trainingvillage.gr/download/Cinfo/Cinfo298/C2C02EN.html#f2.

Don't get me wrong. I am not arguing for a "back to nature" approach, permitting children to engage their curiosity "freely" without the encumbrance of adults' conceptions of what is important and what is not. Children rarely "discover" reading and perhaps never discover algebra (although Newton and Leibniz somehow "discovered" calculus). Children may not have evolved for school learnin', but they are capable of it, and the perpetuation of our culture is dependent upon their continued mastery of the basic technological skills of writing and mathematics. In fact, I have sometimes been disturbed by claims of cross-cultural psychologists who argue that Western societies should adopt the more "natural" style of education found in traditional societies. Given the need to mass-educate children, I see little alternative to modern schools; however, educators need to consider different ways of getting the important cultural messages across, grounded in relevant cognitive developmental theory and research that takes into consideration not only how children's brains process information, but also why the brains evolved to function as they do.

Achievement-oriented Schools and Parents

If you asked most any parent, teacher, or person on the street what the function of school was, I'd imagine that the first answer you'd get would be "to prepare children for the future." They may mention that the preparation was for getting a good job, getting into college, or perhaps even for becoming a good citizen, but "preparation" would be included somewhere in the answer. Other responses, likely lower on the list, might include socializing children, and perhaps a handful of people would mention something about nurturing children's interests, talents, and curiosity. I'm in general agreement with this perspective. It's hard to argue against the role of schools in "preparing" children for adulthood. But I think modern schooling has taken the concept of preparation too far, often at the expense of "nurturing interests, talents, and curiosity." Remember, childhood is not solely a preparation for adulthood, but is a time in development that has it own integrity; childhood is worthwhile living for its own right. If our eyes are always looking to the future, what does one see in the present? At the extreme, we have people whose entire lives are in preparation for an afterlife. Just as adults hope to get something "for now" out of an experience, children should be able to expect to get something "for now" out of going to school.

This is not to abandon a future-oriented perspective, however. Much of childhood *is* preparation for adulthood, and that adulthood

191

is often delayed well past the age of majority. Children, and adolescents especially, must not sacrifice the future for "good times" in the present. Success in modern culture goes to those who can see beyond the here and now, or the upcoming weekend. I heard a country singer recently who sang of "working for the weekend." At least the song's protagonist had a job, but one that would not likely improve much without a more farsighted perspective.

Preparing children for the future and nurturing talent and curiosity do not have to be at odds. For instance, nurturing children's *present* interests and curiosity not only may serve them well in the here and now, but may also set the stage for later interests and learning. Preparation doesn't always have to be boring and drain a child's enthusiasm for learning. Unfortunately, it often is, and is becoming increasingly so in the schools of the early 21st century.

Part of the reason for school's notorious reputation as a motivation killer is that much that needs to be learned is not acquired by simple exposure. David Geary makes the distinction between *biologically primary* and *biologically secondary* cognitive abilities. The former are cognitive skills that are universal, acquired spontaneously without need of special instruction, and evolved to solve recurrent problems faced by our predecessors over hundreds of thousands of years. Language is a good example of a biologically primary ability. In contrast, biologically secondary abilities, although built upon biologically primary abilities, are products of culture. As a result, they are not universal and often require deliberate practice, instruction, and extrinsic motivation to acquire.[40] Reading is a good example of a biologically secondary ability. Many of the skills taught in school are biologically secondary abilities, such as reading and all but the most simple of mathematics. Some children are enthusiastic about reading and math from an early age, but many are not, and they must be prodded to practice these skills. The result is often tedium and a very task-oriented approach to learning. Learning to read doesn't have to be tedious; but the process of learning to read can be laborious, especially for children who do not have a background of believing that reading can be fun and rewarding (for instance, children who are not read to by parents as preschoolers). If formal reading instruction is begun too early, it may involve more of a child's limited mental resources than he or she cares to expend and swamp the motivation to learn.

Children in contemporary society must learn to read and to do basic mathematical computations, whether they enjoy it or not. But little is gained if in the process of teaching reading or arithmetic children lose their intellectual curiosity and a positive attitude about learning new things in general. Children have a thirst for knowledge, reflected in the frequent "why" questions of 3-year-olds. Humans retain this motivation for the rest of their lives, but some experiences can foster love of knowledge more than others, and some can make pursuing the unknown a truly aversive activity.

As I discussed earlier in this chapter, preschool children respond well to developmentally appropriate practice, and this is no less true for older children. Although some children will learn to read and calculate on their own via discovery learning, most will not, and direct instruction and practice may be inevitable. But modern schools, rather than minimizing the negative consequences that acquiring necessary biologically secondary abilities produce, seem to be exacerbating the effects, all in the belief that early achievement is preparation for later achievement.

Most developed countries today are extremely achievement oriented. Our standard of living is dependent upon having an educated and productive society. American workers are the most productive in the world (that is, greatest output per capita, in part because we take fewer vacation days than workers in other developed countries), and American ingenuity from the arts and medicine to science and engineering leads the world. But the gap is getting smaller. In fact, many of America's skilled professionals such as doctors, nurses, scientists, and engineers are recruited from abroad, and many of the United States' more recent Nobel laureates are émigrés. American political and social leaders, along with American parents, worry that future generations may not be sufficiently prepared for the challenges of the 21st century. As a result, there has been a push in the US to enhance academic achievement beginning early on. Middle-class parents worry that their children may not be getting the most out of their education. Each accomplishment is a stepping-stone for the next, and anything that can help their children should be pursued, and anything that wastes their children's time should be avoided. I recall getting a call from a woman whose son brought home a letter from school, seeking permission for him to participate in a study of memory development my students and I were conducting. The woman admitted that the procedures were described well in the letter, and she had no questions about what it was we wanted her son to do. Seemed harmless. But, she wanted to know, would her second-grade son's participation in this study in any way either help or hurt him get into a good college?

This isn't a brand-new phenomenon but can be traced back at least to 1956 and *Sputnik*, the first space satellite ever launched from Earth. The thing was, it was launched by the Soviet Union – the then arch-enemy of the United States. The space race was on, and with it the ratcheting up of primary education. Over the next 50 years the spotlight never really left the topic of educational achievement. American children have been tested and found wanting, educationally speaking, relative to children in other developed nations. The result has been an increasing emphasis on academics in school, with a corresponding decrease in other topics that were once a regular part of the school curriculum. Art, music, and physical education have not been totally excised from most elementary schools, but they have been seriously cut back and have been eliminated in some programs. In their place is an increased focus, beginning ever earlier in the curriculum, on "the basics," mainly reading and math. In 2002 the federal *No Child Left Behind Act* mandated assessment of progress in these core subjects for children in grades 3 through 8. Schools whose children do not make the grade suffer some consequences. In Florida where I live, schools are given grades from A to F depending on how many of their children pass the FCAT (Florida Comprehensive Assessment Test). Scores on the FCAT can affect school budgets and teacher and principal assignments, and if a school receives a grade of F for too many years in a row, there can be serious consequences.

The emphasis on assessment – on meeting specified standards – impacts teaching. The politically wise thing to do is teach to the test. Teachers may not know what specific test items will be, but they know what children are expected to master, and so their instruction is geared to what will be on the test. This should result in improved reading and math scores, and correspondingly improved reading and math abilities, the primary emphasis of the law. This sounds like a good thing, exactly what the "standards movement" was meant to accomplish. There are things, particularly skills such as reading and mathematics, that kids need to know, and it only makes sense that schools should be held accountable for teaching children these critically important technological skills. But there is a downside. Given limited time and a focus on assessment, teachers are reluctant to spend too much time on topics on which children will not be tested. This isn't only music, art, and PE, but also science and history, or any other part of the curriculum that isn't going to be assessed. They may "officially" have to cover these traditional topics, but if your reputation, and perhaps your job, were on the line, what would you focus on?

The goal of education, it seems, is no longer even to prepare children for the future, but to prepare them for the test.[iv]

A second casualty of the focus on assessment is the child. More than ever, school has become a high-stress environment. Teachers with "slow" children meet with parents and emphasize to them how important it is for their children to improve in these core skills. After-school tutoring is available, as are private tutors – some tutors are moonlighting school teachers and others are tutoring companies that, for a fee, will guarantee advancement to the next grade and a passing score on the upcoming test. This, too, may seem to be a step in the right direction (particularly for children who have parents who can afford the private lessons), but it produces increased stress in some of the youngest students, and with it a loss of enthusiasm for school and learning.

Gradually over the past 50 years, early elementary school has become increasingly demanding. First-grade children who do not know something about reading by the time school starts are already behind. Children must achieve and achieve early! If we wait, our kids will fall behind and may never catch up. But 5- and 6-year-old children may not have the maturational competence to handle the more demanding curriculum, and this makes the task all the more difficult. With practice and effort they may reach the federal, state, or county goals, but it makes their heads hurt and sucks the joy of learning right out of them. City College of New York developmental psychologist William Crain in his book, *Reclaiming Childhood*, stated it nicely: "Historically, children seem to have never liked school very much. It has always taken a toll on the natural curiosity and enthusiasm for learning with which children began life. But today, as the standards movement rolls on, the pressure on children is becoming quite oppressive." Crain takes the

---

[iv] The emphasis on assessment has also influenced the school calendar. In my home county of Palm Beach, Florida, children start school in early August, and thus end school in late May. The (unofficial) rationale for starting the school year so early is that it will give teachers extra time in the beginning of the year to prepare children for the FCAT in March. No sense having them in school for too long *after* the test is given. In addition, all out-of-class activities, such as field trips, school assemblies, and athletics, are banned during school hours for two months before the mid-March FCAT assessment so children can devote their full attention to preparing for the test. As one high school principal stated in a January 21, 2006 interview with the *Palm Beach Post*, "It's a balance. I'm sure our world history classes would love to go see [the King Tut exhibit showing this spring in nearby Fort Lauderdale], but they're pretty strapped for time with writing."

195

current school emphasis on preparedness even further, writing "we are so obsessed with preparing children for the future that we are depriving them of the chance to develop their artistic orientation, ties to nature, and other distinctive traits of the childhood years…[W]e are, in effect, stunting their growth, and future research may show that the effects show up in increased depression, suicidal ideation, restlessness, and other symptoms of unfulfilled lives."[41]

Let's Recess: a Simple Alternative

It's not just children's thinking that is at odds with the demands of modern schooling, but also aspects of their social and physical development. As I noted in an earlier chapter, children learn a lot through play, much of which is vigorous and, at times, a bit raucous. Such rough-and-tumble play, particularly characteristic of boys, does not fit well with spending hours sitting in seats, minding one's own business, and concentrating on paper work. Not surprisingly, school discourages this type of activity. In fact, much of the disruptive behavior in elementary school classrooms can be attributed to young children's need for more physical activity. On top of this, young children in particular may require breaks from academic activity, needing to "re-charge" their mental batteries between bouts of focused attention.

The obvious solution is an old one: recess. Unfortunately, long a part of American and British school systems, recess is falling by the wayside. University of Minnesota educational psychologist Anthony Pellegrini has inveighed against the loss of recess in American and British schools over the past 20 years.[42] Recess is seen as the ultimate waste of precious school time. If "optional" subjects such as music, art, and physical education are being replaced by more classes devoted to core academics, what chance does recess have? Recess is fun, but having fun is not the purpose of school. The purpose of school is to provide children with basic technological skills and cultural knowledge and to inculcate societal values in our children. How can a school system justify recess?

As it turns out, recess is a good investment given the social and intellectual characteristics of young children. As discussed previously, school-age children enjoy (and many would say need) physical exercise, something that is not possible in most classrooms, but is during outdoor recess. Well-controlled studies have shown that recess improves elementary school children's attention to school tasks and enhances school learning.[43] For example, Pellegrini and his colleagues varied the timing of a recess break for kindergarten, grade-2, and grade-4 children in two Georgia schools. For two days a week, recess was delayed 30 minutes and attention to seatwork was assessed, both before and after recess. At each grade, children were more attentive after recess than before, and the effects of recess deprivation were significantly greater for the younger than for the older children.

There should be nothing surprising about the enhanced benefits of recess on young children. Young children's ability to concentrate on, or selectively attend to, academic tasks is well known, as are their difficulties with inhibiting speech, thoughts, and behavior. Young children often say the first thing that comes into their heads, and many a second-grade boy has struggled with the urge to stick his foot out as a classmate walks down the aisle. Recess, particularly when it involves physical activity, can help children focus on the task at hand and reduce distraction, increasing the amount learned per minute of study.

Perhaps somewhat ironically, many Asian schools, known for their more rigorous curricula, seem aware of young children's needs for frequent breaks. Developmental psychologists Harold Stevenson and Shin-Ying Lee looked at the structure of the school day in first and fifth grades in Minneapolis, Minnesota, Taipei, Taiwan, and Sendai, Japan. Children in the Asian schools had more recesses (4 versus 2 for first graders; 4 or 5 versus 2 [or fewer] for the fifth graders), and the number of hours spent in school was actually less for the two Asian schools than for the American school for first-grade children. The Chinese and Japanese schools apparently recognized the cognitive and behavioral limitations of young children better than the Minneapolis school and structured the day to take these limitations into consideration.[44]

Recess is not an antiquated and perhaps romanticized practice, thought of in the same quaint context as single-room schoolhouses, ink wells, and boys in knickers. It should be a regular part of the modern school curriculum. Recess acknowledges children's need for physical and social stimulation. Addressing these needs through recess is not the antithesis of good educational practice, but actually fosters school achievement and may help maintain children's enthusiasm for learning.

Old Brain, New Curriculum

The cognitive demands of modern society are far different from the cognitive demands children evolved to handle. Reading and mathematics are the foundation of modern intellectual and economic life, yet these biologically secondary abilities are cultural inventions, foreign to our ancestors. Children require careful tutelage to master these evolutionarily novel skills, beginning early in life. Children will not likely acquire such skills on their own, and hours of practice, over many years, will be necessary for these important technological skills to be mastered. But preschool children do not require formal instruction and drill, in part because we should not expect them to display "expert" competence but only the "emergent" reading and numeracy skills that will serve as the basis for later, more sophisticated abilities. Such practices may indeed be necessary for older children, but they have the cognitive wherewithal to handle them. And even then, children are best educated when their motivation to learn is high and when the pedagogic methods take into consideration their interests, abilities, and natural dispositions.

Younger children's cognitive systems have evolved to learn more effectively by less rigorous methods. Children of all ages can learn. As we've seen, this is true even of fetuses. But there are differences in how children of different ages learn as well as what they can learn with understanding. The techniques that are effective for teaching reading or arithmetic to (many) 7-year-olds may be ineffective for most 4-year-olds. And even if 4-year-olds can learn by formal instruction, this does not mean that they will maintain their advantage in the years ahead or develop a positive disposition toward school learning.

Human beings are the most educable of animals, with the roots of learning extending to infancy. Young children's cognition is well suited to learning about their world and has been for eons. But the world has changed, and so has the complexity of what children need to learn. We as a culture have accepted that children need to be prepared years before the start of formal school to compete adequately for the economic rewards that our society affords. This does not mean accelerating development "above children's cognitive and emotional level," but enriching their lives with experiences properly suited to their learning style and also pertinent to the life they will lead in a post-industrial world. In the words of Deborah Stipek, "We would do much greater service to children if we focused more on making schools ready for children than on making children ready for school."[45]

8

The Changing Face of Childhood

The concept of childhood, so vital to the traditional American way of life, is threatened with extinction in the society we have created. Today's child has become the unwilling, unintended victim of overwhelming stress – the stress borne of rapid, bewildering social change and constantly rising expectation.

David Elkind, *The Hurried Child*

It is human to have a long childhood; it is civilized to have an even longer childhood.

Erik H. Erikson, *Childhood and Society*

Twelve-year old Dylan is a seventh-grade honor student at a private school in south Florida. He takes his Ritalin each morning, climbs into the back of the van with his sister, and completes his homework on the 20-minute drive to school. After school on Mondays, Wednesdays, and Fridays he waits for a chartered bus that takes him and a few other children from his school to gymnastics lessons. On Mondays and Wednesdays he finishes gymnastics around 4:00 and his mother, father, or Denise, the high-school girl his parents sometimes pay to drive him and sister around in the afternoons, takes him to cello lessons, which begin at 4:30. Tuesdays and Thursdays he stays after school and does homework or helps younger kids with their schoolwork as part of the "Learning through Collaboration" program. Someone picks him up around 3:30, takes him home, and he's ready for soccer practice at 5:00. He has Scouts most Wednesday nights. Dinner is often fast food or take-out, sometimes eaten in the car on the way home, sometimes eaten at home with one or both of his parents and his sister, sometimes eaten alone. He watches a little TV most evenings and then does anywhere from half an hour to two hours of homework. Soccer games are Saturday mornings and gymnastics meets and cello recitals the occasional Saturday or Sunday afternoon. He goes to Sunday school and church on Sunday mornings. Dylan's sister Meghan is in the fourth grade and has a similar schedule.

Dylan and Meghan's schedules may seem hectic, and they are, but they're not atypical. Some children are even more overscheduled than this pair, having lessons or activities of some type well into the evening. And this means that mom and dad's lives are overscheduled, too.[i] Modern parents have their own work schedules but believe that caring for their children means more than simply providing food, shelter, and material things, but also "activities." Being "frantically busy" is a badge of honor among many middle-class families. Children with time on their hands seem to reflect a negligent parent. (I recall a *Doonesbury* cartoon in which one mother is complaining to another about what a hectic summer her daughter had: theater camp, swimming practice, French lessons. When she asked the other mother what her daughter had done that summer she responded "Nothing. She played at the pond a lot, and built a tree fort, but basically nothing." After a moment of silence the first mother replied, "Well, I guess technically that's not child abuse.")

In this chapter, I first document a "rushing" of children through childhood. Children are often busier, more knowledgeable about "adult ways," and generally less able to exercise their childlike dispositions than they were in decades past. I next provide a brief history of the sociological concept of childhood, beginning with medieval Europe, where the distinction between children and adults was less distinct than it is today, through the modern area, where the special status of children was emphasized, and to the current postmodern era, where children are viewed as "competent" and capable of substantial independence and maturity of judgment. I then examine the well-being of America's children and note that, although by some measures children's lots are improving relative to the recent

---

[i] I am actually an advocate of schedules. For parents with children and jobs, the lack of some semblance of a schedule is a certain recipe for chaos. I've argued before that children function best when they know what to expect, when they can predict what they'll be doing, and what's going to happen to them – and so do adults (B. Bjorklund & D. Bjorklund, 1990). Schedules are not the problem; in fact they are often the solution to managing a hectic life. The problem is having too many activities to fit in one's schedule, thus the term "overscheduling."

past, in other ways, such as mental health and use of prescription medication, they are not. I conclude that juveniles are being viewed as more independent than they once were, similar in some ways to the perspective of medieval Europe. Although juveniles may be capable of such independence, I argue that there would be greater benefits of slowing the rate at which we in modern society force kids to grow up.

Pushing Children through Childhood

Childhood is not what it once was. Children of course still play, although the structure of play has changed some. Preschoolers and young elementary school children have "play dates," where mothers arrange their schedules so their children can play together, perhaps at a park but more often at one of the children's homes. As I mentioned in a previous chapter, outdoor play is on the decline in many communities, replaced by more sedentary indoor activities, usually centered around a TV or computer. Physical activity is typically scheduled. Lessons in karate, gymnastics, or diving may serve as children's weekly exercise, or perhaps competitive team sports, such as soccer or baseball. The latter activities are almost solely organized by adults and include specified (and limited) times to practice and play the game. Rarely does one see pick-up games of baseball or soccer, in which children choose the teams, make the rules, and play until they tire or someone gets upset and takes the ball and goes home. (The exception to this seems to be basketball, a game that can be played with as few as two people by anyone with the strength to throw a ball to the 10-foot basket, which usually excludes children much below the age of 10 years or so.)

What do parents think they're doing? First they are filling their children's lives with meaningful activities in structured, safe surroundings. Parents worry about their children's safety – from cars on the street to pedophiles lurking behind bushes. Whether life is more dangerous for children today than it was in the past is debatable, but reports in the media make it seem so, and parents are understandably concerned. Second, they are improving their children's résumés. Extra-curricular activities look good on a college application, and who knows, maybe gymnastics lessons will pay off in a college scholarship. Third, they are teaching their children how to cope in a busy world. There's every reason to believe that children will grow up to find an adult world that's every bit as hectic and demanding as the one their parents are living in, and the spoils go to the well prepared, in this case to multi-taskers who know how to use their time effectively. In many ways, modern parents are doing their best to provide for their children and to prepare them for the future, just as parents always have. They are simply preparing them for a very different world and have a different perspective on what their children are able to accomplish than parents of previous generations.

Arguments that these practices are preparing children for a competitive future and thus are necessary sacrifices children must make (or parents must make children make) certainly have some merit, but only some. What happens early in life is only partly important for what happens later in life. Many of children's experiences, emotions, and thoughts will have no long-term consequences of any significant degree, but do influence their lives *now*, as they are experiencing, feeling, and thinking them. Justifying that we do things to children because it will be good for them in the future may not always be justifiable. Children have a right (as do adults) to feel good and enjoy themselves in the here and now. When children are overly stressed and pushed to excel, there may or may not be positive (or negative) long-term effects. But there are clearly immediate effects. Are the potential long-term benefits worth the immediate stress and anguish children experience? And might the stress of childhood actually be associated with long-term negative effects?

Don't get me wrong. I am not arguing for eliminating parental responsibility for preparing a child for life in the 21st century. Nor am I advocating an immediate gratification – an "if it feels good do it" approach to life and child rearing. There are many things in life that children need to do that they do not want to do. They need to learn to regulate their own behavior, to be mindful of the rights and feelings of others, and to master the technological skills of our society, among many other things. They need to learn self-discipline. I am not an advocate of namby-pamby parenting. But children do not necessarily need to acquire these many skills all at once. They shouldn't have to sacrifice play, the joy of discovery learning, and the companionship of other children to achieve these things. In fact, it is play, discovery learning, and the fellowship of their peers that is often the best means for developing the skills needed to succeed in the modern world.

Childhood has changed in another way over the past 50 years or so, and that is in a blurring of the distinction between children and adults. Children become wise to adult ways much earlier than in decades past. Clothing for little boys and girls often resembles that worn by teenagers and young adults. The distinction between adult dress and child dress has almost disappeared. There's *The GAP*, *Kids' GAP*, and *Baby GAP*, all in a row at the local mall. Children are more knowledgeable about sex than they once were. Even parents who want to "protect" children from the secrets of carnal knowledge have a difficult time censuring television commercials for the latest bras from *Victoria's Secret* or explaining ads about drugs for erectile dysfunction. Children are more self-sufficient. Many are likely to spend time without supervision at home, operating the microwave to fix themselves an after-school snack or early dinner, while they lock themselves in the house, waiting for their parents to get home from work. Children often engage in more adult behavior at earlier ages than in decades past. Rates of sexual activity among teenagers are high (as are rates of sexually transmitted diseases), and drug use, including alcohol, is common among preteens in many communities. People reading this book who are much younger than 40 may not recognize much of a change, and may in fact see a decline in some "early adult" behaviors (rates of smoking, drug use, and teen pregnancy are down in the past decade, for instance); but compared to mid-20th-century America, and the many decades that preceded it, the change is drastic.

Scholars and social commentators started noticing and writing about this trend in the early 1980s. Particularly influential were writer Marie Winn's 1981 book, *Children without Childhood*, New York University Educator Neil Postman's 1982 book, *The Disappearance of Childhood*, and Tufts University developmental psychologist David Elkind's 1981 book, *The Hurried Child*. Each author had a slightly different take on the phenomenon of children growing up too fast, but all agreed that the change had been rapid and drastic, occurring over a span of just decades, between 1950 and the early 1970s. Among the culprits identified for this change were television, sexual liberation, women entering the workforce in large numbers, an increasing divorce rate, the Vietnam War, *Sputnik*, Watergate, the popularity of Freud's psychosexual theory of development, explicit sex and violence in movies, and *Mad* magazine, among others. In subsequent re-publication or revision of their books, both Postman and Elkind see their initial interpretations and the consequences of "hurrying" children unchanged. Nor has this phenomenon been lost on contemporary writers, social commentators, educators, and psychologists. More than a dozen popular (or wannabe popular) books have been written in the past decade commenting on aspects of children's accelerated educations, lifestyles, or jump-starts into adulthood, and providing advice how to be an effective parent in such a "hurry up and grow up" world.[ii]

In this chapter, I do not plan to make long-winded statements about how societal changes have ruined childhood as we once knew it with the concomitant ruination of children, or to blame parents for failing to do what's best for their offspring. Nor do I intend to document how self-centered (or lazy, or disrespectful, or rudderless) children and adolescents have become. I really don't believe that conditions and teenagers are so terrible today. In fact, I generally like teenagers and have some sympathy for them. I was actually a teenager once myself. I do think, however, that childhood has changed over the past several decades and that society affords children fewer opportunities to exercise their childlike abilities for their current enjoyment and possibly future betterment. By slowing the pace of growing up and keeping children's natural proclivities for learning in mind, I believe that we can not only make childhood more enjoyable for children, but also better prepare them for life as adults.

A Brief History of Childhood

In documenting the "loss of childhood," it's necessary to be a bit more precise about what it is we're losing, as well as the history of childhood. I'm referring here to the *concept* of childhood to distinguish it from the biological *fact* of childhood.

In Chapter 2 I presented anthropologist Barry Bogin's description of the life stages of humans. Like other mammals, *Homo sapiens* have a period of *infancy* that extends from birth to the end of weaning, a *juvenile period* when children are relatively independent of their parents but are not yet sexually active, and *adulthood*. What is unique about humans, Bogin believes, are two additional life stages, *childhood* and

---

[ii] A partial list of some of these books includes: *Einstein Never Used Flash Cards: How Children REALLY Learn and Why They Need to Play More and Memorize Less* by Kathy Hirsh-Pasek and Roberta Golinkoff; *Reinventing Childhood: Raising and Educating Children in a Changing World* by David Elkind; *Reclaiming Childhood: Letting Children Be Children in Our Achievement-Oriented Society* by William Crain; *The Over-Scheduled Child: Avoiding the Hyper-Parenting Trap* by Alvin Rosenfeld and Nicole Wise; *Home-Alone America: The Hidden Toll of Day Care, Behavioral Drugs, and Other Parent Substitutes*, by Mary Eberstadt; *The Pressured Child: Helping Your Child Find Success in School and Life* by Michael Thompson; *Ready or Not: What Happens When We Treat Children As Small Adults* by Kay Hymowitz.

adolescence. Childhood spans from the end of infancy to the beginning of the juvenile period and represents a stage of life when children are no longer nursing but still require special care from others (for example, they are not able to obtain and prepare food without considerable help). Adolescence is, of course, the time between the end of the juvenile period and adulthood and is marked by certain anatomical and physiological changes, most obviously the development of secondary sexual characteristics.[1]

As I mentioned in Chapter 2, Bogin's view of childhood and adolescence as being unique to humans may be a bit overstated (other primates show features similar to those proposed by Bogin for these stages). Nonetheless, these stages are defined in terms of physical characteristics and behavioral abilities. They are, essentially, biological categories. However, Bogin's definition of childhood, in particular (whether unique to humans or not), does not correspond to what most people mean when they speak of "childhood." If we're losing anything it's certainly not the "post-weaning/pre-independence" life stage between infancy and juvenility. It is the *sociological* meaning of childhood, and not the biological one, that is the focus of this chapter. The sociological concept of childhood refers to how people in a society view children at different times in their development – how adults perceive children and the extent to which they provide them special status, unique from that of the wholly dependent infant and the wholly independent adult.

Regardless of what many people (including me) believe about the changing perception of children in contemporary culture, modern societies afford children special status. They are, if nothing else, the segment of society that must attend school. We also do not hold them accountable for their actions to the same extent that we hold adolescents or adults, and we have laws that restrict them from certain activities judged to be for "grown-ups only" (for example, sex with adults; the purchase and consumption of cigarettes, alcohol, or sexually explicit material; making legally binding contracts). Although parents are the legal guardians of their children, there are laws against child abuse, neglect, and filicide, and parents who violate these laws risk incarceration or the removal of their children from the home by the State. Societies vary in their views of children, but all afford them special status.

Before There Was "Childhood"

This has not always been the case. Archaeological research dating back to 7000 BC has shown that children were killed as religious sacrifices

205

and sometimes buried in walls of buildings to "strengthen" the structures. This does denote a "special status" of children, but hardly one reflecting modern sensibilities. In many societies, infant girls were killed to provide higher ratios of males in the population. Up until the fourth century AD in Europe, parents routinely (and legally) killed their newborns if they were not perfectly healthy at birth, if there were too many children in the family, if the child was a female, or if the child was illegitimate. In AD 374 the Romans outlawed infanticide. For the next thousand years or more, parents simply abandoned their unwanted infants to die outside city gates. Children were also sold into slavery and used as collateral for loans.[2]

In the 1600s, child abandonment was outlawed in most parts of Europe and foundling homes were established to provide for the basic needs of unwanted children. When Vincent de Paul established the first foundling home in Paris, the response was so great that the home was filled within the first week and laws had to be written against transporting infants into the city from surrounding areas. A century later, one-quarter of the infants born in Paris became foundlings.[iii] The Catholic Church later canonized Vincent de Paul, and today in many US cities St. Vincent de Paul Societies run shelters, soup kitchens, and thrift shops to "alleviate the suffering of the poor."[3]

Many scholars have argued that the historical pattern just described reflects the fact that Dark and Middle Age Europeans had no concept of "childhood." Following infancy (or more literally, I assume, the end of Bogin's childhood period, around 7 years of age), children were regarded as miniature adults. They likely worked for a living, many doing farm work alongside their parents, and shared in the social intercourse of adult life. They ate what adults ate, dressed as adults dressed, witnessed (and even partook in) the sexual activity of adults, and were privy to all the conversations of grown-ups. More recent scholarship suggests that the erasure of childhood was not complete, and that medieval adults realized that children had some special needs beyond those of grown-ups. Their special status was recognized in law

---

[iii] *Oblation*, leaving a child in the custody of some religious institution, was an alternative to infanticide or abandoning an infant for many European women between the 15th and 18th centuries. Mothers could leave their infants, anonymously, at the church, believing that their babies would be well cared for. This was rarely the case, however. In days before baby formula, wet nurses were hard to find; infants were fed a diet consisting mostly of gruel, and death rates often exceeded 60% (Hrdy, 1999).

and by the Church. They played with other children and were not viewed as being as responsible for their actions as were adults. Medieval children were certainly treated more like adults than children are today, however. This is most apparent in the age of majority, which was as low as 12 years for some purposes. But despite the exaggerated claims by some scholars of an absence of a notion of childhood in medieval Europe, childhood during this time was substantially different than we think of it today.[4]

The Transformation of Childhood

What prompted the transformation of childhood? The most provocative proposal is the one presented by Neil Postman in *The Disappearance of Childhood*. Postman proposed that for a society to have a concept of childhood it must have secrets. There must be some important aspects of society that children are not privileged to. That was not the case, Postman suggests, in Middle Ages Europe. Postman traces the beginning of childhood to the invention of moveable type in Mainz, Germany by Johann Gutenberg in the 1440s. Prior to the printing press and the possibility to mass-produce the written word, literacy was limited to the elite. The printing press changed this, as first the Bible, and later books, pamphlets, and newspapers became commonplace. There was now a new means of conveying messages and obtaining information, and successful adults were those who possessed the skill of reading. It also served to mark a distinction between adults and children, the former being literate and the latter not, or at least not formerly so.

Becoming an adult was now viewed as a prolonged process, accomplished through formal schooling. At school, children spent much of their waking hours with other children and *not* in the contact of their parents or other "working" adults. As more children began to attend school, their special status became more obvious. The 7- or 8-year-old was no longer a miniature adult, but an incomplete one who needed to be educated in the ways of adulthood. Although illiteracy was the initial defining characteristic of childhood, once classified as "different," other distinctions were noted. Children didn't think like adults and didn't have the same sensibilities or drives (particularly sexual) as adults. The language of adults was not always viewed as appropriate for the ears of children, and certainly the sexual activities of adults were no longer appropriate for their eyes. These were the secrets of adulthood, which were kept from children until they had the physical, emotional, and intellectual maturity to deal with them. Major

Enlightenment philosophers, such as John Locke in England and Jean Jacques Rousseau in France, saw an increasing distinction – and purpose – for childhood. For Locke, children were viewed as blank slates (*tabula rasa*), and it was the responsibility of parents and other adults to fill those slates appropriately. Rousseau was perhaps the most ardent advocate of childhood, believing that children are important in themselves, and are not merely a means to an end.[iv] Through the 18th, 19th, and into the 20th centuries, the concept of childhood was increasingly ingrained into the fabric of Western society.

Despite an increased awareness of the special status of children, this did not translate to an idyllic life for most of Europe's (or America's) children. Education was limited to the children of the middle class and aristocracy. Children of the poor and working classes were valuable as farm laborers or factory workers. The industrial revolution made use of children's unskilled labor, and many children in the 18th and 19th centuries spent long hours working in factories, mills, and mines. Such treatment, while accepted as "normal" by many, was viewed as crimes against children by others, and movements to improve the lot of children began. For example, in 1836 Massachusetts passed the first state child labor law, requiring that children under 15 years of age working in factories attend school at least three months a year. Even if 19th century Europe and America were not ideal places for children, many recognized the "specialness" of children, and society was moving to give all of its children such recognition.

The beginning of the 20th century has been called the high point of childhood in Western culture. Great works of literature were centered around children, including *Alice's Adventures in Wonderland* by Lewis Carroll and James Barrie's *Peter Pan*, and great composers wrote music for children's amusement, including Robert Schumann's *Kinderscenen* and Felix Mendelssohn's *Kinderstucke*. In the United States, the 20th century saw the move away from farms to cities, and a beginning of a shift in the structure of family life. Women, whose labor was as critical as that of men on farms, began to stay at home and care for children, as men/husbands became the primary breadwinners. Children came to be viewed as vulnerable, in need of active protection, guidance, and encouragement, especially by mothers, and nuclear families (that is, mother, father, children) were viewed as the ideal setting for bringing up children. By the 1910s and 20s child advocates were cropping up all over Europe and America, as was a

---

[iv] It is ironic then that Rousseau placed all five of his children in foundling homes because they would otherwise interfere with his work.

new group of child development and parenting experts. More children attended school for longer periods. Universal education approached reality. Child labor laws were passed in many states (although the first US federal law regulating minimum age of employment and hours of work per week for children wasn't passed until 1938). By mid-century, the view that children needed to be protected and nurtured, ideally in a two-parent family with a stay-at-home mom, was well established and a reality for a majority of American children.

I must make it clear that the childhood I'm talking about is a Western invention, and although developed countries everywhere provide children with special status, children in many parts of the world still experience life much as children did in the Middle Ages. Where there is poverty, children join their parents in the fields or beg on the streets to make a living; young girls work as prostitutes; millions of children in parts of Asia and Africa are sold into slavery; in some South American cities "street children" roam in gangs trying to stay alive; where there is war, children are recruited (often abducted) to serve as soldiers. The modern conception of childhood is not universal. In 1989 the United Nations approved *The Convention on the Rights of the Child*, which has now been signed by all but two of the 192 members of the United Nations (the United States and Somalia being the exceptions). This international treaty "recognizes the human rights of children, defined as persons up to the age of 18 years...[I]t establishes in international law that States Parties must ensure that all children – without discrimination in any form – benefit from special protection measures and assistance; have access to services such as education and health care; can develop their personalities, abilities and talents to the fullest potential; grow up in an environment of happiness, love and understanding; and are informed about and participate in, achieving their rights in an accessible and active manner."[5] Essentially, the United Nations adopted as a standard the view of childhood that evolved in the West over the past 500 years. Recognizing that children deserve special status is an important step, but, unfortunately, such treaties are difficult, or impossible, to enforce.

Postmodern Parenting

Childhood is a function of society, and societies are in constant states of flux, and this was especially true for American society in the latter half of the 20th century. How has American society changed in the past 50 years? Let me count the ways: the civil rights movement, women's liberation, the sexual revolution, the increased divorce rate, the increase in single-parent homes, the de-stigmatization of child-birth out of wedlock, the recognition of alternative lifestyles, HIV/AIDS, easy access to drugs, accelerating crime rates, television, the personal computer, and the global economy, to name a few of the major phenomena that influenced, directly or indirectly, how society views children. With the advent of new forms of mass communication, most notably television, sociological changes spread rapidly. Soon after its introduction to the American market, few families were without a TV in their homes, and by the 1970s most homes boasted several sets. With television, parochialism died. Even more than radio before it, what happened in the metropolitan centers of the world traveled quickly to suburbia and rural America. This was the case not simply for news, but for fashion and lifestyle practices, as reflected on entertainment shows. With television and its immediate images, cultural trends became wildfires, leaving no part of the nation untouched.

It was television, more so than anything else, that was responsible for the "disappearance of childhood," at least according to Neil Postman. Recall that Postman proposed that childhood required secrets – things that adults knew that children didn't. (It was another type of communication revolution – the invention of moveable type – that made literacy a defining characteristic of adulthood and led to the invention of childhood in Renaissance Europe.) With television, Postman stated, the secrets of adulthood disappeared. Children now saw what adults saw; they heard what adults heard; their innocence quickly vanished as they became privy to adult knowledge. It didn't happen all at once, of course, but slowly the distinction between what adults know and do and what children know and do diminished. This, by itself, did not bring about the change in society's view of children that has occurred in the past five or six decades, but it surely sped the change.

We have moved into what David Elkind in his book *Reinventing Childhood* calls *postmodern parenting*. Families have adjusted to divorce and a variety of family relationships, which makes leaving existing families and joining new ones easier. More women with children work outside the home (full or part time) than stay at home, and preschool children increasingly spend much of their time in daycare or preschool programs. Mothers are no longer viewed as the primary caretaker of children, but parenting responsibilities are shared between parents. "Good fathers" no longer simply bring home the bacon, providing their children with opportunities to do better than their parents did, only occasionally spending time with their children. Good fathers, whether married to their children's mother or not, devote time to their children, change diapers, read bedtime stories, help with homework, as well as throw the ball around. (This, of course, is the new ideal, not the new reality. Mothers, whether working outside the home or not, still spend significantly more time caring for their children than fathers do. And although many men are taking greater responsibility for childcare than fathers of past generations, as many are abandoning their children, leaving mothers to fend entirely for themselves.[6])

Perhaps the greatest change in parenting in this postmodern age is the very nature of how children are viewed. The "modern," circa 1950, perspective held that children were innocent and in need of protection. The postmodern view, claims Elkind, holds that children are *competent.* This is consistent with the new findings from psychology, discussed in the previous chapter, suggesting that infants and young children are smarter than we had previously believed. But this postmodern view of the competent child stemmed not only (or even primarily) from new research findings. Rather, Elkind argues, "it developed because postmodern families need competent children. We need children who can adapt to out-of-home parenting, and who will not be unduly upset by the graphic violence and lurid sexuality so prominent on our television screens."[7]

The Costs of Ignoring Immaturity: The Well-Being of America's Children

Are children being adversely affected by the changing nature of childhood and the increased stress associated with our "hurry up and grow up" society? I cannot provide any scientifically certain cause-and-effect statements here. There have been many changes in society over the past 30 or 50 years, and stating that any one particular change is responsible for any one particular outcome cannot be done. But we can look at the general well-being of children now and see how things have changed over the years.

Some things haven't changed all that much in the past 30 years. For example, 87% of children completed high school in 2003; this is only a slight rise from the 1980 rate of 84%.[8] Similarly, the percentage of children living in poverty has fluctuated slightly from year to year, but the 1980 and 2003 rates were the same at 16%.

Other things have changed for the better. The percentage of children whose parents evaluate them as being in very good or excellent health has increased from about 79% in 1984 to 83% in 2003, with most of the gain being among poor children (62% to 71%). Childhood mortality rates (for children aged 1 to 4 years) have been cut more than in half since 1980, and the adolescent death rate has declined by nearly a third over that same time. Although serious crimes committed both by and against juveniles went up slightly in 2003 relative to 2002, the overall rates are significantly down from the previous decade. Cigarette smoking, alcohol abuse, and illicit drug use among teens were also all down from peak years in the 1980s or 90s.[v] And the teenage birth rate in 2003 was 22 per 1,000 women 15 to 17 years of age, the lowest in the nation's history. (This rate is still higher, however, than for most other developed countries.)

In other ways, children are not doing so well. Although children are rated by their parents as overall healthier than 30 years ago, they are also fatter. The percentage of children 6 to 18 years of age considered overweight for the years 1999–2002 was 11%, up from 6% 20 years earlier. One result of this increasing trend in obesity in American children is that rates of diabetes are on the rise. It is estimated that an American child born in 2000 has a one in three chance of developing diabetes in his or her lifetime.[9] More American children become sexually active before the age of 15 than in most other developed countries such as Canada, France, the United Kingdom, and Sweden, and they have more sexual partners in a year than teens from these other nations.[10] Related to earlier and more promiscuous sexuality, the rates of sexually transmitted diseases (STDs) are exceptionally high in American adolescents and young adults. A 2004 study reported that of the approximately 18.9 million new cases of STDs in the United States in the year 2000, 9.1 million of them (48%) were contracted

---

[v] For those interested in the numbers: There were 15 crimes committed *by* juveniles per every 1,000 juveniles between the ages of 12 and 17 in 2003, down from a peak of 55 per 1,000 in 1993; the rates of crimes *against* juveniles showed a similar decline from the peak year of 1993 (44/1,000 to 15/1,000). The rate of 12th graders reporting having five or more drinks in a row within the last two weeks decreased from a high in 1980 of 41% to 29% in 2004. However, rates for 8th and 10th graders have stayed essentially unchanged since they were first measured in the early 1990s at about 10% and 20%, respectively. Rates of smoking for 12th graders declined from 21% in 1980 to 16% in 2004. Rates of illicit drug use in 12th graders declined from a peak of 37% in 1980 to 23% in 2004; rates for 8th and 10th graders were 8% and 18%, respectively, in 2004, down from peaks in the 1990s of 15% and 23%. Data from *America's Children, Key National Indicator of Well-Being*, 2005.

by people between the ages of 15 and 24 years old.[11] Although rates of syphilis are down, rates of Chlamydia and human papillomavirus (HPV) have increased since the 1970s; these infections are associated with problems of fertility, birth complications, and even cancer, especially in women.

With respect to mental health, about 5% of children between the ages of 4 and 17 years had definite or severe difficulties with emotions, concentration, behavior, or being able to get along with other children, according to parents' reports in 2003. Other studies put the level of mental disturbance higher. For example, University of Texas researcher Robert Roberts and his colleagues conducted a meta-analysis (a study that summarizes the findings of many previous studies) of the prevalence of psychopathology among children and adolescents (1 to 18 years) between 1963 and the mid-1990s, mostly in the United States and the United Kingdom. They reported that the average (median) rates of psychopathology were 8% for preschoolers, 12% for preadolescents, and 15% for adolescents. They also examined changes in the overall rates of psychopathology over time. They divided the studies (52 in all) into four categories and computed the average psychopathology rates: for studies conducted in 1970 or earlier the rate was 15.4%; the rates were 14.1% for the years 1971–80 and 13.8% for the years 1981–90. For studies conducted since 1990 the rate jumped to 26%.[12]

Children are also being medicated at all-time levels. As of the late 1990s, about 6% of youths younger than 20 years were taking some type of mood- or behavior-altering (psychotropic) medication, including stimulants, such as Ritalin (mostly for attention-deficit disorder, with and without hyperactivity, ADHD, ADD), antidepressants, such as Prozac, and other "mood stabilizer" drugs, often used to treat conduct disorders. Between 1987 and 1996, the rate at which these drugs were prescribed to youth tripled. Since then, the rates have continued to climb, not just in the US but in all developed countries where it has been investigated. In a large-scale study of seven countries (USA, Canada, Mexico, Brazil, Argentina, UK, Spain, Germany, France), the rates that youths 18 and younger were prescribed psychotropic drugs increased in all countries between the years 2000 and 2002, with the smallest increase being in Germany (13%) and the largest in the UK (68%). The rate of increase in the US was approximately 33%. Rates of medication for preschoolers, ages 2 to 4 years, are still low (about 1% in the US), but these, too, increased three-fold over the past decade, mostly for stimulants, but rates also increased for antidepressants.[13]

American teenagers also experience greater stress associated with school than teenagers in some other developed nations. For example, research by University of Michigan developmental psychologist Harold Stevenson and his colleagues reported, somewhat ironically, that American teenagers experienced greater stress related to their school work than Chinese and Japanese children. It is ironic because in this 1993 study, American children spent less time doing homework and lagged far behind their Asian counterparts in school achievement (especially mathematics). Despite their poorer performance, the parents of these American high-school kids were generally pleased with their children's achievement and their education. A more recent international comparison revealed that although American adolescents scored below the average level in mathematics achievement among 40 developed nations, they ranked first in math self-concept.[14] That is, despite mediocre achievement levels at best, they felt good about their math knowledge and abilities.

If an over-demanding school curriculum were the primary source of stress, one would expect the Chinese and Japanese students to top the charts. But it was the American teenagers who experience the most school-associated stress. Stevenson and his colleagues suggested that this is because, unlike Asian students, American students are unclear how much importance they should place on academics. Parents and the culture at large make it clear to Japanese and Chinese students that they are to devote themselves to their studies. American students, in comparison, have distracting concerns: they date earlier and more frequently than Japanese and Chinese students and are more likely to have jobs. Stevenson and his colleagues wrote: "The motivation for economic independence and broad social experience, as well as the desire to engage in sports, and to assist with family chores, make it difficult for American high school students to devote themselves wholeheartedly to their studies."[15] The point I wish to make here is that the problem American high schoolers face is not one narrowly focused on educational practices (although these are certainly at issue), but with broader societal views of what teenagers are "supposed" to be doing and what both their short-term and long-term goals are expected to be.

Affluence and the Postmodern Child

No one pretends (or should) that children in the United States are a homogeneous population. There is great economic and educational diversity among children in America, usually greater than found in most European countries. While an increasing number of children live in affluence, many others live in poverty, or close to it. To some extent, all children in Western society are subject to the same forces that are producing a loss of childhood, namely the increasing divorce rate and the greater exposure to what were previously adult-only topics. But in other respects, children of the affluent may be more prone to the pressures of the postmodern child – pressures to succeed, to become over-scheduled, and alienation from adults – than their less-affluent peers.

Columbia University psychologist Suniya Luthar and her colleagues have conducted research comparing middle- and high-school children from affluent, suburban families, where median family income is often over $100,000, to children from the inner city, with family incomes around $30,000.[16] Psychologists and educators have long known about the association between poverty and negative educational, sociological, and psychological outcomes. Children living in poverty do more poorly in school, are more apt to be involved in the use of illegal drugs and in criminal behavior, and show signs of poor psychological adjustment, all compared to the general population. What Luthar found in three samples of affluent children, then, came as somewhat of a surprise. These children from well-to-do homes had a higher incidence of cigarette smoking, alcohol use, and marijuana and hard-drug use than the national norm, *and* their inner-city counterparts. They also reported higher levels of anxiety and somewhat higher levels of depression than the inner-city youth. These effects tended to get larger (or first appear) as children moved from middle school to high school.

Luthar and her colleagues speculated on the reasons for such problems in these privileged adolescents. One fact seems to be what they called *achievement pressure*. Children who viewed achievement failures (for instance, doing poorly in school) as personal failures had relatively high levels of anxiety, depression, and substance use; so, too, did children whose parents overemphasized their accomplishments at the expense (from the children's point of view) of emphasizing their personal character. A second factor Luthar identified was *isolation from adults*, both literal and emotional. Analyses of their data showed that youth who felt distant from their parents, either in time spent with them or in emotional closeness, showed more distress and greater substance abuse than less-isolated teens.

In general, Luthar's research indicates that adolescents at the socioeconomic extremes are more similar in many ways than they are different. Substance abuse, delinquency, lack of interest in school, and poor academic performance were found in both groups, all greater than typically observed in the general population of adolescents. Luthar concludes a recent summary of her work: "The American dream spawns widespread beliefs that Ivy League educations and subsequently lucrative careers are critical for children's long-term happiness. In the sometimes single-minded pursuit of these goals, let us not lose sight of the possible costs to mental health and well-being of all concerned."[17] Although one always has to be cautious of simple explanations for complex problems, one contributing factor for the distress that many affluent children experience is the stress and alienation associated with an accelerated childhood.

The Independent Human Juvenile: A New View of Childhood?

When social commentators talk about "the loss of childhood," or children having too much freedom, information, or even stress, they are not generally talking about preschoolers (although this may be the case for many children with respect to adult-directed education as we saw in the previous chapter). Rather it is school-age children, preteens, and teenagers who are losing their innocence and increasing their stress levels relative to earlier times. Going back to Bogin's anthropological classification of human lifestyles, it is young people in the *juvenile* stage of life, roughly between 7 and 12 years of age, who are being especially accelerated, along with adolescents.

If we can back off a bit and view human juveniles as we view juvenile members of other species, the present state of children may not seem so strange. Juvenile animals can fend for themselves – usually not as well as adults, but they no longer need, and rarely get, help from their parents in obtaining food, finding their way around their environment, avoiding predators, and fending off assaults from other members of their own species. The juvenile period in many mammals seems to be a time when the young are learning to "make it" on their own, to acquire knowledge about their environment and other members of their social group, often through play. Why should humans be so different? Humans are the most behaviorally flexible of animals, especially during the early years of life. Human 7- and 8-year-olds in some traditional societies work alongside their parents, and although they may not be treated as adults, they seem to have a more demanding life than children in developed countries today. As we've seen, children in medieval Europe apparently led lives more similar to those of adults than children do today. Most lived in a family and worked with their parents, but work they did, and we have every reason to believe that they had access to adult conversation and knowledge of adult activities, much as children today do. They likely began sexual activity early, and my guess is that they drank grog or beer or wine at an early age, often to intoxication. Yet they survived to become our ancestors.

It may seem harsh, but in many ways medieval parents may be models for modern moms and dads. We may not like it, having developed over the intervening centuries a view of children as being very different from adults, requiring protection and shielding from the harsh realities of grown-up life. But the hallmark of *Homo sapiens* is our intelligence, particularly our ability to modify our behavior to the varying demands of the environment. We have achieved ecological domination not because we are well adapted to any one environment, but because we can adapt to almost any ecology the Earth has to offer. And it is children who are most plastic and can most easily adjust their behavior and ways of thinking to new worlds. Rather than lamenting the "loss of childhood," perhaps we should view children's responses to the changing landscape of childhood as evidence that children, once past the age of 7 or so, are capable of adapting to new environments and displaying the innovation that makes our species so special.

Maybe, but I'm not ready to surrender the modern (as opposed to postmodern) concept of childhood just yet. Just because juveniles are capable of a substantial degree of self-sufficiency doesn't mean we need to afford it to them. Juveniles *can* fend for themselves more easily than we once thought, especially in a world of refrigerators, microwaves, cell phones, and computers. But the presence of these modern conveniences shouldn't deceive us into thinking that children's lives are any less complex than they were a few generations ago, or even a few eons ago. Modern life is enormously complicated. We may not need to learn how hunt gazelle, forage for nutritious tubers, or start a fire with flint; but we do need to learn how to read, to calculate, to operate modern machinery, to drive, and to buy plane tickets online. We need to learn how to negotiate with one another, to avoid fights, to woo members of the opposite sex, and get along with our neighbors and bosses, who may very likely be from a different tribe than we are. It is because we have so much to learn that we need an extended period of immaturity to learn it.

217

Racing to Adulthood, Prolonging Adolescence

Precocious children may get exposed to the problems of adulthood sooner, and may even learn to solve some of them; but they do not necessarily achieve maturity sooner. One of the ironies of the societal drive to rush children through childhood is that it is accompanied by a prolongation of adolescence. The requirements of modern cultures that oblige children to forgo a more casual and hands-on education for a more formal one also extend our functional period of immaturity. It wasn't all that long ago that eight years of schooling made you an educated person. By then you could read, write, and do basic "figurin'," more than enough skills to handle a small family farm or business. As more jobs required more knowledge, more people needed more education. In the United States today, most good jobs require some college, either a four-year degree or a two- or three-year technical degree or certification. Nearly half of American children attend some college. The most prestigious jobs go to people who earn graduate or professional degrees. Would-be physicians attend four years of college, another four years of medical school, then several years of internships and residencies before they are ready to strike it out "on their own." Their adolescence is extended well into their 20s or 30s. All this education keeps people out of the workforce and postpones their entry into "real" adult life. I, for instance, didn't get my first "real" job until I was 27, something my younger brothers and cousins would remind me of from time to time, noting, in so many words, my less-than-adult status despite my age.

Most parents provide support for their college-age children, often well past the four years it takes to get a college degree. Although teens may be sexually active earlier on average than in years past, they are marrying later and having children later. And many parents, rather than experiencing the empty nest syndrome once their children graduate from high school and leave home, find themselves living with their adult children who have returned "home," sometimes with their own children in tow, because of economic difficulties associated with divorce, a sputtering job market, or the high cost of home ownership in some parts of the country. Many parents never get to experience the empty nest syndrome, as their adult children continue to live "at home," often well into to their 30s. (This is even more common in some European countries than in the US.)

We also live a long time and are healthier later in life than generations past. I remember my grandparents when they were in their 60s. They were old. My parents are now in their early 80s and are much younger in appearance and action than their parents were in their 60s. If 80 is the new 60, 60 is the new 40. We have time for multiple careers if we want them. We have time to develop our talents and pursue our interests. Yes, there are economic realities, and young adults must make a living. But we don't have to be in such a rush. More to the point, I believe that if we can slow down the pace of growing up over the period we still call childhood, we'll be better prepared to make the important decisions of young adulthood. We may not get there as fast, but we may be better prepared for living our adult lives. And we will be happier as children.

Epilogue: *Homo Juvenalis*

May your hands always be busy
May your feet always be swift
May you have a strong foundation
When the winds of changes shift
May your heart always be joyful
May your song always be sung
May you stay forever young
Bob Dylan

◆   ◆   ◆   ◆

I assume that anyone who even bothered opening this book was already convinced that development is something that one must take seriously. It's not really a very controversial position. Perhaps more controversial, or at least less encountered, is the idea that aspects of youth are important in their own right – to help deal with life at a particular time in development – in addition to, or instead of, preparing children for the life they will lead as adults. And perhaps most counterintuitive of all is the idea that children's immature thought and behavior can sometimes be adaptive – provide children real benefits – either in coping with their current environment, or in directing them to experiences that will serve to prepare them for the future. Let me reiterate that I do not believe that immaturity should be praised for its own sake. It is quite often maladaptive, and the goal of development is still maturity – physical, intellectual, emotional, and social. But infants' and children's less-than-adult ways seem well suited to the demands placed on a slow-developing, big-brained, social animal, despite the perils they may bring.

I believe that we would not be the creatures we are today if it weren't for our immaturity. (Of course, our extended immaturity could just as easily have been the death – or extinction – of us, but we were lucky and it wasn't.) Slow growth played a significant role in human evolution, including evolution of the brain; neural immaturity

221

is associated with our species' behavioral and cognitive plasticity and to our high degree of educability, which accounts in large part for our species' ecological dominance. Perhaps rather than *Homo sapiens*, Our Kind should be called *Homo juvenalis*.

Revisiting Childhood

The immaturity of infants and children may very well have initially been an evolutionary by-product of a big-brained animal that lives a long time. Big brains and longevity go together. The former are good for learning, but are expensive to build and maintain and take time to develop. These costs can only be afforded by an animal with a plastic mind and flexible behavior that lives long enough to reap the resulting benefits. A shorter-lived animal would be long dead before a big brain could do it much good. Whereas some animals, such as 17-year locusts, can hide away, nearly dormant, underground or in tree bark during highly vulnerable stages of pre-adult life, most mammals, including humans and our near-human relatives, don't have that luxury. They must somehow solve the problem of surviving the pre-adult years, and the longer that time is, the more critical it becomes to develop, and eventually evolve, adaptive ways to get through childhood. The theme of this book has been that our ancestors developed a suite of behaviors, cognitions, and dispositions that increased the chances that youngsters would grow up and have the opportunity to put the neural machinery they were blessed with to good purposes. Immaturity may have been a necessary side effect of increased brain size in our forebears, but we only survived to rule the Earth because our infants and children evolved means of using that immaturity to get through the niche of childhood and to better prepare themselves to use their enhanced neural apparatus effectively as adults.

Children born in the current millennium have brains and the accompanying dispositions, abilities, and adaptations nearly identical to those of children born 40 or 100 or 200 millennia before them. Life has changed for Our Kind especially rapidly over the past 10,000 years or so, but the brains we inherit have not. The minds we *develop* over childhood, however, are different from those developed by our ancestors. They must be if we are to survive in environments so different from those in which early humans lived and evolved. Humans are able to adapt so readily to rapid and radical cultural changes only through the special abilities associated with childhood. Children's

222

immaturity is accompanied by a brain that stays pliable – able to acquire new technologies unimaginable to our ancestors – long past the time when the brains of other species have become (essentially) fixed in their ways. Children have ways of learning and knowing, through discovery and play, that permit them to master new skills easily and to invent new knowledge (such as language if the conditions are right). We owe a substantial debt to our childhoods. We could not be the adults we become if children were more like us in how they see and learn about the world.

This view of development makes childhood more than a training school for adulthood. Childhood has an integrity of its own. Children are not simply little, incomplete adults, but people whose minds and behaviors are well suited to the demands of their young lives. It should be our jobs as adults to promote children's development, putting their youthful ways of learning and knowing to good use, not only to prepare them for the adults they will become, but to foster the children they are.

Visiting Adulthood

But what has immaturity done for us lately, specifically as adults? Sure, it may have played a role in getting us through childhood (ontogenetic adaptations) and it may have helped prepare us for adulthood (deferred adaptations); but does it continue to have a role in adult functioning? I think it does. Our neural flexibility, quest for novelty and meaning, and our constant need to learn result in an animal that is never complete. As the Reverend Jesse Jackson once said, "God's not finished with me yet"; and that's true not only of politicians and preachers, but of us all. What is unique about *Homo sapiens* is that we are in a constant state of development. In a real sense, humans, like Peter Pan, never fully grow up.

I write this being fully aware that aspects of human cognitive functioning decline in adulthood and old age. Starting in our 30s, the speed with which we process information begins to slow down, imperceptibly at first, but it's quite noticeable by the time we reach our 60s or 70s. So do other "elementary cognitive abilities," such as how many ideas we can keep in mind at once (termed *working memory*) and our ability to inhibit, or keep out of working memory, unwanted information. Brain cells also die as we age. Despite these losses, the healthy adult brain continues to develop. The brain retains much of its earlier plasticity; new synaptic connections develop well into old age. The

223

losses in speed of processing and working memory are often compensated by increases in vocabulary, world knowledge, and "wisdom." Old brains and old people can learn, and they often display a remarkable proficiency at solving real-world (as opposed to laboratory) problems.[1] Yes, we may become a bit set in our ways as we get older, but it's not inevitable. Human adults, more than any other adult animal, have the capacity to learn and change. What we make of that youthful capacity depends to a large extent on the degree to which we remain "young at heart."

Adult immaturity is perhaps most readily seen in play. Humans are not the only animals that play in adulthood, but we are more involved in play throughout our lives than any other species. Play in adulthood (and even in childhood, I'd venture) goes beyond the conventional categories of physical, object, and symbolic play. It is also expressed in a sense of humor, in laughter, and in discovery learning. Play in adulthood is not isolated from work or social relationships, so it might never seem "purposeless." But then again, it never really was purposeless, even in childhood.

Play may be the work of children, but it is clearly optional for adults. Adults are obligated to work in one way or another – to gain resources in order to feed, clothe, protect, and house themselves and their families. This can all be done without the need to play. In fact, play may interfere with the successful accomplishment of work (and get one fired if the boss catches you). But all modern cultures expect their adult members to play. How much we play varies with how burdensome achieving the essentials of life is.

In developed countries today, adult play has been elevated to an art form. We look for ways to spend our leisure time and for opportunities for "recreation." (Break the word down – re-creation, essentially reinventing ourselves through play.) Exercise play, from golf, bicycling, and dancing to tennis, softball, and rock climbing, consume much of adults' leisure time. We tell ourselves we do it for the health benefits associated with the exercise, and I'm sure that's true; but we could just as easily walk or run or go to the gym if staying fit is all there was to it (which many people do). However, we enjoy the social interaction, the competition, or challenges that exercise play, and especially games, provide us. We read for fun, travel to have new experiences, and seek out entertainment or interactions that make us smile and laugh.

Play extends into old age. Exercise play is common among older adults. Golf and tennis communities for "active seniors" are quite common. For instance, my father took up golf at the age of 68 and continues to play 13 years later. The short course at my parents' winter condo at Leisureville in Pompano Beach, Florida is always busy, with residents (55 and older) and their occasional guests. I recall playing one day with my father and a man in his late 80s, who walked the course pulling an oxygen tank. (He beat me.) Softball, and even basketball, leagues are not uncommon for the older crowd. As a south Florida resident, I am perhaps more attuned to the "active senior lifestyle" than most people, but hiking, canoeing, bicycling, and dancing are common activities among the retired set across the country and the world.

More sedentary play is also common among older adults, usually in the company of others. Playing cards is one frequent form of social play. At other times, senior citizens mingle at the community club house or a local restaurant to visit and "play" with one another. Michael Cheang of the Center of Aging at the John A. Burns School of Medicine in Honolulu spent nine months observing a group of 26 senior citizens, half men and half women, as they met each morning at a fast food restaurant. The group formed slowly, but these older adults came to the restaurant to socialize, play, and laugh. Cheang writes that "They were there to have fun, and not to seek social support ... Stated simply, these older adults came to the restaurant to 'play' and, for the most part, they came to the restaurant to be with their playmates."[2] These older adults, who ranged in age from 57 to 83 (average age, 73), related stories both about recent events and from "the old days," told jokes, commented on other people in the restaurant, and laughed a lot. It, of course, was a social group, but most of these people had social support outside of the restaurant, specifically spouses and other family members. This social group was for play, and the people were happier (and I'd bet healthier) because of it. George Vaillant, Director of the Harvard Study of Adult Development, stated that one significant finding of his research was the importance of learning to play and create after retirement.[3]

Adult play has a more serious, or productive, side as well. Although most folks today distinguish between work and play, some of us are fortunate to have work that we play at. I'm not talking about professional athletes (although it is certainly true for them), but for more mundane jobs such as teachers, scientists, artists, computer programmers, writers, actors, and anyone who "plays" with ideas, objects, or other people in the course of their daily duties. There is a pleasure one gets from manipulating words, ideas, mathematical symbols, parts of a car engine, colors on a canvas, or musical notes. People lucky enough to be in these jobs get paid to "play." Granted, it is often a special type of play that more sane people may wisely avoid. I never got a lot of pleasure from my *Erector Set* as a child, so I can't imagine what fun it would be to design a bridge, car, or building, either on paper, a computer, or in real life. But I do know what it feels like to have a germ of an idea and convert it into a practical experiment; to "play" with research data ("make the data confess," as a colleague of mine says); to give a lecture on a topic I'm excited about; or to craft a sentence I think really rocks! (It often sinks like a stone the following day, but that's what editing is for.) The cave painters of 30,000 years ago were not only talented artists and conveyers of symbolic meaning, but players. As children we playfully fancy the world as it might be, no holds barred. We need to be a bit more practical as adults, to be in touch with our abilities and shortcomings. But adult *Homo juvenalis* retain some of the fantasy play they practiced as children and with it create realities that our ancestors could not have imagined.

Any scientist, even a psychologist, who can cite the 20th century's most heralded thinker jumps at the self-serving chance to do so. So let me conclude this book with a quote from Albert Einstein, who seemed to realize the value of remaining young at heart (and mind):

> I sometimes ask myself how it came about that I was the one to develop the theory of relativity. The reason, I think, is that a normal adult never stops to think about problems of space and time. These are things which he has thought of as a child. But my intellectual development was retarded, as a result of which I began to wonder about space and time only when I had already grown up. Naturally, I could go deeper into the problem than a child with normal abilities.[4]

Notes

Chapter 1

1 Palm Beach Post, "Close-up study finds family life child-oriented, frantic," 20 March 2005 (Associated Press); www.celf.ucla.edu
2 Bjorklund, 1997; Bjorklund & Green, 1992
3 deferred adaptations, Hernández Blasi & Bjorklund, 2003
4 See Geary, 1998; Bjorklund & Pellegrini, 2002
5 Maestripieri & Pelka, 2002
6 Blakemore, 1990
7 See Maestripieri & Roney, 2006
8 See Suomi, 1978; Fairbanks, 1990; Maestripieri & Roney, 2006
9 Caspi et al., 2002
10 industrial pollutants, Blanck et al., 2000; effects of father absence, Ellis, 2004
11 Berenbaum & Hines, 1992; Berenbaum & Snyder, 1995
12 parental investment theory, Trivers, 1972; applied to humans, Buss & Schmidt, 1993; Bjorklund & Shackelford, 1999
13 ontogenetic adaptations, Oppenheim, 1981; Bjorklund, 1997
14 Gelfand & Drew, 2003
15 Meltzoff & Moore, 1977, 1985; neonatal imitation declines, Jacobson, 1979
16 "Alternate views of neonatal imitation," Bjorklund, 1987; Jacobson, 1979; Legerstee, 1991; Heimann, 1989
17 See Gottlieb (1992), Gould (1977), and Schwartz (1999) for discussion of preDarwinian ideas about evolution
18 B. R. Grant & Grant, 1989, 1993; P. R. Grant & Grant, 2002, 2006
19 Quotes from Huxley and Galton can be found in Shipman (1994); quote from Dobzhansky, 1973

Chapter 2

1 As translated from the German, cited in Gould, 1977, p. 361
2 The Chimpanzee Sequencing and Analysis Consortium, 2005
3 Diamond, 1992
4 For descriptions of human evolution see Eccles, 1989; Johanson & Edgar, 1996; Olson, 2002; Stringer & Andrews, 2005; Tattersal, 1998
5 See, for example, Balter, 2001; Galik et al., 2004
6 Goren-Inbar et al., 2004; Haile-Selassie, Suwa, & White, 2004
7 Swisher et al., 1996
8 "what was so intriguing about *H. floresiensis* is that the fossils date back to just 12,000 years ago," Morwood et al., 2005; Brown et al., 2004; Wong, 2005; "Recent analysis of the endocast," Falk et al., 2005
9 Lieberman, 2005
10 McDougall, Brown, & Fleagle, 2005
11 Krings et al., 1997
12 See Culotta, 2005; Krings et al., 1997; Serre et al., 2004
13 Goodall, 1986; Wrangham & Peterson, 1996
14 Potts, 1998
15 Nesse & Williams, 1994
16 For fuller discussion of the lifestyle of our ancestors and their consequences for interpreting modern development, see Bjorklund & Pellegrini, 2002
17 Poirier & Smith, 1974
18 Bogin, 1997, 1999, 2003
19 tool use in chimpanzees, Goodall, 1986; McGrew, 1992; chimpanzee teaching, Boesch, 1991; sex differences in chimpanzee attention; Lonsdorf, Eberly, & Pusey, 2004
20 Spear, 2000
21 Bullough, 1981; Tanner, 1981; earlier estimates by Tanner, 1962 of menarche occurring between 16 and 16.5 years for women in the mid-19th century are widely known, but apparently based on uncertain data, see Bullough, 1981
22 "earlier onset of puberty in U.S.," Herman-Giddens et al., 1997; "possible factors associated with early onset," Herman-Giddens et al., 1997; Blanck et al., 2000; Windham et al., 2004; Ellis, 2004
23 Bogin, 2003
24 Antón & Leigh, 2003; Bermúdez de Castro et al., 2003
25 Akazawa et al., 1995; Zollikofer et al., 1995; Stringer, Dean, & Martin, 1990; but see Trinkaus & Tompkins, 1990 for an alternative interpretation
26 Mithen, 1996
27 See Gould, 1977
28 de Beer, 1958; Garstang, 1922; Bolk, 1926

29 Bolk, 1926, p. 470
30 See Gould, 1977; Hattori, 1998; Montagu, 1989; Schwartz, 1999; Wesson, 1991. However, few would argue that neoteny, or paedomorphosis in general, is an adequate description of human evolution. Rather, retarded development was one of many influences on the evolution of human form, see McKinney & McNamara, 1991; Shea, 1989
31 See Gottlieb, 1992; Gould, 1977; Mayr, 1982 for historical reviews
32 de Beer, 1958
33 Wesson, 1991, p. 205
34 Gould, 1977, p. 375
35 Martin et al., 1974; Sherrod et al., 1984
36 Haldane, 1932, p. 150
37 Antón & Leigh, 2003
38 See Gould, 1977; Montagu, 1989
39 See Allman, 1999; Crook, 1980; Gould, 1977; Hattori, 1998; Wesson 1991
40 Eccles, 1989; Deacon, 1997
41 Finlay & Darlington, 1995; Finlay, Darlington, & Nicastro, 2001
42 "We continue the pace of brain development begun prenatally through our second year of postnatal life," Gould, 1977; brain weight at different ages, Tanner, 1978
43 See Gould, 1977
44 Trevathan, 1987
45 See Langer, 2000; Parker & McKinney, 1999
46 See Bolk, 1926; Montagu, 1962, 1989

Chapter 3

1   Age of first childbirth in traditional and ancestors: Hill & Hurtado, 1996; Kaplan et al., 2000
2   Gies & Gies, 1987
3   Ambrose, 1998; Olson, 2002
4   Bonner, 1988
5   See, for example, Alexander, 1989; Bjorklund & Harnishfeger, 1995; Bjorklund, Cormier, & Rosenberg, 2005; Byrne & Whiten, 1988; Crook, 1980; Dunbar, 1995; Geary & Flinn, 2001; Humphrey, 1976
6   Bjorklund & Bering, 2003; Bjorklund, Cormier, & Rosenberg, 2005; Dunbar, 1995
7   Joffe, 1997
8   Kaplan et al., 2000
9   Humphrey, 1976
10 Alexander, 1989
11 "Belle, was shown the source of some hidden food," Menzel, 1974; "male chimps would sometimes suppress their distinctive cry," Goodall,

1986; "male chimpanzees that serve to grab and maintain social status," de Waal, 1982; for other examples of deception in monkeys and apes see Whiten & Byrne, 1988

12 Burghardt, 2005

13 Hrdy, 1986, p. 152

14 Wesson, 1991

15 Cited in Gould, 1977, p. 403

16 "A single neuron can have as many as 10,000 synapses," Huttenlocher, 2002; "In fact, by the end of the first year, the infant brain has nearly twice as many synapses as the adult brain," Huttenlocher, 2002

17 Gould et al., 1999; Eriksson et al., 1998

18 Greenough et al., 1987

19 Crabtree & Riesen, 1979; Timney, Mitchell, & Cynader, 1980

20 Sur, Pallas, & Roe, 1990

21 Hebb, 1949; Hymovitch, 1952; Turner & Greenough, 1985; see Geary, 2005 for a review

22 Giedd et al., 1999

23 "In other research Beatriz Luna and her colleagues," Luna et al., 2001; "teenagers were less apt to activate the frontal cortex," Baird et al., 1999; "For example, the excitatory neurotransmitter GABA," Spear, 2000

24 See Beckman, 2004

25 Flynn effect, Flynn, 1987, 1998, 1999; "The effects seem to be larger for people on the low end of the IQ range," Teasdale & Owen, 1989, 2000; "there is some evidence that the effect is slowing down or has stopped in recent decades," Lynn & Hampson, 1986; Teasdale & Owen, 2000

26 Flynn, 1998, 1999

27 Greenfield, 1998

28 Demetriou et al., 2005

29 For discussion of the Flynn effect see Neisser, 1998

30 Harlow, Dodsworth, & Harlow, 1965; Harlow & Harlow, 1962; Harlow & Zimmerman, 1959

31 "The negative effects of such child rearing were apparent by 3 or 4 months of age, and became progressively worse over infancy," Goldfarb, 1945, 1947; Spitz, 1945; "infants as feeling 'something like sawdust dolls; they moved, they bent easily at the proper joints, but they felt stiff or wooden'," Provence & Lipton, 1962, p. 56; "Wayne Dennis followed the outcomes of children reared in the Crèche," Denis, 1973

32 Suomi & Harlow, 1972

33 Provence & Lipton, 1962, p. 145

34 Skeels, 1966; Skeels & Dye, 1939

35 Clark & Hanise, 1982; see also Winik, Meyer, & Harris, 1975

36 O'Connor et al., 2000; see also Juffer & IJzendoorn, 2005 and Rutter et al., 1998

37 Feuerbach, 1833; see http://www.feralchildren.com/en/pager.php?df =feuerbach1833 for an English translation of Feuerbach's book. The story of Kasper Hauser is documented in the interesting film by Werner Herzog, *The Enigma of Kasper Hauser*

38 Curtiss, 1977

39 McCall, 1981, p. 5

40 Greene, 1996

41 See, for example, Baldwin, 1902; Bateson, 1988; Bjorklund, 2006; Bjorklund, Grotuss, & Csinady, in press; Gottlieb, 1992; Harper, 2005; West-Eberhard, 2003

42 See Bjorklund & Rosenberg, 2005 for review of theory and data

Chapter 4

1 Turkewitz & Kenny, 1982

2 Turkewitz & Kenny, 1982; "The various sensory systems develop in a constant order," Gottlieb, 1971; "neural Darwinism," Edelman, 1987

3 Lorenz, 1937

4 See Gottlieb, 1997

5 Lickliter, 1990

6 McBride & Lickliter, 1994; Lickliter & Hellewell, 1992; Radell & Gottlieb, 1992; Kenny & Turkewitz, 1986

7 Spear, 1984, p. 335

8 Lickliter, 2000; Als, 1995, pp. 451, 462

9 Borke, 1975; Flavell et al., 1981

10 Lord, 1980; for other examples, see Kail & Levine, 1976; Nadelman, 1974; Pratkanis & Greenwald, 1985

11 Mood, 1979

12 Foley & Ratner, 1998; Foley, Ratner, & Passalacqua, 1993; Ratner, Foley, & Gimbert, 2002

13 Piaget, 1955

14 Bakeman & Brownlee, 1980; these play categories were modified from those originally developed by Parten, 1932

15 Vygotsky, 1962: Vygotsky's work was not translated from Russian until nearly 30 years after his death

16 See Berk, 1992; Winsler, 2003

17 Elkind, 1967; Elkind & Bowen, 1979; Gray & Hudson, 1984; see also Arnett, 1992; Inhelder & Piaget, 1958

18 Crook, 1980

19 See Weisfeld, 1999

20 Bickerton, 1990

21 Senghas, Kita, & Ozyürek, 2004; Senghas & Coppola, 2001

22 Thomas, 1993

23 Locke & Bogin, 2006

24   Newport, 1990, p. 24
25   Newport, 1991; Elman, 1994; Kersten & Earles, 2001
26   Bruner, 1983; Fernald, 1992; Bjorklund & Schwartz, 1996
27   "adults consistently view children with immature facial features as cuter, more in need of 'parental' caregiving and protection," Alley, 1981, 1983a, 1983b; Zebrowitz, Kendall-Tackett, & Fafel, 1991; "This preference for 'babyness' is first seen in girls between the ages of 12 and 14 years," Fullard & Reiling, 1976; "There is a caveat to this effect, however," Zebrowitz et al., 1991
28   Guthrie (1993) describes at length adults' tendencies to attribute life characteristics to living things (animism) and human characteristics to nonhuman things (anthropomorphism)
29   Rosenberg, Hernández Blasi, Shin, & Bjorklund, 2005

Chapter 5

1   See, for example, Mazzoni & Nelson, 1998; Schneider & Lockl, 2002
2   Bjorklund & Bjorklund, 1985; Bjorklund & Zeman, 1982, 1983
3   See Bjorklund, 2005; Flavell, 1978; Schneider, 1985
4   Bandura, 1989, 1997
5   Yussen & Levy, 1975
6   "children's achievement motivation," Stipek, 1984; Stipek & MacIver, 1989; "When children are given very explicit and salient feedback," see Stipek & Daniels, 1988
7   Stipek, Recchia, & McClintic, 1992
8   Stipek, 1981, 1984; Stipek & Hoffman, 1980; Stipek, Roberts, & Sanborn, 1984; see also Spinath & Spinath, 2005
9   Rozenbilt & Keil, 2002
10   Mills & Keil, 2004
11   Bjorklund, Gaultney, & Green, 1993
12   Lockhart, Chang, & Tyler, 2002
13   Seligman, 1995
14   "Young children have the basic competencies," see Bjorklund, 2005; "There is some suggestion that using an advanced strategy is so mentally effortful," see Bjorklund, Muir-Broaddus, & Schneider, 1990
15   "Young children seem to enjoy performing a task for its own sake," Stipek, 1984; Siegler, 1996; "Deborah Stipek suggested such latitude allows preschool children," Stipek et al., 1992, pp. 78–79
16   "The message that most preschool children are likely to get," Stipek & MacIver, 1989; "A parallel finding," Dweck & Elliott, 1983; Harter & Pike, 1984
17   "Stipek has proposed an explanation of young children's overestimations based on Piaget's idea of 'wishful thinking'," Stipek, 1984; Piaget, 1930; "For example, Wolfgang, Schneider found," Schneider, 1998

18 See Hawley, 1999; Weisfeld, 1999; Weisfeld & Janisee, 2005
19 See Weisfled & Janisee, 2005 for a review
20 Boulton & Smith, 1990; Edelman & Omark, 1973; Humphreys & Smith, 1987; Omark & Edelman, 1975, 1976; Pickert & Wall, 1981
21 Bjorklund et al., 1993
22 "it is well established that bright young children (as measured by IQ scores) usually maintain their intellectual advantage in later childhood, for example," Honzik, MacFarlane, & Allen, 1948
23 "One robust and not too surprising finding," see Bjorklund, 2005; "Also, proficiency of strategy use," see Schneider, Körkel, & Weinert, 1987
24 "utilization deficiency," Miller, 1990; Miller & Seier, 1994; Bjorklund et al., 1997; "children were shown a series of boxes with doors on top," DeMarie-Dreblow & Miller, 1988; Miller et al., 1986; Miller et al., 1991
25 Bjorklund, Coyle, & Gaultney, 1992; Bjorklund, Schneider, Cassel, & Ashley, 1994; Coyle & Bjorklund, 1996
26 Wellman, 1988, p. 26
27 Shin & Bjorklund, 2005; Shin, Bjorklund, & Beck, in press
28 Plumert, 1995; Plumert & Schwebel, 1997; Schwebel & Plumert, 1999
29 "By 8 years of age, however, the relation between estimation ability and accident proneness was not significant": correlations between estimation accuracy and need for medical attention, in Plumert, 1995: 6 years, −.44, Experiment 1, −.48, Experiment 2; 8 years, .10, Experiment 1, −.02, Experiment 2; Plumert & Schwebel, 1997: 6-year-old boys, −.51; 6-year-old girls, .05; 8-year-old boys, −.01; 8-year-old girls, −.10
30 Plumert, Kearney, & Cremer, 2004
31 Schwebel & Plumert, 1999
32 Plumert, 1995, p. 875
33 Bandura, 1989, 1997
34 Stipek, 1984, p. 53
35 Seligman, 1998
36 Stipek et al., 1992

Chapter 6

1 Huizinga, 1950
2 Gosso et al., 2005, pp. 240, 241
3 See Pellegrini & Smith, 2005
4 Parten, 1932
5 Piaget, 1962; Smilansky, 1968; see Rubin, Fein, & Vandenberg, 1983; Pellegrini & Smith, 2005
6 See Bjorklund & Pellegrini, 2002 for children's play; see Fagen, 1981 for animal play

7   Fry, 2005
8   Harris, 1989, p. 256
9   Spinka, Newbury, & Bekoff, 2001
10 Connor & Serbin, 1977; see also Yan, Thomas, & Downing, 1998 and Bjorklund & Brown, 1998 for reviews and commentaries
11 Burghardt, 1984; Pellis et al., 1996; Pellegrini & Davis, 1993; Pellegrini, Huberty, & Jones, 1995
12 "Gosso and her colleagues believe that the benefits of skilled fighting likely declined in early human history," Gosso et al., 2005; "Others would disagree," see Geary, 1998; Keeley, 1996
13 Groos, 1901; Piaget, 1962; Vygotsky, 1978; Bruner, 1972
14 See Cairns, 1983
15 Hawley, 1999; Mazur, 2005; Savin-Williams, 1979
16 Gosso et al., 2005
17 Bock & Johnson, 2004
18 Lancy, 1996
19 Smith, 1982, p. 151
20 Cheyne & Rubin, 1983; Smith & Dutton, 1979; Sylva, 1977
21 Gredlein & Bjorklund, 2005
22 Geary, 1998, p. 238
23 sex differences in play; see Geary, 1998; Pellegrini & Bjorklund, 2004
24 See Pellegrini, Galda, et al., 1995; Pellegrini et al., 1998
25 See Smith, 2005 for summary of findings between the relationship of fantasy play and theory of mind
26 Gosso et al., 2005, p. 238
27 Gosso et al., 2005
28 Lumeng et al., 2006
29 Pellegrini et al., 2002
30 Bjorklund, Hubertz, & Reubens, 2004
31 Popper & Eccles, 1977, p. 446
32 Kawai, 1965; but see Tomasello and Call, 1997 for criticisms of this research
33 Piaget, 1972, p. 27
34 Green & Bavelier, 2003; Subrahmanyam & Greenfield, 1996; see also Subrahmanyam et al., 2000; improvements in mental rotation, McClurg & Chaillé, 1987
35 Harris, 1995

Chapter 7

1   Sigel, 1987, p. 145
2   OECD, 2004
3   Perie & Morn, 2005
4   Geary et al., 1996

5   OECD, 2004

6   See Berk, 2001; Bredekamp & Copple, 1997; Hirsh-Pasek & Golinkoff, 2003; Kagan & Ziegler, 1987

7   "that there is a positive relation between time spent in school and IQ," Ceci, 1991; "other research has shown that one year of schooling has a greater impact on IQ and certain areas of academic achievement than does one year of age," Bisanz, Morrison, & Dunn, 1995; Cahan & Cohen, 1989; Morrison, Griffith, & Frazier, 1996

8   quote from Vygotsky, 1978, p. 86; Rogoff, 1990; quote from Gauvin, 2001, p. 63

9   See Bruer, 1999

10   DeCasper & Fifer, 1980; see also Spence & Freeman, 1996

11   Kisilevsky et al., 2003

12   Mehler et al., 1988; see also Nazzi, Bertoncini, & Mehler, 1998

13   DeCasper & Spence, 1986

14   DeCasper et al., 1994

15   Logan, 1991

16   Lafuente et al., 1997; but see Huttenlocher, 2002, who claims that the study suffers from reporting biases on the part of the mothers

17   Huttenlocher, 2002, p. 214

18   "They can identify their mothers on the basis of smell by 10 days," Macfarlane, 1975; "and perhaps as soon on the basis of vision," Bushnell, Sai, & Mullin, 1989

19   Friedman, 1972; but this effect may be limited to only the neurologically most developed newborns

20   Bauer et al., 2000; Collie & Hayne, 1999

21   Rudy, Vogt, & Hyson, 1984; quote from Spear & Hyatt, 1993, p. 189

22   Harlow, 1959, p. 472

23   Papousek, 1977

24   Bredekamp & Copple, 1997; see also Elkind, 1987; Hirsh-Pasek & Golinkoff, 2003; Sigel, 1987

25   Piaget, 1977, cited in Rogoff, 1998, p. 38

26   See an evaluation of Piaget's theory in Bjorklund, 2005

27   www.naeyc.org/about/positions/dap4.asp, National Association for the Education of Young Children, Guidelines for decisions about developmentally appropriate practice: Developmentally Appropriate Practice in Early Childhood Programs Serving Children from Birth through Age 8

28   See Barnett, 1995

29   "Many early childhood educators and developmental psychologists thought the latter," see chapters in Kagan & Ziegler, 1987; "miseducation," Elkind, 1987

30   "differences favoring developmentally appropriate programs," Marcon, 1999; Stipek et al., 1998; "differences favoring directed-instructional

programs," Stipek et al., 1995; "no differences," Hirsh-Pasek, Hyson, & Rescorla, 1990; Schweinhart & Weikart, 1988; van Horn & Ramey, 2003

31   "no long-term effects," Hirsh-Pasek et al., 1990; "long-term effects for children who attended the developmentally appropriate preschools," Burts et al., 1993; Marcon, 1992

32   See van Horn et al., 2005 who cite methodological difficulties with many of the studies and claim that there is no evidence of superior outcomes for children attending developmentally appropriate programs

33   Burts et al., 1990, 1992; Hirsh-Pasek et al., 1990; Schweinhart & Weikart, 1988; Stipek et al., 1995, 1998

34   Stipek et al., 1995

35   Hirsh-Pasek et al., 1990, p. 42

36   Sigel, 1987, pp. 135

37   Goodman, 1992, p. 254

38   See Bjorklund & Bering, 2002; Geary, 1995, 2002b, in press

39   See Rogoff, 1990; Rogoff et al., 1993

40   Geary, 1995

41   Quotes from Crain, 2003, p. 199 and p. 6

42   See Pellegrini, 2005

43   Pellegrini & Davis, 1993; Pellegrini, Huberty, & Jones, 1995; see Pellegrini & Bjorklund, 1997 and Pellegrini, 2005 for reviews

44   Stevenson & Lee, 1990

45   Stipek, 2002, p. 14

Chapter 8

1   Bogin, 1999

2   de Mause, 1974; Hrdy, 1999

3   Katz, 1986

4   See Ariès, 1962; Borstelmann, 1983; Orme, 2001

5   http://www.unicef.org/crc/convention.htm

6   See Collins et al., 2000

7   Elkind, 1998, p. 15

8   Unless otherwise noted, data reported in this section come from *America's Children, Key National Indicator of Well-Being*, 2005

9   Narayan et al., 2003

10   Guttmacher Institute, *Teenagers' Sexual and Reproductive Health: Developed Countries*, http://www.agi-usa.org/pubs/fb_teens.html

11   Weinstock, Berman, & Cates, 2004

12   "With respect to mental health, parents reported that about 5% of children between the ages of 4 and 17 years," *America's Children, Key National Indicator of Well-Being*, 2005; "Robert Roberts and his col-

leagues conducted a meta-analysis," Roberts, Attkisson, & Rosenblatt, 1998

13 "Between 1987 and 1996, the rate at which these drugs were prescribed to youth tripled, with most of the increase occurring after 1991," Zito et al., 2003; "Since then, the rates have continued to climb, not just in the U.S. but in all developed countries," Wong et al., 2004; "Rates of medication for preschoolers," ages 2 to 4 years. Zito et al., 2000

14 Stevenson, Chen, & Lee, 1993; "A more recent international comparison," OECD, 2004

15 Stevenson et al., 1993, p. 57

16 See Luthar, 2003; Luthar & Latendresse, 2005; Luthar & Sexton, 2004

17 Luthar & Latendresse, 2005, p. 52

Epilogue

1 See B. Bjorklund & Bee, 2007
2 Cheang, 2002, p. 314
3 Vaillant, 2002
4 From Clark, 1971, p. 10

References

Akazawa, T., Muhesen, S., Dodo, Y., Kondo, O., & Mizouguchi, Y. (1995). Neanderthal infant burial. *Nature, 377*, 585–586.

Alexander, R. D. (1989). Evolution of the human psyche. In P. Mellers & C. Stringer (Eds.), *The human revolution: Behavioural and biological perspectives on the origins of modern humans* (pp. 455–513). Princeton, NJ: Princeton University Press.

Alley, T. R. (1981). Head shape and the perception of cuteness. *Developmental Psychology, 17*, 650–654.

Alley, T. R. (1983a). Growth-produced changes in body shape and size as determinants of perceived age and adult caregiving. *Child Development, 54*, 241–248.

Alley, T. R. (1983b). Infantile head shape as an elicitor of adult protection. *Merrill-Palmer Quarterly, 29*, 411–427.

Allman, J. M. (1999). *Evolving brains.* New York: Scientific American Library.

Als, H. (1995). The preterm infant: A model for the study of fetal brain expectation. In J-P. Lecanuet, W. P. Fifer, N. A. Krasnegor, & W. P. Smotherman (Eds.). *Fetal development: A psychobiological perspective* (pp. 439–471). Hillsdale, NJ: Erlbaum.

Ambrose, S. H. (1998). Late Pleistocene human population bottlenecks, volcanic winter, and differentiation of modern humans. *Journal of Human Evolution, 35*, 115–118.

America's Children, Key National Indicator of Well-Being (2005). Federal Interagency Forum on Child and Family Statistics. Washington, DC: US Government.

Anderson, C. A., & Bushman, B. J. (2001). Effects of violent video games on aggressive behavior, aggressive cognition, aggressive affects, physiological arousal, and prosocial behavior: A meta-analytic review of the scientific literature. *Psychological Science, 12*, 353–359.

Antón, S. C., & Leigh, S. R. (2003). Growth and life history in Homo erectus. In J. L. Thompson, G. E. Krovitz, & A. J. Nelson (Eds.), *Patterns of growth and development in the genus* Homo (pp. 219–245). Cambridge, UK: Cambridge University Press.

Ariès, P. (1962). *Centuries of childhood: A social history of family life.* New York: Knopf.

Arnett, J. (1992). Reckless behavior in adolescence: A developmental perspective. *Developmental Review, 12,* 339–373.

Asfaw, B., White, T., Lovejoy, O., Latimer, B., Simpson, S., & Suwa, G. (1999). *Australopithecus garhi*: A new species of early hominid from Ethiopia. *Science, 284* (April 23), 629–635.

Baird, A. A., et al. (1999). Functional magnetic resonance imaging of facial affect recognition in children and adolescents. *Journal of the American Academy of Child & Adolescent Psychiatry, 38,* 195–199.

Bakeman, R., & Brownlee, J. R. (1980). The strategic use of parallel play: A sequential analysis. *Child Development, 51,* 873–878.

Baker, R. R., & Bellis, M. A. (1995). *Human sperm competition.* London: Chapman & Hall.

Baldwin, J. M. (1902). *Development and evolution.* New York: Macmillan.

Balter, M. (2001). Scientists spar over claims of earliest human ancestor. *Science, 291* (23 February), 1460–1461.

Bandura, A. (1989). Regulation of cognitive processes through perceived self-efficacy. *Developmental Psychology, 25,* 729–735.

Bandura, A. (1997). *Self-efficacy: The exercise of control.* New York: Freeman.

Barnett, W. S. (1995). Long-term effects of early childhood programs on cognitive and school outcomes. *The Future of Children, 5* (No. 3, Winter), 25–50.

Bateson, P. P. G. (1988). The active role of behaviour in evolution. In M.-W. Ho & S. Fox (Eds.), *Process and metaphors in evolution* (pp. 191–207). Chichester, UK: Wiley.

Bauer, P. J., Wenner, J. A., Dropik, P. L., & Wewerka, S. S. (2000). Parameters of remembering and forgetting in the transition from infancy to early childhood. *Monographs of the Society for Research in Child Development, 65* (Serial No. 263).

Beckman, M. (2004). Crime, culpability, and the adolescent brain. *Science, 305,* 596–599.

Berenbaum, S. A., & Hines, M. (1992). Early androgens are related to childhood sex-typed toy preferences. *Psychological Science, 3,* 203–206.

Berenbaum, S. A., & Snyder, E. (1995). Early hormonal influences on childhood sex-types activity and playmate preferences: Implications for the development of sexual orientation. *Developmental Psychology, 31,* 31–42.

Berk, L. E. (1992). Children's private speech: An overview of theory and the status of research. In R. M. Diaz & L. E. Berk (Eds.), *Private speech: From social interaction to self-regulation* (pp. 17–53). Hillsdale, NJ: Erlbaum.

240

Berk, L. E. (2001). *Awakening children's minds: How parents and teachers can make a difference*. New York: Oxford University Press.

Bermúdez, de Castro, J. M., Ramírez Rozzi, F., Martinón-Torres, M., Sarmientoérez, S., & Rosas, A. (2003). Patterns of dental development in Lower and Middle Pleistocene hominins from Atapuerca (Spain). In J. L. Thompson, G. E. Krovitz, & A. J. Nelson (Eds.), *Patterns of growth and development in the genus* Homo (pp. 246–270). Cambridge, UK: Cambridge University Press.

Bering, J. M., Bjorklund, D. F., & Ragan, P. (2000). Deferred imitation of object-related actions in human-reared juvenile chimpanzees and orangutans. *Developmental Psychobiology, 36,* 218–232.

Bickerton, D. (1990). *Language and species.* Chicago: University of Chicago Press.

Bisanz, J., Morrison, F. J., & Dunn, M. (1995). Effects of age and schooling on the acquisition of elementary quantitative skills. *Developmental Psychology, 31,* 221–235.

Bjorklund, B. R., & Bee, H. L. (2007). *The journey of adulthood* (6th edn). Upper Saddle River, NJ: Prentice Hall.

Bjorklund, B. R., & Bjorklund, D. F. (1990). *Parents' book of discipline.* New York: Ballantine.

Bjorklund, D. F. (1987). A note on neonatal imitation. *Developmental Review, 7,* 86–92.

Bjorklund, D. F. (1997). The role of immaturity in human development. *Psychological Bulletin, 122,* 153–169.

Bjorklund, D. F. (2005). *Children's thinking: Cognitive development and individual differences* (4th edn). Belmont, CA: Wadsworth.

Bjorklund, D. F. (2006). Mother knows best: Epigenetic inheritance, maternal effects, and the evolution of human intelligence. *Developmental Review, 26,* 213–242.

Bjorklund, D. F., & Bering, J. M. (2002). The evolved child: Applying evolutionary developmental psychology to modern schooling. *Learning and Individual Differences, 12,* 1–27.

Bjorklund, D. F., & Bering, J. M. (2003). Big brains, slow development, and social complexity: The developmental and evolutionary origins of social cognition. In M. Brüne, H. Ribbert, & W. Schiefenhövel (Eds.). *The social brain: Evolutionary aspects of development and pathology* (pp. 133–151). Wiley: New York.

Bjorklund, D. F., & Bjorklund, B. R. (1985). Organization versus item effects of an elaborated knowledge base on children's memory. *Developmental Psychology, 21,* 1120–1131.

Bjorklund, D. F., & Brown, R. D. (1998). Physical play and cognitive development: Integrating activity, cognition, and education. *Child Development, 69,* 604–606.

Bjorklund, D. F., Cormier, C., & Rosenberg, J. S. (2005). The evolution of theory of mind: Big brains, social complexity, and inhibition. In W.

Schneider, R. Schumann-Hengsteler, & B. Sodian (Eds.), *Young children's cognitive development: Interrelationships among executive functioning, working memory, verbal ability and theory of mind* (pp. 147–174). Mahwah, NJ: Erlbaum.

Bjorklund, D. F., Coyle, T. R., & Gaultney, J. F. (1992). Developmental differences in the acquisition and maintenance of an organizational strategy: Evidence for the utilization deficiency hypothesis. *Journal of Experimental Child Psychology, 54,* 434–448.

Bjorklund, D. F., Gaultney, J. F., & Green, B. L. (1993). "I watch, therefore I can do": The development of meta-imitation over the preschool years and the advantage of optimism in one's imitative skills (pp. 79–102). In R. Pasnak & M. L. Howe (Eds.), *Emerging themes in cognitive development.* Vol. 1. New York: Springer-Verlag.

Bjorklund, D. F., & Green, B. L. (1992). The adaptive nature of cognitive immaturity. *American Psychologist, 47,* 46–54.

Bjorklund, D. F., Grotuss, J., & Csinady, A. (in press). Maternal effects, social cognitive development, and the evolution of human intelligence. In D. Maestripieri (Ed.), *Maternal effects in mammals.* Chicago: Chicago University Press.

Bjorklund, D. F., & Harnishfeger, K. K. (1995). The role of inhibition mechanisms in the evolution of human cognition and behavior. In F. N. Dempster & C. J. Brainerd (Eds.), *New perspectives on interference and inhibition in cognition* (pp. 141–173). New York: Academic Press.

Bjorklund, D. F., Hubertz, M. J., & Reubens, A. C. (2004). Young children's arithmetic strategies in social context: How parents contribute to children's strategy development while playing games. *International Journal of Behavioral Development, 28,* 347–357.

Bjorklund, D. F., Miller, P. H., Coyle, T. R., & Slawinski, J. L. (1997). Instructing children to use memory strategies: Evidence of utilization deficiencies in memory training studies. *Developmental Review, 17,* 411–442.

Bjorklund, D. F., Muir-Broaddus, J. E., & Schneider, W. (1990). The role of knowledge in the development of children's strategies. In D. F. Bjorklund (Ed.), *Children's strategies: Contemporary views of cognitive development* (pp. 93–128). Hillsdale, NJ: Erlbaum.

Bjorklund, D. F., & Pellegrini, A. D. (2002). *The origins of human nature: Evolutionary developmental psychology.* Washington, DC: American Psychological Association.

Bjorklund, D. F., & Rosenberg, J. S. (2005). The role of developmental plasticity in the evolution of human cognition. In B. J. Ellis & D. F. Bjorklund (Eds.), *Origins of the social mind: Evolutionary psychology and child development* (pp. 45–75). New York: Guilford.

Bjorklund, D. F., Schneider, W., Cassel, W. S., & Ashley, E. (1994). Training and extension of a memory strategy as a function of knowledge base and IQ: Evidence for utilization deficiencies in the acquisition of an organizational strategy. *Child Development, 65,* 951–965.

Bjorklund, D. F., & Schwartz, R. (1996). The adaptive nature of developmental immaturity: Implications for language acquisition and language disabilities. In M. Smith & J. Damico (Eds.), *Childhood language disorders* (pp. 17–40). New York: Thieme Medical Publishers.

Bjorklund, D. F., & Shackelford, T. K. (1999). Differences in parental investment contribute to important differences between men and women. *Current Directions in Psychological Science, 8*, 86–89.

Bjorklund, D. F., & Zeman, B. R. (1982). Children's organization and metamemory awareness in their recall of familiar information. *Child Development, 53*, 799–810.

Bjorklund, D. F., & Zeman, B. R. (1983). The development of organizational strategies in children's recall of familiar information: Using social organization to recall the names of classmates. *International Journal of Behavioral Development, 6*, 341–353.

Blakemore, J. E. O. (1990). Children's nurturant interactions with their siblings: An exploration of gender differences and maternal socialization. *Sex Roles, 22*, 43–57.

Blanck, H. M., Marcus, M., Tolbert, P. E., Rubin, C., Henderson, A. K., Hertzberg, V. S., Zhang, R. H., & Cameron, L. (2000). Age at menarche and Tanner stage in girls exposed *in utero* and postnatally to polybrominated biphenyl. *Epidemiology, 11*, 641–647.

Bock, J., & Johnson, S. E. (2004). Play and subsistence ecology among the Okavango Delta Peoples of Botswana. *Human Nature, 15*, 63–81.

Boesch, C. (1991). Teaching among wild chimpanzees. *Animal Behavior, 41*, 530–532.

Bogin, B. (1997). Evolutionary hypotheses for human childhood. *Yearbook of Physical Anthropology, 40*, 63–89.

Bogin, B. (1999). *Patterns of human growth* (2nd edn). Cambridge, UK: Cambridge University Press.

Bogin, B. (2003). The human pattern of growth and development in paleontological perspective. In J. L. Thompson, G. E. Krovitz, & A. J. Nelson (Eds.), *Patterns of growth and development in the genus* Homo (pp. 15–44). Cambridge, UK: Cambridge University Press.

Bolk, L. (1926). On the problem of anthropogenesis. *Proc. Section Sciences Kon. Akad. Wetens. Amsterdam, 29*, 465–475.

Bonner, J. T. (1988). *The evolution of complexity by means of natural selection.* Princeton, NJ: Princeton University Press.

Borke, H. (1975). Piaget's mountains revisited: Changes in the egocentric landscape. *Developmental Psychology, 11*, 240–243.

Boulton, M. J., & Smith, P. K. (1990). Affective bias in children's perceptions of dominance relations. *Child Development, 61*, 221–229.

Bredekamp, S., & Copple, C. (Eds.). (1997). *Developmentally appropriate practice in early childhood programs* (rev. edn). Washington, DC: National Association for the Educational of Young Children.

243

Brown, P. et al. (2004). A new small-bodied hominin from the Late Pleistocene of Flores, Indonesia. *Nature, 431,* 1055–1061.

Bruer, J. T. (1999). *The myth of the first three years: A new understanding of early brain development and lifelong learning.* New York: Free Press.

Bruner, J. S. (1972). The nature and uses of immaturity. *American Psychologist, 27,* 687–708.

Bruner, J. S. (1983). *Child's talk: Learning to use language.* New York: Norton.

Bullough, V. L. (1981). Age at menarche: A misunderstanding. *Science, 213,* 356–366.

Burghardt, G. (1984). On the origins of play. In P. K. Smith (Ed.), *Play in animals and humans* (pp. 5–42). Oxford: Blackwell.

Burghardt, G. (2005). *The genesis of animal play.* Cambridge, MA: MIT Press.

Burts, D. C., Hart, C. H., Charlesworth, R., DeWolf, D. M., Ray, J., Manuel, K., & Fleege, P. O. (1993). Developmental appropriateness of kindergarten programs and academic outcomes in first grade. *Journal of Research in Childhood Education, 8,* 23–31.

Burts, D. C., Hart, C. H., Charlesworth, R., Fleege, P. O., Mosley, J., & Thomasson, R. H. (1992). Observed activities and stress behaviors of children in developmentally appropriate and inappropriate kindergarten classrooms. *Early Childhood Research Quarterly, 7,* 297–318.

Burts, D. C., Hart, C. H., & Kirk, L. (1990). A comparison of frequencies of stress behaviors observed in kindergarten children in classrooms with developmentally appropriate versus developmentally inappropriate instructional practices. *Early Childhood Research Quarterly, 5,* 407–423.

Bushnell, I. W. R., Sai, F., & Mullin, J. T. (1989). Neonatal recognition of the mother's face. *British Journal of Developmental Psychology, 7,* 3–15.

Buss, D. M., & Schmidt, D. P. (1993). Sexual strategies theory: An evolutionary perspective on human mating. *Psychological Review, 100,* 204–232.

Byrne, R., & Whiten, A. (Eds.). (1988). *Machiavellian intelligence: Social expertise and the evolution of intellect in monkeys, apes, and humans.* Oxford: Clarendon.

Cahan, S., & Cohen, N. (1989). Age versus schooling effects on intelligence development. *Child Development, 60,* 1239–1249.

Cairns, R. B. (1983). The emergence of developmental psychology. In W. Kessen (Ed.), *History, theory, and methods* (pp. 41–102), Vol. 1 of P. H. Mussen (Gen. Ed.), *Handbook of child psychology* (4th edn). New York: Wiley.

Caspi, A., McClay, J., Moffitt, T. E., Mill, J., Martin, J., Craig, I. W., Taylor, A., & Poulton, R. (2002). Role of genotype in the cycle of violence in maltreated children. *Science, 297* (2 August), 851–854.

Ceci, S. J. (1991). How much does schooling influence general intelligence and its cognitive components? A reassessment of the evidence. *Developmental Psychology*, *27*, 703–722.

Cheang, M. (2002). Old adults' frequent visits to a fast-food restaurant: Non-obligatory social interaction and the significance of play in a "third place." *Journal of Aging Studies*, *16*, 303–321.

Cheyne, J. A., & Rubin, K. H. (1983). Playful precursors of problem solving in preschoolers. *Developmental Psychology*, *19*, 577–584.

The Chimpanzee Sequencing and Analysis Consortium. (2005). Initial sequence of the chimpanzee genome and comparison with human genome. *Nature*, *437* (1 September), 69–88.

Clark, E. A., & Hanisee, J. (1982). Intellectual and adaptive performance of Asian children in adoptive American settings. *Developmental Psychology*, *18*, 595–599.

Clark, R. W. (1971). *Einstein: The life and times*. New York: The World Publishing Co.

Collie, R., & Hayne, R. (1999). Deferred imitation by 6- and 9-month-old infants: More evidence for declarative memory. *Developmental Psychobiology*, *35*, 83–90.

Collins, W. A., Maccoby, E. E., Steinberg, L., Hetherington, E. M., & Bornstein, M. H. (2000). Contemporary research on parenting: The case for nature *and* nurture. *American Psychologist*, *55*, 218–232.

Connor, J. M., & Serbin, L. A. (1977). Behaviorally based masculine and feminine-activity-preference scales for preschoolers: Correlates with other classroom behaviors and cognitive tests. *Child Development*, *48*, 1411–1416.

Coyle, T. R., & Bjorklund, D. F. (1996). The development of strategic memory: A modified microgenetic assessment of utilization deficiencies. *Cognitive Development*, *11*, 295–314.

Crabtree, J. W., & Riesen, A. H. (1979). Effects of the duration of dark rearing on visually guided behavior in the kitten. *Developmental Psychobiology*, *12*, 291–303.

Crain, W. (2003). *Reclaiming childhood: Letting children be children in our achievement-oriented society*. New York: Holt.

Crook, J. M. (1980). *The evolution of human consciousness*. Oxford: Clarendon Press.

Culotta, E. (2005). The question of sex. *Science*, *307* (11 February), 841.

Curtiss, S. (1977). *Genie: A psycholinguistic study of a modern day "wild child."* New York: Academic.

Darwin, C. (1859). *The origin of species*. New York: Modern Library.

Deacon, T. W. (1997). *The symbolic species: The co-evolution of language and the brain*. New York: Norton.

de Beer, G. (1958). *Embryos and ancestors* (3rd edn). Oxford: Clarendon Press.

DeCasper, A. J., & Fifer, W. P. (1980). Of human bonding: Newborns prefer their mother's voice. *Science, 208*, 1174–1176.

DeCasper, A. J., Lecanuet, J.-P., Busnel, M.-C., Granier-Deferre, C., & Maugeais, R. (1994). Fetal reactions to recurrent maternal speech. *Infant Behavior & Development, 17*, 159–164.

DeCasper, A. J., & Spence, M. J. (1986). Prenatal maternal speech influences newborns' perception of speech sounds. *Infant Behavior & Development, 9*, 133–150.

DeMarie-Dreblow, D., & Miller, P. H. (1988). The development of children's strategies for selective attention: Evidence for a transitional period. *Child Development, 59*, 1504–1513.

de Mause, L. (1974). The evolution of childhood. In L. de Mause (Ed.), *The history of childhood* (pp. 1–73). New York: Psychohistory Press.

Demetriou, A., Xiang Kui, Z., Spanoudis, G., Christou, C., Kyriakides, L., & Platsidou, M. (2005). The architecture, dynamics, and development of mental processing: Greek, Chinese, or Universal? *Intelligence, 33*, 109–141.

Dennis, W. (1973). *Children of the Crèche*. New York: Appleton-Century-Crofts.

de Waal, F. B. M. (1982). *Chimpanzee politics: Power and sex among apes*. London: Jonathan Cape.

Diamond, J. M. (1992). *The third chimpanzee: The evolution and future of the human animal*. New York: Perennial.

Dobzhansky, T. (1973). Nothing in biology makes sense except in the light of evolution, *American Biology Teacher, 35*, 125–129.

Dunbar, R. I. M. (1995). Neocortex size and group size in primates: A test of the hypothesis. *Journal of Human Evolution, 28*, 287–296.

Duyme, M., Dumaret, A-C., & Tomkiewicz, S. (1999). How can we boost IQs of "dull" children?: A late adoption study. *Proceedings of the National Academy of Science, 96*, 8790–8794.

Dweck, C. S., & Elliott, E. S. (1983). Achievement motivation. In E. M. Hetherington (Vol. Ed.), *Socialization, personality, and social development* (pp. 643–691). In P. H. Mussen (Gen. Ed.), *Handbook of child psychology* (vol. 4). New York: Wiley.

Eberstadt, M. (2004). *Home-alone America: The hidden toll of day care, behavioral drugs, and other parent substitutes*. New York: Sentinel.

Eccles, J. C. (1989). *Evolution of the brain: Creation of the self*. New York: Routledge.

Edelman, G. M. (1987). *Neural Darwinism: The theory of neuronal group selection*. New York: Basic Books.

Edelman, M. S., & Omark, D. R. (1973). Dominance hierarchies in young children. *Social Sciences Information, 12*, 103–110.

Elkind, D. (1967). Egocentrism in adolescence. *Child Development, 38*, 1025–1034.

Elkind, D. (1981). *The hurried child: Growing up too fast too soon*. Reading, MA: Addison-Wesley.

Elkind, D. (1987). *The miseducation of children: Superkids at risk*. New York: Knopf.

Elkind, D. (1998). *Reinventing childhood: Raising and educating children in a changing world*. Rosemont, NJ: Modern Learning Press.

Elkind, D., & Bowen, R. (1979). Imaginary audience behavior in children and adolescents. *Developmental Psychology, 15*, 38–44.

Ellis, B. J. (2004). Timing of pubertal maturation in girls: An integrated life history approach. *Psychological Bulletin, 130*, 920–958.

Elman, J. (1994). Implicit learning in neural networks: The importance of starting small. In C. Umilta and M. Moscovitch (Eds.), *Attention and performance XV: Conscious and nonconscious information processing* (pp. 861–888). Cambridge, MA: MIT Press.

Enard, W., Khaitovich, P., Klose, J., Zöllner, S., Heissig, F., Giavalisco, P., Nieselt-Struwe, K., Muchmore, E., Varki, A., Ravid, R., Doxiadis, G. M., Bontrop, R. E., & Pääbo, S. (2002). Intra- and interspecific variation in primate gene expression patterns. *Science, 296*, 340–343.

Erikson, E. H. (1950). *Childhood and society*. New York: Norton.

Eriksson, P. S., Perfilieva, E., Bjoerk-Eriksson, T., Alborn, A-M., Nordborg, C., Peterson, D. A., & Gage, F. H. (1998). Neurogenesis in the adult human hippocampus. *Nature Medicine, 4*, 1313–1317.

Evans, P. D., Gilbert, S. L., Mekel-Bobrov, N., Vallender, E. J., Anderson, J. R., Vaez-Azizi, L. M., Tishkoff, S. A., Hudson, R. R., & Lahn, B. T. (2005). *Microcephalin*, a gene regulating brain size, continues to evolve adaptively in humans. *Science, 309* (9 September), 1717–1720.

Fagen, R. (1981). *Animal play behavior*. New York: Oxford University Press.

Fairbanks, L. A. (1990). Reciprocal benefits of allomothering for female vervet monkeys. *Animal Behaviour, 40*, 553–562.

Falk, D., Hildebolt, C., Smith, K., Morwood, M. J., Sutikna, T., Brown, P., Jatmiko, Wayhu Saptomo, E., Brunsden, B., & Prior, F. (2005). The brain of LB1, *Homo floresiensis. Science Express* [www.sciencexpress.org], (3 March).

Fernald, A. (1992). Human maternal vocalizations to infants as biologically relevant signals: An evolutionary perspective. In J. H. Barkow, L. Cosmides, & J. Tooby (Eds.), *The adaptive mind: Evolutionary psychology and the generation of culture* (pp. 391–428). New York: Oxford University Press.

Feuerbach, A. von (1833). *An ACCOUNT of an individual kept in a dungeon, separated from all communication with the world, from early childhood to about the age of seventeen*. London: Simpkin and Marshall.

Finlay, B. L., & Darlington, R. D. (1995). Linked regularities in the development and evolution of mammalian brains. *Science, 268* (16 June), 1579–1584.

Finlay, B., L., Darlington, R. B., & Nicastro, N. (2001). Developmental structure in brain evolution. *Behavioral and Brain Sciences, 24*, 263–308.

Flavell, J. H. (1978). Metacognitive development. In J. M. Scandura, & C. J. Brainerd (Eds.), *Structural/process theories of complex human behavior* (pp. 213–247). Alphen a. d. Rijn, The Netherlands: Sijthoff & Noordhoff.

Flavell, J. H., Everett, B. A., Croft, K., & Flavell, E. (1981). Young children's knowledge about visual perception: Further evidence for level 1–level 2 distinction. *Developmental Psychology, 17,* 99–107.

Flynn, J. R. (1987). Massive IQ gains in 14 nations: What IQ tests really measure. *Psychological Bulletin, 101,* 171–191.

Flynn, J. R. (1998). IQ gains over time: Toward finding the causes. In U. Neisser (Ed.), *The rising curve: Long-term gains in IQ and related measures* (pp. 25–66). Washington, DC: American Psychological Association.

Flynn, J. R. (1999). Searching for justice: The discovery of IQ gains over time. *American Psychologist, 54,* 5–20.

Foley, M. A., & Ratner, H. H. (1998). Children's recoding in memory for collaboration: A way of learning from others. *Cognitive Development, 13,* 91–108.

Foley, M. A., Ratner, H. H., & Passalacqua, C. (1993). Appropriating the actions of another: Implications for children's memory and learning. *Cognitive Development, 8,* 373–401.

Friedman, S. (1972). Habituation and recovery of visual response in the alert human newborn. *Journal of Experimental Child Psychology, 13,* 339–349.

Fry, D. P. (2005). Rough-and-tumble social play in humans. In A. D. Pellegrini & P. K. Smith (Eds.), *Play in humans and great apes* (pp. 54–85). Mahwah, NJ: Erlbaum.

Fullard, W., & Reiling, A. M. (1976). An investigation of Lorenz's "Babyness." *Child Development, 47,* 1191–1193.

Galik, K., Senut, B., Pickford, M., Gommery, D., Treil, J., Kuperavage, A. J., & Eckhardt, R. B. (2004). External and internal morphology of the BAR 1002'00 *Orrorion tugenensis* femur. *Science, 305* (3 Sept.), 1450–1454.

Gallup Poll (May 8–11, 2006). Origin of human life. Uploaded from: http://www.pollingreport.com/science.htm, July 12, 2006.

Garstang, W. (1922). The theory of recapitulation: A critical restatement of the biogenetic law. *Journal of the Linnaean Society (Zoology), 35,* 81–101.

Gauvain, M. (2001). *The social context of cognitive development.* New York: Guilford.

Geary, D. C. (1995). Reflections of evolution and culture in children's cognition: Implications for mathematical development and instruction. *American Psychologist, 50,* 24–37.

Geary, D. C. (1998). *Male, female: The evolution of human sex differences.* Washington, DC: American Psychological Association.

Geary, D. C. (2002a). Sexual selection and human life history. In R. Kail (Ed.), *Advances in child development and behavior* (vol. 30, pp. 41–101). San Diego, CA: Academic Press.

Geary, D. C. (2002b). Principles of evolutionary educational psychology. *Learning and Individual Differences, 12,* 317–345.

Geary, D. C. (2005). *The origin of mind: Evolution of brain, cognition, and general intelligence.* Washington, DC: American Psychological Association.

Geary, D. C. (in press). Educating the evolved mind: Conceptual foundations for an evolutionary psychology. In J. S. Carlson & J. R. Levin (Eds.), *Psychological perspectives on contemporary educational issues.* Greenwich CT: Information Age Publishing.

Geary, D. C., & Flinn, M. V. (2001). Evolution of human parental behavior and the human family. *Parenting: Science and Practice, 1,* 5–61.

Geary, D. C., Salthouse, T. A., Chen, G-P., & Fan, L. (1996). Are East Asian versus American differences in arithmetical ability a recent phenomenon? *Developmental Psychology, 32,* 254–262.

Gelfand, D. M., & & Drew, C. J. (2003). *Understanding child behavioral disorders.* Belmont, CA: Wadsworth.

Giedd, J. N., et al. (1999). Brain development during childhood and adolescence: A longitudinal MRI study. *Nature Neuroscience, 2,* 861–863.

Gies, F., & Gies, J. (1987). *Marriage and family in the middle ages.* New York: Harper & Row.

Goldfarb, W. (1945). Effects of psychological deprivation in infancy and subsequent stimulation. *American Journal of Psychiatry, 102,* 18–33.

Goldfarb, W. (1947). Variations in adolescent adjustment of institutionally reared children. *American Journal of Orthopsychiatry, 17,* 449–457.

Gómez, J-C., & Martín-Andrade, B. (2005). Fantasy play in apes. In A. D. Pellegrini & P. K. Smith (Eds.), *The nature of play* (pp. 139–172). New York: Guilford.

Goodall, J. (1986). *The chimpanzees of Gombe.* Cambridge, MA: Belknap.

Goodman, J. F. (1992). *When slow is fast enough: Educating the delayed preschool child.* New York: Guilford.

Goren-Inbar, N., Alperson, N., Kislev, M. E., Simchoni, O., Melamed, Y., Ben-Nun, A., & Werker, E. (2004). Evidence of hominin control of fire at Gesher Benot Ya'agov, Isreal. *Science, 304* (30 April), 725–727.

Gosso, Y., Otta, E., de Lima Salum e Morais, M., Leite Ribeiro, F. J., & Raad Bussab, V. S. (2005). Play in hunter-gatherer society. In A. D. Pellegrini & P. K. Smith (Eds.), *Play in humans and great apes* (pp. 213–253). Mahwah, NJ: Erlbaum.

Gottlieb, G. (1971). Ontogenesis of sensory function in birds and mammals. In E. Tobach, L. R. Aronson, & E. Shaw (Eds.), *The biopsychology of development* (pp. 67–128). New York: Academic Press.

Gottlieb, G. (1992). *Individual development & evolution: The genesis of novel behavior.* New York: Oxford.

Gottlieb, G. (1997). *Synthesizing nature–nurture: Prenatal roots of instinctive behavior.* Mahwah, NJ: Erlbaum.

Gould, E., Beylin, A., Tanapat, P., Reeves, A., & Shors, T. J. (1999). Learning enhances adult neurogenesis in the hippocampal formation. *Nature Neuroscience, 2,* 260–265.

Gould, S. J. (1977). *Ontogeny and phylogeny.* Cambridge, MA: Harvard University Press.

Grant, B. R., & Grant, P. R. (1989). Natural selection in a population of Darwin's finches. *American Naturalist, 133,* 377–393.

Grant, B. R., & Grant, P. R. (1993). Evolution of Darwin's finches caused by rare climate event. *Proceedings of the Royal Society of London B, 251,* 111–117.

Grant, P. R., & Grant, B. R. (2002). Unpredictable evolution in a 30-year study of Darwin's finches. *Science, 296* (April 26), 707–711.

Grant P. R., & Grant, B. R. (2006). Evolution of character displacement in Darwin's finches. *Science, 313* (July 14), 224–226.

Gray, W. M., & Hudson, L. M. (1984). Formal operations and the imaginary audience. *Developmental Psychology, 20,* 619–627.

Gredlein, J. M., & Bjorklund, D. F. (2005). Sex differences in young children's use of tools in a problem-solving task: The role of object-oriented play. *Human Nature, 16,* 97–118.

Green, C. S., & Bavelier, D. (2003). Action video game modifies visual attention. *Nature, 423,* 534–537.

Greene, E. (1996). Effect of light quality and larval diet on morph induction in the polymorphic caterpillar Nemoria arizonaria (*Lepidoptera: Geometridae*). *Biological Journal of the Linnean Society, 58,* 277–285.

Greenfield, P. M. (1998). The cultural evolution of IQ. In U. Neisser (Ed.), *The rising cure: Long-term gains in IQ and related measures* (pp. 81–123). Washington, DC: American Psychological Association.

Greenough, W. T., Black, J. E., & Wallace, C. S. (1987). Experience and brain development. *Child Development, 58,* 539–559.

Groos, K. (1898). *The play of animals.* New York: Appleton.

Groos, K. (1901). *The play of man.* New York: Appleton.

Guthrie, S. E. (1993). *Faces in the clouds: A new theory of religion.* New York: Oxford University Press.

Guttmacher Institute, *Teenagers' Sexual and Reproductive Health: Developed Countries,* http://www.agi-usa.org/pubs/fb_teens.html.

Haile-Selassie, Y., Suwa, G., & White, T. D. (2004). Late Miocene teeth from Middle Awash, Ethiopia, and early hominid dental evolution. *Science, 303* (5 March), 1503–1505.

Haldane, J. B. S. (1932). *The causes of evolution.* New York: Harper & Brothers.

Harlow, H. F. (1959). The development of learning in the Rhesus monkey. *American Scientist,* 459–479.

Harlow, H. F., Dodsworth, R. O., & Harlow, M. K. (1965). Total isolation in monkeys. *Proceedings of the National Academy of Science, 54,* 90–97.

Harlow, H., & Harlow, M. (1962). Social deprivation in monkeys. *Scientific American, 207,* 136–146.

Harlow, H., & Zimmerman, R. R. (1959). Affectional responses in the infant monkey. *Science, 130,* 421–432.

Harper, L. (2005). Epigenetic inheritance and the intergenerational transfer of experience. *Psychological Bulletin, 131,* 340–360.

Harris, J. R. (1995). Where is the child's environment? A group socialization theory of development. *Psychological Review, 102,* 458–489.

Harris, P. (1989). *Children and emotion: The development of psychological understanding.* Oxford, UK: Blackwell.

Harter, S., & Pike, R. (1984). The pictorial scale of perceived competence and social acceptance for young children. *Child Development, 55,* 1969–1982.

Hattori, K. (1998). Drivers of intelligence evolution in Homo: Sexual behavior, food acquisition and infant neoteny. *The Mankind Quarterly, 39,* 127–146.

Hawley, P. A. (1999). The ontogenesis of social dominance: A strategy-based evolutionary perspective. *Developmental Review, 19,* 97–132.

Hebb, D. O. (1949). *The organization of behavior.* New York: Wiley.

Heimann, M. (1989). Neonatal imitation gaze aversion and mother–infant interaction. *Infant Behavior & Development, 12,* 495–505.

Herman-Giddens, M. E., Slora, E. J., Wasserman, R. C., Bourdony, C. J., Bhapkar, M. V., Koch, G. G., & Hasemeir, C. M. (1997). Secondary sexual characteristics and menses in young girls seen in office practice: A study from the pediatric research in office settings network. *Pediatrics 99,* 505–512.

Hernández Blasi, C., & Bjorklund, D. F. (2003). Evolutionary developmental psychology: A new tool for better understanding human ontogeny. *Human Development, 46,* 259–281.

Hill, K., & Hurtado, A. M. (1996). *Ache life history: The ecology and demography of a foraging people.* New York: Aldine de Gruyter.

Hirsh-Pasek, K., & Golinkoff, R. M. (2003). *Einstein never used flash cards: How children REALLY learn and why they need to play more and memorize less.* Emmaus, PA: Rodale Press.

Hirsh-Pasek, K., Hyson, M. C., & Rescorla, L. (1990). Academic environments in preschool: Challenge or pressure? *Early Education and Development, 1,* 401–423.

Honzik, M. P., MacFarlane, J. W., & Allen, L. (1948). Stability of mental test performance between 2 and 18 years. *Journal of Experimental Education, 17,* 309–324.

Hrdy, S. B. (1986). Sources of variation in the reproductive success of female primates. *Proceedings of the International Meeting on Varia-*

251

bility and Behavioral Evolution (pp. 191–203). Problemi Attuali di Scienza e di Cultura, N. 259. Rome: Adademia a Nazionale dei Lincei.

Hrdy, S. B. (1999). *Mother nature: A history of mothers, infants, and natural selection.* New York: Pantheon Books.

Huizinga, J. (1950). *Homo ludens: A study of the play-element in culture.* Boston, MA: Beacon Press.

Humphrey, N. K. (1976). The social function of intellect. In P. P. G. Bateson & R. A. Hinde (Eds.), *Growing points in ethology* (pp. 303–317). Cambridge, UK: Cambridge University Press.

Humphreys, A. P., & Smith, P. K. (1987). Rough and tumble, friendship, and dominance in schoolchildren: Evidence for continuity and change with age. *Child Development, 58,* 201–212.

Huttenlocher, P. (2002). *Neural plasticity: The effects of environment on the development of the cerebral cortex.* Cambridge, MA: Harvard University Press.

Hymovitch, B. (1952). The effects of experimental variations on problem solving in the rat. *Journal of Comparative and Physiological Psychology, 45,* 313–321.

Hymowitz, K. (2000). *Ready or not: What happens when we treat children as small adults.* San Francisco: Encounter Books.

Inhelder, B., & Piaget, J. (1958). *The growth of logical thinking from childhood to adolescence.* New York: Basic Books.

Jacobson, S. W. (1979). Matching behavior in the young infant. *Child Development, 50,* 425–430.

Jerison, H. J. (1973). *Evolution of the brain and intelligence.* New York: Academic Press.

Jerison, H. J. (2002). On theory in comparative psychology. In R. J. Sternberg & J. C. Kaufman (Eds.), *The evolution of intelligence* (pp. 251–288). Mahwah, NJ: Erlbaum.

Joffe, T. H. (1997). Social pressures have selected for an extended juvenile period in primates. *Journal of Human Evolution, 32,* 593–605.

Johanson, D., & Edgar, B. (1996). *From Lucy to language.* New York: Simon & Schuster.

Juffer, F., & IJzendoorn, M. (2005). Behavior problems and mental health referrals of international adoptees: A meta-analysis. *Journal of the American Medical Association, 293* (25 May), 2501–2515.

Kagan, S. L., & Ziegler, E. F. (Eds.). (1987). *Early schooling: The national debate.* New Haven, CT: Yale University Press.

Kail, R. V., & Levine, L. E. (1976). Encoding processes and sex-role preferences. *Journal of Experimental Child Psychology, 21,* 256–263.

Kaplan, H., Hill, K., Lancaster, J., & Hurtado, A. M. (2000). A theory of human life history evolution: Diet intelligence, and longevity. *Evolutionary Anthropology, 9,* 156–185.

Katz, M. B. (1986). *In the shadow of the poor house: A social history of welfare in America.* New York: Basic Books.

Kawai, M. (1965). Newly acquired pre-cultural behavior of natural troop of Japanese monkeys. *Primates, 6*, 1–30.

Keeley, L. H. (1996). *War before civilization: The myth of the peaceful savage.* New York: Oxford University Press.

Kenny, P., & Turkewitz, G. (1986). Effects of unusually early visual stimulation on the development of homing behavior in the rat pup. *Developmental Psychobiology, 19*, 57–66.

Kersten, A. W., & Earles, J. L. (2001). Less really is more for adults learning a miniature artificial language. *Journal of Memory and Language, 44*, 250–273.

Kisilevsky, B. S., Hains, S. M. J., Lee, K., Xie, X., Huang, H., Ye, H. H., Zhang, K., & Wang, Z. (2003). Effects of experience on fetal voice recognition. *Psychological Science, 14*, 220–224.

Krings, M., Stone, Am Schmitz, R. W., Krainitzki, H., Stoneking, M., & Pääbo, S. (1997). Neandertal DNA sequences and the origins of modern humans. *Cell, 90*, 19–30.

Lafuente, M. J., Grifol, R., Segerra, J., Soriano, J., Gorba, M. A., & Montesinos, A. (1997). *Pre- & Peri-Natal Psychology Journal, 11*, 151–162.

Lancy, D. F. (1996). *Playing on the mother-ground: Cultural routines for children's development.* New York: Guilford Press.

Langer, J. (2000). The heterochronic evolution of primate cognitive development. In S. T. Parker, J. Langer, & M. L. McKinney (Eds.), *Biology, brains, and behavior: The evolution of human development* (pp. 215–235). Santa Fe, NM: School of American Research Press.

Legerstee, M. (1991). The role of person and object in eliciting early imitation. *Journal of Experimental Child Psychology, 51*, 423–433.

Lickliter, R. (1990). Premature visual stimulation accelerates intersensory functioning in bobwhite quail neonates. *Developmental Psychobiology, 23*, 15–27.

Lickliter, R. (2000). The role of sensory stimulation in perinatal development: Insights from comparative research for care of the high-risk infant. *Developmental and Behavioral Pediatrics, 21*, 437–447.

Lickliter, R., & Hellewell, T. B. (1992). Contextual determinants of auditory learning in bobwhite quail embryos and hatchlings. *Developmental Psychobiology, 25*, 17–24.

Locke, J. L., & Bogin, B. (2006). Language and life history: A new perspective on the development and evolution of human language. *Behavioral and Brain Sciences, 29*, 259–280.

Lockhart, K. L., Chang, B., & Tyler, S. (2002). Young children's belief about the stability of traits: Protective optimism. *Child Development, 73*, 1408–1430.

Logan B. (1991). Infant outcomes of a prenatal stimulation pilot study. *Pre and Perinatal Psychology Journal, 6*, 7–31.

Lonsdorf, E. L., Eberly, L. E., & Pusey, A. E. (2004). Sex differences in learning in chimpanzees. *Nature, 428* (15 April), 715–716.

Lord, C. G. (1980). Schemas and images as memory aids: Two modes of processing social information. *Journal of Personality and Social Psychology*, *38*, 257–269.

Lorenz, K. (1937). The companion in the bird's world. *Auk*, *54*, 245–273.

Louv, R. (2005). *Last child left in the woods: Saving our children from nature-deficit disorder*. Chapel Hill, NC: Algonquin Books of Chapel Hill.

Lumeng, J. C., Appugliese, D., Cabral, H. J., Bradley, R. H., & Zuckerman, B. (2006). Neighborhood safety and overweight status in children. *Archives of Pediatric & Adolescence Medicine*, *160*, 25–31.

Luna, B., Thulborn, K. R., Munoz, D. P., Merriam, E. P., Garve, K. E., Minshew, N. J., Keshavan, M. S., Genovese, C. R., Eddy, W. F., & Sweeney, J. A. (2001). Maturation of widely distributed brain function subserves cognitive development. *NeuroImage*, *13*, 786–793.

Luthar, S. S. (2003). The culture of affluence: Psychological costs of material wealth. *Child Development*, *74*, 1581–1593.

Luthar, S. S., & Latendresse, S. J. (2005). Children of the affluent: Challenges to well-being. *Current Directions in Psychological Science*, *14*, 49–53.

Luthar, S. S., & Sexton, C. (2004). The high price of affluence. In R. V. Kail (Ed.), *Advances in child development* (vol. 32, pp. 126–162). San Diego, CA: Academic Press.

Lynn, R., & Hampson, S. (1986). The rise of national intelligence: Evidence from Britain, Japan, and the U.S.A. *Personality and Individual Differences*, *7*, 23–32.

Macfarlane, A. (1975). Olfaction in the development of social preferences in the humane neonate. *CIBA Foundation Symposium 33: Parent–infant interaction*. Amsterdam, The Netherlands: Elsevier.

Maestripieri, D., & Pelka, S. (2002). Sex differences in interest in infants across the lifespan: A biological adaptation for parenting? *Human Nature*, *13*, 327–344.

Maestripieri, D., & Roney, J. R. (2006). Evolutionary developmental psychology: Contributions from comparative research with nonhuman primates. *Developmental Review*, *26*, 120–137.

Marcon, R. A. (1992). Differential effects of three preschool models on inner-city 4-year-olds. *Early Childhood Research Quarterly*, *7*, 517–530.

Marcon, R. A. (1999). Differential impact of preschool models on development and early learning of inner-city children: A three cohort study. *Developmental Psychology*, *35*, 358–375.

Martin, H., Beezley, P. C., Conway, E., & Kempe, H. (1974). The development of abused children: A review of the literature. *Advances in Pediatrics*, *21*, 119–134.

Mayr, E. (1982) *The growth of biological thought: Diversity, evolution, and inheritance*. Cambridge, MA: Belknap Press.

Mazur, A. (2005). *Biopsychology of dominance and deference*. New York: Rowan & Littlefield.

Mazzoni, G., & Nelson, T. O. (1998). *Metacognition and cognitive neuro-psychology: Monitoring and control processes.* Mahwah, NJ: Erlbaum.

McBride, T., & Lickliter, R. (1994). Specific postnatal auditory stimulation interferes with species-typical responsiveness to maternal visual cues in bobwhite quail chicks. *Journal of Comparative Psychology, 107,* 320–327.

McCall, R. B. (1981). Nature–nurture and the two realms of development: A proposed integration with respect to mental development. *Child Development, 52,* 1–12.

McClurg, P. A., & Chaillé, C. (1987). Computer games: Environments for developing spatial cognition? *Journal of Educational Computing Research, 3,* 95–111.

McDougall, I., Brown, F. H., & Fleagle, J. G. (2005). Stratigraphic placement and age of modern humans from Kibish, Ethiopia. *Nature, 433* (17 Feb), 733–736.

McGrew, W. C. (1992). *Chimpanzee material culture: Implication for human evolution.* Cambridge, UK: Cambridge University Press.

McKinney, M. L., & McNamara, K. (1991). *Heterochrony: The evolution of ontogeny.* New York: Plenum.

Mehler, J., Jusczyk, P., Lambertz, G., Halsted, N., Bertoncini, J., & Amiel-Tison, C. (1988). A precursor of language acquisition in young infants. *Cognition, 29,* 143–178.

Mekel-Bobrov, N., Gilbert, S. L., Evans, P. D., Vallender, E. J., Anderson, J. R., Hudson, R. R., Tishkoff, S. A., & Lahn, B. T. (2005). Ongoing adaptive evolution of *ASPM*, a brain size determinant in *Homo sapiens. Science, 309* (9 September), 1720–1722.

Meltzoff, A. N., & Moore, M. K. (1977). Imitation of facial and manual gestures by human neonates. *Science, 198,* 75–78.

Meltzoff, A. N., & Moore, M. K. (1985). Cognitive foundations and social functions of imitation and intermodal representation in infancy. In J. Mehler & R. Fox (Eds.), *Neonate cognition: Beyond the booming buzzing confusion.* Hillsdale, NJ: Erlbaum.

Menzel, E. W., Jr. (1974). A group of young chimpanzees in a 1-acre field: Leadership and communication. In A. M. Schrier & F. Stollnitz (Eds.), *Behavior of nonhuman primates* (vol. 5, pp. 83–153). New York: Academic Press.

Miller, P. H. (1990). The development of strategies of selective attention. In D. F. Bjorklund (Ed.), *Children's strategies: Contemporary views of cognitive development* (pp. 157–184). Hillsdale, NJ: Erlbaum.

Miller, P. H., Haynes, V. F., DeMarie-Dreblow, D., & Woody-Ramsey, J. (1986). Children's strategies for gathering information in three tasks. *Child Development, 57,* 1429–1439.

Miller, P. H., & Seier, W. L. (1994). Strategy utilization deficiencies in children: When, where, and why. In H. W. Reese (Ed.), *Advances in child development and behavior* (vol. 25, pp. 108–156). New York: Academic.

255

Miller, P. H., Seier, W. L., Probert, J. S., & Aloise, P. A. (1991). Age differences in the capacity demands of a strategy among spontaneously strategic children. *Journal of Experimental Child Psychology*, 52, 149–165.

Mills, C. M., & Keil, F. C. (2004). Knowing the limits of one's understanding: The development of an awareness of an illusion of explanatory depth. *Journal of Experimental Child Psychology*, 87, 1–32

Mithen, S. (1996). *The prehistory of the mind: The cognitive origins of art, religion and science*. London: Thames and Hudson.

Montagu, A. (1989). *Growing young* (2nd edn). Grandy, MA: Bergin & Garvey.

Montagu, M. F. A. (1962). Time, morphology, and neoteny in the evolution of man. In M. F. A. Montagu (Ed.), *Culture and the evolution of man* (pp. 324–342). New York: Oxford University Press.

Mood, D. W. (1979). Sentence comprehension in preschool children: Testing an adaptive egocentrism hypothesis. *Child Development*, 50, 247–250.

Morrison, F. J., Griffith, E. M., & Frazier, J. A. (1996). Schooling and the 5–7 shift: A natural experiment. In A. Sameroff & M. M. Haith (Eds.), *Reason and responsibility: The passage through childhood* (pp. 161–186). Chicago, IL: University of Chicago Press.

Morwood, M. J., Brown, P., Jatmiko, Sutikna, T., Wahyu Saptomo, E., Westaway, K. E., Rokus Awe Due, Roberts, R. G., Maeda, T., Wasisto, S., & Djubiantono, T. (2005). Further evidence for small-bodied hominins from the late Pleistocene of Flores, Indonesia. *Nature*, 437 (13 October), 1012–1017.

Nadelman, L. (1974). Sex identity in American children: Memory, knowledge, and preference tests. *Developmental Psychology*, 10, 413–417.

Narayan, K. M., Boyle, J. P., Thompson, T. J., Sorensen, S. W., & Williamson, D. F. (2003). Lifetime risk for diabetes mellitus in the United States. *Journal of the American Medical Association*, 290, 1884–1890.

National Association for the Education of Young Children. *Guidelines for decisions about developmentally appropriate practice: Developmentally appropriate practice in early childhood programs serving children from birth through age 8*: www.naeyc.org/about/positions/dap4.asp.

Nazzi, T., Bertoncini, J., & Mehler, J. (1998). Language discrimination by newborns: Toward an understanding of the role of rhythm. *Journal of Experimental Psychology: Human Perception and Performance*, 24, 756–766.

Neisser, U. (Ed.). (1998). *The rising curve: Long-term gains in IQ and related measures*. Washington, DC: American Psychological Association.

Nesse, R. M., & Williams, G. C. (1994). *Why we get sick: The new science of Darwinian medicine*. New York: Times Books.

Newport, E. L. (1990). Maturational constraints on language learning. *Cognitive Science*, 14, 11–28.

Newport, E. L. (1991). Constraining concepts of the critical period for language. In S. Carey & R. Gelman (Eds.), *The epigenesis of mind: Essays on biology and cognition* (pp. 111–130). Hillsdale, NJ: Erlbaum.

Nunn, C. L., Gittleman, J. L., & Antonovics, J. (2000). Promiscuity and the primate immune system. *Science*, *290* (November 10), 1168–1170.

OECD. (2004). *Learning for tomorrow's world: First results from PISA 2003*. Paris: Organization for Economic Co-operation and Development.

O'Connor, T. G., Rutter, M., Beckett, C., Keaveney, L., Kreppner, J. M., and the English and Romanian Adoptees Study Team. (2000). The effects of global severe privation on cognitive competence: Extension and longitudinal follow-up. *Child Development*, *71*, 376–390.

Olson, S. (2002). *Mapping human history: Genes, race, and our common origins*. Boston, MA: Houghton Mifflin.

Omark, D. R., & Edelman, M. S. (1975). A comparison of status hierarchies in young children: An ethological approach. *Social Sciences Information*, *14*, 87–107.

Omark, D. R., & Edelman, M. S. (1976). The development of attention structures in young children. In M. R. A. Chance & R. R. Larson (Eds.), *The social structure of attention* (pp. 119–151). London: Wiley.

Oppenheim, R. W. (1981). Ontogenetic adaptations and retrogressive processes in the development of the nervous system and behavior. In K. J. Connolly & H. F. R. Prechtl (Eds.), *Maturation and development: Biological and psychological perspectives* (pp. 73–108). Philadelphia: International Medical Publications.

Orme, N. (2001). *Medieval children*. New Haven, CT: Yale University Press.

Palm Beach Post, "Close-up study finds family life child-oriented, frantic," March 20, 2005 (Associated Press).

Papousek, H. (1977). The development of learning ability in infancy (Entwicklung der Lernfähigkeit im Säuglingsalter). In G. Nissen (Ed.), *Intelligence, learning, and learning disabilities (Intelligenz, Lernen und Lernstörungen)* (pp. 75–93). Berlin: Springer-Verlag.

Parker, S. T., & McKinney, M. L. (1999). *Origins of intelligence: The evolution of cognitive development in monkeys, apes, and humans*. Baltimore, MD: The Johns Hopkins University Press.

Parten, M. (1932). Social participation among preschool children. *Journal of Abnormal and Social Psychology*, *27*, 243–269.

Pellegrini, A. D. (2005). *Recess: Its role in education and development*. Mahwah, NJ: Erlbaum.

Pellegrini, A. D., & Bjorklund, D. F. (1997). The role of recess in children's cognitive performance. *Educational Psychologist*, *32*, 35–40.

Pellegrini, A. D., & Bjorklund, D. F. (2004). The ontogeny and phylogeny of children's object and fantasy play. *Human Nature*, *15*, 23–43.

Pellegrini, A. D., & Davis, P. (1993). Confinement effects on playground and classroom behavior. *British Journal of Educational Psychology*, *63*, 88–95.

Pellegrini, A. D., Galda, L., Bartini, M., & Charak, D. (1998). Oral language and literacy learning in context: The role of social relationships. *Merrill-Palmer Quarterly, 44*, 38–54.

Pellegrini, A. D., Galda, L., Shockley, B., & Stahl, S. (1995). The nexus of social and literacy events at home and school: Implications for primary school oral language and literacy. *British Journal of Educational Psychology, 65*, 273–285.

Pellegrini, A. D., & Gustafson, K. (2005). Boys' and girls' uses of objects for exploration, play, and tools in early childhood. In A. D. Pellegrini & P. K. Smith (Eds.), *Play in humans and great apes* (pp. 113–135). Mahwah, NJ: Erlbaum.

Pellegrini, A. D., Huberty, P. D., & Jones, I. (1995). The effects of play deprivation on children's recess and classroom behaviors. *American Educational Research Journal, 32*, 845–864.

Pellegrini, A. D., Kato, K., Blatchford, P., & Baines, E. (2002). A short-term longitudinal study of children's playground games across the first year of school: Implications for social competence and adjustment to school. *American Educational Research Journal, 39*, 991–1015.

Pellegrini, A. D., & Smith, P. K. (Eds.). (2005). *Play in humans and great apes*. Mahwah, NJ: Erlbaum.

Pellis, S. M., Field, E. F., Smith, L. K., & Pellis, V. C. (1996). Multiple differences in the play fighting of male and female rats. *Neuroscience and Biobehavioral Reviews, 21*, 105–120.

Perie, M., & Morn, R. (2005). *NAEP 2004 trends in academic progress: Three decades of student performance* [NCES 2005-464]. US Department of Education, National Center for Education Statistics, Washington, DC.

Piaget, J. (1930). *The child's conception of physical causality*. London: Routledge & Kegan Paul.

Piaget, J. (1955). *The language and thought of the child*. New York: World.

Piaget, J. (1962). *Play, dreams, and imitation*. New York: Norton.

Piaget, J. (1972). *Play and development*. Maria W. Piers (Ed.). New York: Norton.

Pickert, S. M., & Wall, S. M. (1981). An investigation of children's perceptions of dominance relations. *Perceptual and Motor Skills, 52*, 75–81.

Plumert, J. M. (1995). Relations between children's overestimation of their physical abilities and accident proneness. *Developmental Psychology, 31*, 866–876.

Plumert, J. M., Kearney, J. K., & Cremer, J. F. (2004). Children's perception of gap avoidances: Bicycling across traffic-filled intersections in an immersive virtual environment. *Child Development, 75*, 1243–1253.

Plumert, J. M., & Schwebel, D. C. (1997). Social and temperamental influences on children's overestimation of their physical abilities: Links to accidental injuries. *Journal of Experimental Child Psychology, 67*, 317–337.

258

Poirier, F. E., & Smith, E. O. (1974). Socializing functions of primate play. *American Zoologist*, *14*, 275–287.

Popper, K. R., & Eccles, J. C. (1977). *The self and its brain*. New York: Springer International.

Postman, N. (1982). *The disappearance of childhood*. New York: Vintage Books.

Potts, R. (1998). Variability selection in Hominid evolution. *Evolutionary Anthropology*, *7*, 81–96.

Pratkanis, A. R., & Greenwald, A. B. (1985). How shall the self be conceived? *Journal for the Theory of Social Behavior*, *15*, 311–328.

Provence, S., & Lipton, R. C. (1962). *Infants in institutions: A comparison of their development with family-reared infants during the first year of life*. New York: International Universities Press.

Radell, P. L., & Gottlieb, G. (1992). Development of intersensory interference: Augmented prenatal sensory experience interferes with auditory learning in duck embryos. *Developmental Psychology*, *28*, 795–803.

Ratner, H. H., Foley, M. A., & Gimpert, N. (2002). The role of collaborative planning in children's source-monitoring errors and learning. *Journal of Experimental Child Psychology*, *81*, 44–73.

Rendell, L., & Whitehead, H. (2001). Culture in whales and dolphins. *Behavioral and Brain Sciences*, *24*, 309–382.

Rilling, J. K., & Insel, T. R. (1999). The primate neocortex in comparative perspective using magnetic resonance imaging. *Journal of Human Evolution*, *37*, 191–223.

Roberts, R. E., Attkisson, C. C., & Rosenblatt, A. (1998). Prevalence of psychopathology among children and adolescents. *American Journal of Psychiatry*, *155*, 715–725.

Rogoff, B. (1990). *Apprenticeship in thinking: Cognitive development in social context*. New York: Oxford University Press.

Rogoff, B. (1998). Cognition as a collaborative process. In D. Kuhn & R. S. Siegler (Vol. Eds.), *Cognition language, and perceptual development*, Vol. 2. In W. Damon (Gen. Ed), *Handbook of child psychology* (pp. 679–744). New York: Wiley.

Rogoff, B., Mistry, J., Göncü, A., & Mosier, C. (1993). Guided participation in cultural activity by toddlers and caregivers. *Monographs of the Society for Research in Child Development*, *58* (Serial No. 236).

Rosenberg, J. S., Hernández Blasi, C., Shin, H-E., & Bjorklund, D. F. (August, 2005). *Why rush growing up? Possible adaptive benefits of cognitive immaturity*. Poster presented at European Conference on Developmental Psychology, Tenerife, Spain.

Rosenfeld, A. & Wise, N. (2000). *The over-scheduled child: Avoiding the hyper-parenting trap*. New York: St. Martin's Griffin.

Rousseau, J. J. (1979). *Emile: Or, on education*, trans. Allan Bloom. New York: Basic Books.

Rozenbilt, L., & Keil, F. (2002). The misunderstood limits of folk science: An illusion of explanatory depth. *Cognitive Science, 26,* 521–562.

Rubin, K. H., Fein, G., & Vandenberg B. (1983). Play. In E. M. Hetherington (Ed.), *Handbook of child psychology* (vol. 4, pp. 693–774). New York: Wiley.

Rudy, J. W., Vogt, M. B., & Hyson, R. L. (1984). A developmental analysis of the rat's learned reactions to gustatory and auditory stimulation. In R. Kail & N. E. Spear (Eds.), *Memory development: Comparative perspectives* (pp. 181–208). Hillsdale, NJ: Erlbaum.

Rutter, M., & the English and Romanian Adoptees study team. (1998). Developmental catch-up, and delay, following adoption after severe global early privation. *Journal of Child Psychology and Psychiatry, 39,* 465–476.

Savin-Williams, R. C. (1979). Dominance hierarchies in groups of early adolescents. *Child Development, 50,* 923–935.

Schneider, W. (1985). Developmental trends in the metamemory–memory behavior relationship: An integrative review. In D. L. Forrest-Pressley, G. E. MacKinnon, & T. G. Waller (Eds.), *Cognition, metacognition, and human performance* (vol. 1, pp. 57–109). New York: Academic Press.

Schneider, W. (1998). Performance prediction in young children: Effects of skill, metacognition and wishful thinking. *Developmental Science, 1,* 291–297.

Schneider, W., Korkel, J., & Weinert, F. E. (1987). The effects of intelligence, self-concept, and attributional style on metamemory and memory behaviour. *International Journal of Behavioral Development, 10,* 281–299.

Schneider, W., & Lockl, K. (2002). The development of metacognitive knowledge in children and adolescents. In T. Perfect & B. Schwartz (Eds.), *Applied metacognition* (pp. 224–257). Cambridge, UK: Cambridge University Press.

Schwartz, J. H. (1999). *Sudden origins: Fossils, genes, and the emergence of species.* New York: Wiley.

Schwebel, D. C., & Plumert, J. M. (1999). Longitudinal and concurrent relations among temperament, ability estimation, and injury proneness. *Child Development, 70,* 700–712.

Schweinhart, L. J., & Weikart, D. P. (1988). Education for young children living in poverty: Child-initiated learning or teacher-directed instruction? *The Elementary School Journal, 89,* 212–225.

Seligman, M. E. P. (with Reivich, K., Jaycox, L., & Gillham, J.). (1995). *The optimistic child.* Boston, MA: Houghton Mifflin.

Seligman, M. E. P. (1998). *Learned optimism: How to change your mind and your life* (2nd edn). New York: Free Press.

Senghas, A., & Coppola, M. (2001). Children creating language: How Nicaraguan Sign Language acquired a spatial grammar. *Psychological Science, 12,* 323–326.

Senghas, A., Kita, S., & Ozyürek, A. (2004). Children creating core properties of language: Evidence from an emerging sign language in Nicaragua. *Science, 305* (17 September), 1179–1782.

Serre, D., Langaney, A., Chech,, M., Teschler-Nicola, M., Paunovic, M., Mennecier, P., Hofreiter, M., Possnert, G., & Svante Pääbo, S. (2004). No evidence of Neanderthal mtDNA contribution to early modern humans. *PLoS Biol., 2*, 313–317.

Shea, B. T. (1989). Heterochrony in human evolution: The case for neoteny revisited. *Yearbook of Physical Anthropology, 32*, 69–101.

Sherrod, K. B., O'Connor, S., Vietz, P. M., & Altmeier, W. A. (1984). Child health and maltreatment. *Child Development, 55*, 1174–1183.

Sherry, J. L. (2001). The effects of violent video games on aggression: A meta-analysis. *Human Communication Research, 27*, 409–431.

Shin, H-E, & Bjorklund, D. F. (April, 2005). *Ontogenetic adaptations of children's overestimation*. Poster presented at meeting of the Society for Research in Child Development, Atlantic, GA.

Shin, H-E., Bjorklund, D. F., & Beck, E. (in press). The adaptive value of children's overestimation in a strategic memory task. *Cognitive Development*.

Shipman, P. (1994). *The evolution of racism: Human differences and the use and abuse of science*. New York: Simon & Schuster.

Short, R. V. (1979). Sexual selection and its component parts, somatic and genital selection, as illustrated by man and great apes. *Advances in the Study of Behavior, 9*, 131–158.

Siegler, R. S. (1996). *Emerging minds: The process of change in children's thinking*. New York: Oxford University Press.

Sigel, I. E. (1987). Early childhood education: Developmental enhancement or developmental acceleration? In S. L. Kagan & E. F. Ziegler (Eds.), *Early schooling: The national debate* (pp. 129–150). New Haven, CT: Yale University Press.

Skeels, H. M. (1966). Adult status of children with contrasting early life experiences. *Monographs of the Society for Research in Child Development, 31* (Serial No. 105).

Skeels H. M., & Dye, H. B. (1939). A study of the effects of differential stimulation on mentally retarded children. *Program of the American Association of Mental Deficiency, 44*, 114–136.

Smilansky, S. (1968). *The effects of sociodramatic play on disadvantaged preschool children*. New York: Wiley.

Smith, P. K. (1982). Does play matter? Functional and evolutionary aspects of animal and human play. *The Behavioral and Brain Sciences, 5*, 139–184.

Smith, P. K. (2005). Social and pretend play in children. In A. D. Pellegrini & P. K. Smith (Eds.), *Play in humans and great apes* (pp. 173–209). Mahwah, NJ: Erlbaum.

Smith, P. K., & Dutton, S. (1979). Play and training in direct and innovative problem solving. *Child Development, 50*, 830–836.

Spear, L. P. (2000). Neurobehavioral changes in adolescence. *Current Directions in Psychological Science, 9*, 111–114.

Spear, N. E. (1984). Ecologically determined dispositions control the ontogeny of learning and memory. In R. Kail & N. E. Spear (Eds.), *Memory development: Comparative perspectives* (pp. 325–358). Hillsdale, NJ: Erlbaum.

Spear, N. E., & Hyatt, L. (1993). How the timing of experience can affect the ontogeny of learning. In G. Turkewitz, & D. A. Devenny (Eds.), *Developmental time and timing* (pp. 167–209). Hillsdale, NJ: Erlbaum.

Spence, M. J., & Freeman, M. S. (1996). Newborn infants prefer the maternal low-pass filtered voice, but not the maternal whispered voice. *Infant Behavior & Development, 19*, 199–212.

Spinath, B., & Spinath, F. M. (2005). Development of self-perceived ability in elementary school: The role of parents' perceptions, teacher evaluations, and intelligence. *Cognitive Development, 20*, 190–204.

Spinka, M., Newbury, R. C., & Bekoff, M. (2001). Mammalian play: Can training for the unexpected be fun? *Quarterly Review of Biology, 76*, 141–168.

Spitz, R. (1945). Hospitalism: An inquiry into the genesis of psychiatric conditions in early childhood. *Psychoanalytic Study of the Child, 1*, 53–74.

Sternberg, R. J. (1997). The concept of intelligence and its role in lifelong learning and success. *American Psychologist, 52*, 1030–1037.

Stevenson, H. W., Chen, C., & Lee, S-Y. (1993). Mathematics achievement of Chinese, Japanese, and American children: Ten years later. *Science, 259*, 53–58.

Stevenson, H. W., & Lee, S-Y. (1990). Context of achievement. *Monographs of the Society for Research in Child Development, 55* (Serial No. 221).

Stipek, D. (1981). Children's perceptions of their own and their classmates' ability. *Journal of Experimental Child Psychology, 73*, 404–410.

Stipek, D. (1984). Young children's performance expectations: Logical analysis or wishful thinking? In J. G. Nicholls (Ed.), *Advances in motivation and achievement: Vol. 3. The development of achievement motivation* (pp. 33–56). Greenwich, CT: JAI Press.

Stipek, D. (2002). At what age should children enter kindergarten? A question for policy makers and parents. *Social Policy Report, 16*, 3–16.

Stipek, D., & Daniels, D. (1988). Declining perceptions of competence: A consequence of changes in the child or the educational environment? *Journal of Educational Psychology, 80*, 352–356.

Stipek, D., Feiler, R., Blyer, P., Ryan, R., Milburn, S., & Salmon, J. M. (1998). Good beginnings: What differences does the program make in preparing children for school? *Journal of Applied Developmental Psychology, 19*, 41–46.

Stipek, D., Feiler, R., Daniels, D., & Milburn, S. (1995). Effects of different instructional approaches on young children's achievement and motivation. *Child Development, 66,* 209–223.

Stipek, D., & Hoffman, J. (1980). Development of children's performance-related judgments. *Child Development, 51,* 912–914.

Stipek, D., & MacIver, D. (1989). Developmental change in children's assessment of intellectual competence. *Child Development, 60,* 521–538.

Stipek, D. J., Recchia, S., & McClintic, S. (1992). Self-evaluation in young children. *Monographs of the Society for Research in Child Development, 57* (Serial No. 226).

Stipek, D., Roberts, T., & Sanborn, M. (1984). Preschool-age children's performance expectations for themselves and another child as a function of the incentive value of success and the salience of past performance. *Child Development, 55,* 1983–1989.

Stringer, C., & Andrews, P. (2005). *The complete world of human evolution.* New York: Thames & Hudson.

Stringer, C. B., Dean, M. C., & Martin, R. D. (1990). A comparative study of cranial and dental development within recent British samples among Neanderthals. In C. J. DeRousseau (Ed.), *Primate life history and evolution* (pp. 115–152). New York: Wiley-Liss.

Stone, L. J., Smith, H. T., & Murphy, L. B. (Eds.). (1973). *The competent infant: Research and commentary.* New York: Basic Books.

Subrahmanyam, K., & Greenfield, P. M. (1994). Effect of video game practice on spatial skills in girls and boys. *Journal of Applied Developmental Psychology, 15,* 13–32.

Subrahmanyam, K., Kraut, R. E., Greenfield, P. M., & Gross, E. F. (2000). The impact of home computer use on children's activities and development. *The Future of Children, 10,* 123–144.

Suomi, S., & Harlow, H. (1972). Social rehabilitation of isolate-reared monkeys. *Developmental Psychology, 6,* 487–496.

Suomi, S. J. (1978). Maternal behavior by socially incompetent monkeys: Neglect and abuse of offspring. *Journal of Pediatric Psychology, 3,* 28–34.

Sur, M., Pallas, S. L., & Roe, A. W. (1990). Cross-modal plasticity in cortical development: Differentiation and specification of sensory neocortex. *Trends in Neuroscience, 13,* 227–233.

Swisher, C. C. III, Rink, W. J., Antón, S. C., Schwarcz, H. P., Curtis, G. H., Suprijo, A., & Widiasmoro. (1996). Latest *Homo erectus* of Java: Potential contemporaneity with *Homo sapiens* in Southeast Asia. *Science, 274,* 1870–1874.

Sylva, K. (1977). Play and learning. In B. Tizard & J. P. Harvey (Eds.), *Biology of play* (pp. 244–257). London: Heinemann.

Tanner, J. M. (1962). *Growth at adolescence* (2nd edn). Oxford: Blackwell.

Tanner, J. M. (1978). *From fetus into man: Physical growth from conception to maturity.* Cambridge, MA: Harvard University Press.

Tanner, J. M. (1981). *A history of the study of human growth.* Cambridge, UK: Cambridge University Press.

Tattersall, I. (1998). *Becoming human: Evolution and human intelligence.* San Diego, CA: Harcourt Brace.

Teasdale, T. W., & Owen, D. R. (1989). Continuing secular increases in intelligence and a stable prevalence of high intelligence levels. *Intelligence, 13,* 255–262.

Teasdale, T. W., & Owen, D. R. (2000). Forty-year secular trends in cognitive abilities. *Intelligence, 28,* 115–120.

Thomas, L. (1993). *The fragile species.* New York: Charles Scribner's Sons.

Thompson, M. (2004). *The pressured child: Helping your child find success in school and life.* New York: Ballantine.

Timney, B., Mitchell, D. E., & Cynader, M. (1980). Behavioral evidence for prolonged sensitivity to effects of monocular deprivation in dark-reared cats. *Journal of Neurophysiology, 43,* 1041–1054.

Tinbergen, N. (1951). *The study of instinct.* New York: Oxford University Press.

Tomasello, M., & Call, J. (1997). *Primate cognition.* New York: Oxford University Press.

Trevathan, W. R. (1987). *Human birth: An evolutionary perspective.* New York: Gruyter.

Trinkus, E., & Tompkins, R. L. (1990). The Neanderthal life cycle: The possibility, probability and perceptibility of contrasts with recent humans. In C. J. DeRousseau (Ed.), *Primate life history and evolution* (pp. 153–180). New York: Wiley-Liss.

Trivers, R. (1972). Parental investment and sexual selection. In B. Campbell (Ed.), *Sexual selection and the descent of man* (pp. 136–179). New York: Aldine de Gruyter.

Turkewitz, G., & Kenny, P. (1982). Limitations on input as a basis for neural organization and perceptual development: A preliminary theoretical statement. *Developmental Psychobiology, 15,* 357–368.

Turner, A. M., & Greenough, W. T. (1985). Differential rearing effects on rat visual cortex synapses. I. Synaptic and neuronal density and synapses per neuron. *Brain Research, 329,* 195–203.

Vaillant, G. E. (2002). *Aging well: Surprising guideposts to a happier life from the Landmark Harvard Study of Adult Development.* Boston, MA: Little, Brown and Company.

Van Horn, M. L., Karlin, E. O., Ramey, S. L., Aldridge, J., & Snyder, S. W. (2005). Effects of developmentally appropriate practices on children's development: A review of research and discussion of methodological and analytic issues. *The Elementary School Journal, 105,* 325–351.

van Schaik, C. P., Ancrenaz, M., Borgen, G., Galdikas, B., Knott, C. D., Singleton, I., Suzuki, A., Utami, S. S., & Merrill, M. (2003). Orangutan cultures and the evolution of material culture, *Science, 299,* 102–105.

Van Horn, K. L., & Ramey, S. L. (2003). The effects of developmentally appropriate practices on academic outcomes among former Head Start students and classmates, grades 1–3. *American Educational Research Journal, 40,* 961–990.

Vygotsky, L. S. (1962). *Thought and language.* Cambridge, MA: MIT Press.

Vygotsky. L. S. (1978). *Mind in society.* Cambridge, MA: Harvard University Press.

Weinstock, H., Berman, S., & Cates, Jr., W. (2004). Sexually transmitted diseases among American youth: Incidence and prevalence estimates, 2000. *Perspectives on Sexual and Reproductive Health, 36,* 6–10.

Weisfeld, G. E. (1999). *Evolutionary principles of human adolescence.* New York: Basic Books.

Weisfeld, G. E., & Janisee, H. C. (2005). Some functional aspects of human adolescence. In B. J. Ellis & D. F. Bjorklund (Eds.), *The origins of the social mind: Evolutionary psychology and child development* (pp. 189–218). New York: Guilford.

Wellman, H. M. (1988). The early development of memory strategies. In F. E. Weinert & M. Perlmutter (Eds.), *Memory development: Universal changes and individual differences* (pp. 3–29). Hillsdale, NJ: Erlbaum.

Wesson, R. (1991). *Beyond natural selection.* Cambridge, MA: MIT Press.

West-Eberhard, M. J. (2003). *Developmental plasticity and evolution.* New York: Oxford University Press.

Whiten, A., & Byrne, R. W. (1988). The manipulation of attention in primate tactical deception. In R. W. Byrne & A. Whiten (Eds.). *Machiavellian intelligence: Social expertise and the evolution of intellect in monkeys, apes, and humans* (pp. 211–223). Oxford: Clarendon Press.

Whiten, A., Goodall, J., McGrew, W. C., Nishida, T., Reynolds, V., Sugiyama, Y., Tutin, C. E. G., Wrangham, R. W., & Boesch, C. (1999). Cultures in chimpanzees. *Nature, 399* (June), 682–685.

Windham, G. C., Bottomley, C., Birner, C., & Fenster, L. (2004). Age at menarche in relation to maternal use of tobacco, alcohol, coffee, and tea during pregnancy. *American Journal Epidemiology, 159,* 862–871.

Winick, M., Meyer, K. K., & Harris, R. C. (1975). Malnutrition and environmental enrichment by early adoption. *Science, 190,* 1173–1175.

Winn, M. (1981). *Children without childhood.* New York: Pantheon.

Winsler, A. (2003). Overt and covert verbal problem-solving strategies: Developmental trends in use, awareness, and relations with task performance in children age 5 to 17. *Child Development, 74,* 659–678.

Wong, I. C. K., Murray, M. L., Camilleri-Novak, D., & Stephens, P. (2004). Increased prescribing trends of paediatric psychotropic medications. *Archives of Disease in Child, 89,* 1131–1132.

Wong, K. (2005). The littlest human. *Scientific American, 292,* 56–65.

Wrangham, R., & Peterson, D. (1996). *Demonic males.* Boston, MA: Houghton Mifflin.

Yan, J. H., Thomas, J. R., & Downing, J. H. (1998). Locomotion improves children's spatial search: A meta-analytic review. *Perceptual and Motor Skills, 87,* 67–82.

Yussen, S., & Levy, V. (1975). Developmental changes in predicting one's own span of short-term memory. *Journal of Experimental Child Psychology, 19,* 502–508.

Zebrowitz, L. A., Kendall-Tackett, K., & Fafel, J. (1991). The impact of children's facial maturity on parental expectations and punishments. *Journal of Experimental Child Psychology, 52,* 221–238.

Zito, J. M., Safer, D. J., dosReis, S., Gardner, J., Boles, M., & Lynch, F. (2000). Trends in the prescribing of psychotropic medications to preschoolers. *Journal of the American Medical Association, 283,* 1025–1030.

Zito, J. M., Safer, D. J., dosReis, S., Gardner, J., Magder, L., Soeken, K., Boles, M., Lynch, F., & Riddle, M. A. (2003). Psychotropic practice patterns for youth. *Archives of Pediatric and Adolescent Medicine, 157,* 17–25.

Zollikofer, C. P. E., Ponce de León, M. S., Martin, R. D., & Stucki, P. (1995). Neanderthal computer skulls. *Nature, 375,* 283–285.

Index

institutionalized infants and
    children, 74, 75–7, 78–9
intelligence, 50, 70–1n
    crystallized, 72
    and education, 171
    evolution of, 58–62
    fluid, 72, 73
    Flynn effect, 71–3
    incremental theory of, 126
    and metacognition, 117–18, 126,
        128–9
    overestimation of, 117–18
    possible increases in children,
        70–3
    and reversal of early deprivation,
        74, 76, 79
    social, 61–2
Intelligent Design, 17–18
inter-species mating, 30–1
intuitive thinking, 108
IQ tests, 70–3, 70–1n, 128, 129

juvenile period, 36, 37, 49
    brain size and length of, 58,
        59–60
    and independent human juvenile,
        216–17

knowledge, overestimation of,
    117–18

Lamarck, Jean Baptiste, 15
language
    acquisition, 101–6
        age differences in ease of, 102
        and child-directed speech, 106
        computer simulations, 105–6
        less-is-more hypothesis, 105
        and limited information-
            processing abilities, 104–6
        sensitive period for, 104
    capacity/potential for, 103
    children and evolution of,
        103–4
    and play, 152

and problem-solving behavior,
    98–9
    second language learning, 102,
        105
lapware, 178
learning readiness, 179
life expectancy, 56–7
literacy, 3–4, 207
    emergent, 167
locomotor play, 143, 144–5
longevity, 222
lure-retrieval task, and object-
    oriented play, 149–50

males
    and family bonds, 64–5
    and parental investment, 10–11,
        101
    risk-taking behavior, 100–1
    and social status, 127
    see also boys; sex differences
mammals
    play in, 143
    postnatal developmental stages,
        36
marginally monogamous/
    marginally polygamous
    species, humans as, 32–3&n,
        64
mathematical abilities, 165–6
medication, 213
medieval Europe, children in,
    206–7
memory, and self-referencing, 95–6
menarche, 38
    age of, 40, 41–2
mental health, 213
metacognition, 112
    benefits of deficiencies in,
        128–35
    bidirectional relationship with
        cognition, 114–15
    development, 113–27
    and failure, 120–2
    and intelligence, 128–9